Economic Games People Play

ECONOMIC GAMES PEOPLE PLAY

Shlomo Maital

&

Sharone L. Maital

Basic Books, Inc., Publishers *New York*

Library of Congress Cataloging in Publication Data

Maital, Shlomo.
    Economic games people play.

    Includes bibliographical references and index.
    1. Game theory. 2. Economics—Psychological
aspects. I. Maital, Sharone L. II. Title.
HB144.M34   1984   330'.01'9   83–45260
ISBN 0–465–01789–4

For Temira, Ronen, and Yochai,

our three best chapters

CONTENTS

Contents

PART V

Nations

ix

ACKNOWLEDGMENTS

I WOULD like to thank all those, too numerous to name, who taught me so much during my undergraduate and graduate studies at Douglass College, Tel Aviv University, and Temple University. I am especially grateful to members of Temple University's Department of School Psychology. With patient good humor, they trained me to think both as a scientist and as a practitioner. I hope what they imparted to me is at least partly visible in our book.

The children and families with whom I worked over the years have enlightened me about human interaction in a manner that no classroom could. I am very thankful to all of them, and to my colleagues at Haifa School Psychological Services.

This book is dedicated to our children, Temira, Ronen, and Yochai, in the hope of changing for the better the economic games they will play in their lifetimes.

Sharone L. Maital
October 1983

As a graduate student at Princeton University, I was inspired by the wise and gentle teaching of W. Arthur Lewis. There was always more to his lectures than met the ear. It took years of reflection, and the writing of this book, for me to understand how *much* more.

Parts of this book were drafted at the Institute for Advanced Studies of the Hebrew University in Jerusalem. I am indebted to the director, Professor Aryeh Dvoretzky, and to Professor Menahem Yaari for enabling me to savor the unique combination of serenity and stimulation the Institute and its fellows provided.

An economic game not mentioned in our book is the competition for grants. I am deeply grateful to the following institutions for including me in their generous coalition: the Ford Foundation, through the Israel Foundations Trustees; Fulbright Research Program on Economic Policy Coordination among Industrial Countries, through the Social Science Research Council; Samuel Neaman Institute for Advanced Study in Science and Technology; and the Technion-Israel Institute of Technology Vice-President's Fund.

Material for the book was gathered in part during a summer at the Woodrow Wilson School of Public and International Affairs at Princeton University. During our stay, we found Princeton University's Psychology Library to be a wonderfully efficient, compact, and helpful research tool.

We are fortunate to have Martin Kessler as our editor and publisher. From the book's inception to the last draft, his skilled hand gave us invaluable guidance, as did our copy editors, Sheila Friedling, Kathleen Antrim, and Maureen Bischoff.

Shlomo Maital
October 1983

PART I

Individuals

If I am not for myself,
Who will be for me?
If I am only for myself,
What am I?
　　　　　—Talmud

CHAPTER 1

Run for Your Money: Game Playing in Our Factious Society

WHOEVER YOU ARE, wherever you live, whatever your ancestry, and however you spend your time and money, one thing is certain—you the reader are an expert, inveterate game player.

True, you may never feed slot machines or roll dice. You may be blissfully unaware of the odds of drawing a worthless poker hand (50-50) or a perfect bridge hand (nearly 160 trillion to 1).[1] Monopoly, Clue, and Go may bore you. You may visit Atlantic City often—to see your aunt. And you may believe Pacman is a shipping clerk. Nonetheless, you play games—tough competitive games with high stakes. Moreover, you have little choice. Not to play is not to live.

The games we all play involve competing for shares of resources whose supplies are limited relative to those who want them. How well and how fairly resources are allocated is the primary focus of economics. Thus we shall call them economic games, even though other disciplines—psychology, mathematics, law, politics, sociology—will be summoned to help us understand them.

Economic games are played every day by individuals, families, small and large groups, and entire nations. They are not confined exclusively to free markets and market economies. Conflicts over wealth and status are just as fierce and frequent in planned economies, only the rules and scene of action differ. And the prizes can range from multibillion-dollar markets down to simply the fun of winning. At times, there are only winners, such as when production teams compete to boost productivity. More often, though, there are mainly losers, when, for instance, people vie for larger shares of a constant, or shrinking, national output. Sometimes, there are *only* losers, as happens when countries destroy international trade and specialization through escalating tariff wars.

An appropriate catchall label for economic games people play is *Run for Your Money,* where money is broadly interpreted as anything people value, including affection and prestige. Most of us do "run for our money," in one way or another. The object of the game is to use our skills, assets, experience, and connections, alone and in collusion with others, to achieve happiness and security for ourselves and for those we love. Whatever the specific context of the game, two features are almost always present. First, interdependence. Our success in the game depends only in part on our own intelligence and diligence. What *others* choose to do can matter just as much to our winnings. And second, doubt. Usually we do not know for sure what other people will do when we choose our own behavior or strategy. These twin key ingredients—uncertainty and interdependence—are to economic games what hot spices are to Indian curries: they add interest, flavor, and variety, but they are often hard to digest.

THE ECONOMY: SICK AND UGLY

Since 1972, the outcomes of economic games have been disappointing for society as a whole. Western economies have behaved erratically. Growth of national output on average has been sluggish, running well below the pace of the 1960s. Inflation and unemployment, which once shunned one another, became reconciled and climbed together. Recessions became unwelcome guests that visited us more frequently and were harder to get rid of, even though they all eventually departed.

Bleak macro performance does not mean everyone becomes a pauper. At the start of this decade, despite years of economic bad news, the average American was quite well off compared to past years and to inhabitants of other countries. Median family income in 1980 was $21,000—nearly 40 percent higher than in 1960. In 1980, one white person in ten, and one black person in three, were poor. The corresponding ratios for 1960 were two in eleven for whites and over one in two for blacks. Since 1960, the fraction of people with high school educations or beyond has risen by nearly half and the number with college degrees has more than doubled. Over the same two decades, ownership of the comforts of life grew enormously—for example, passenger car registrations doubled. In 1979, 56 percent of all households had air conditioners, compared with 15 percent in 1960. Forty-three percent had dishwashers (7 percent in 1960); 45 percent had freezers (23 percent in 1960); 93 percent had food mixers (56 percent in 1960); 77 percent had washing machines (55 percent in 1960); and 90 percent had color TVs (none in 1960). People were freer to travel. Three million passports were issued in 1980, three-and-one-half times more than in 1960. Over 52 million households made trips by air. Ninety-eight percent of households had telephone service in 1980, compared with 79 percent in 1960. And of the world's 400 million telephones, Americans had a full 40 percent.[2]

These claims hide an essential fact: most of the gains in standards of living were attained in the fast growth of the 1960s. To a society accustomed to growth, the fact that there was no absolute decline offers little solace.

A curious aspect of the slumping economy is the expectational schizophrenia it spawned. When asked, "Do you expect to be financially better off or worse off a year from now?," 44 percent told Gallup interviewers in August 1979 that they expected to be better off. For the same group, only 11 percent felt economic conditions in the country *as a whole* would be better. When asked to look five years ahead, 51 percent said they personally would be better off, while only 20 percent said the country as a whole would have more good times than bad.[3] (Since that poll, the degree of personal optimism has eroded considerably; 230 million bright individual prospects cannot long coexist with a limping macro economy.)

Our economic ailments recall Henny Youngman's crisp humor. A skeptic visits his doctor. "You're ill," the doctor warns. "I want a second opinion," the man asserts. "O.K.," the doctor responds. "You're ugly, too." The economy is not just sick, it is also ugly. Its ugliness derives from the numerous parochial factions that split society, factions that compete hard for more wealth or more esteem or more power. Such clashes sow rivalry and reap rancor, heartache, and ill will. Some writers depict economic games as ones in which my loss is your gain. A more accurate portrayal is: my loss is your loss.

What underlies the non-zero-sum dilemma? Why have economic games metamorphosed? People have always struggled to better themselves and to get ahead. America, and England before it, was built on vigorous competition. Generally, and over the long run, successful entrepreneurs' gains pulled others ahead with them. When and why did economic games become malevolent? One theory points to a kind of vicious circle now afflicting us. Suppose, for some reason, national income stops growing. When one person or group manages to

7

grab more income than before, it follows logically that somebody, somewhere, gets less. No one likes to get less or to live less well. Therefore, aggrieved losers react aggressively to restore what they see as their fair share. Soon, others react; the battle is joined. The end result of this destructive competition may well be that everyone gets less. (This process is described in detail in later chapters.) Businessmen know this game well. Countless times "marketers strive to take away [market] share from competing brands rather than look to expansion" during slow growth.[4] The same script is replicated in thousands of different contexts: on shop floors, around bargaining tables, and in banks and brokerage houses, with leading roles played by powerful multinationals or just you and me. The less there is, the fiercer the game. When growth slows, a host of emotional problems emerge. Anomie, alienation, and helplessness dominate the national mood. Those who are lambs find themselves lying down with those who are lions, as Isaiah prophesied; but, as P. T. Barnum once warned, to make this possible, you need a lot of lambs.

Run for Your Money changes ominously. Where society once rewarded those who competed to be most able, it now elevates those most able to compete. Once, the price society paid for various types of labor truly reflected the skills and ability of that labor and its contribution to national output. In such a society, competition for wealth was competition of abilities, a game in which nearly all made gains, though some much more than others. Now, society rewards those whose chief skill is in securing economic rents—incomes that do not arise from productive labor—and in appropriating wealth at the expense of others.

THE SYNTAX SOCIETY

From time to time, scholars produce works of social criticism whose titles use the syntax, "The Something Society," where "Something" usually fingers a major social failing. Tawney's *The Acquisitive Society* deplores greed and materialism; Galbraith denounces favoring fins over fellowships in *The Affluent Society;* Johansen notes our passion for negotiation in "The Bargaining Society"; Aharoni's *The No-Risk Society* decries attempts to shift private risk onto public shoulders; Krueger, in "The Rent-Seeking Society," analyzes the channeling of economic energies into unproductive endeavors; Thurow dissects how we carve up GNP, and each other, in *The Zero-Sum Society;* and Lieberman's *Litigious Society* asks why we sue, instead of soothe, each other.[5] This syntax is notably asymmetric. It is hard to find books titled "The Loving Society," "The Helping Society," "The Caring Society," or "The Together Society." (Lyndon Johnson's label for his legislative program, "The Great Society," doesn't qualify; it wasn't.) We were tempted to call our book "The Factious Society" or "The Game-Playing Society," but the temptation was resisted.

Despite the gloomy perspective from which we have just viewed society and economy, this is *not* principally a book about what is wrong with economics or with the economy or both—though we do intend to discuss those important issues. This is a book about *people*—how they interact and interrelate, especially in situations involving choice. How people relate to one another is, we contend, what matters most and what should interest

9

us most as lay persons and scientists alike. There are few things wrong with the economy that a strong cohesive society cannot cure. And there are surprisingly few social ills that a strong economy cannot alleviate. Social and economic strength flows ultimately from bonds among people. It is these bonds that most concern us in this book.

The framework we found most suitable for unifying a study of interpersonal relations is that of games—specifically, economic games. Alfred North Whitehead once said that while we think in generalities, we live in specifics. Few thinkers thought more generally than Whitehead; in partnership with Bertrand Russell, Whitehead's great work on the foundations of mathematics gets around to proving one plus one makes two only on page 83—of volume 2.[6] Perhaps, in the study of humanity we ought to *think* in specifics. Game theory is a superb way to do so. The case for game theory as a tool for synthesizing and integrating the study of behavior rests on several pillars, any one of them alone strong enough to support our claim.

- Game theory adapts with ease and grace to empirical test and observation.
- The two features game theory stresses, uncertainty and interdependence, are also prime features of modern societies and economies.
- Game settings *suggest* norms and customs society might adopt for resolving its problems, instead of assuming them from the outset. In other words, social institutions are an *output* of game theory, not an *input* as in conventional social and economic theory.
- Games are universal phenomena, found in virtually all societies and eras, and played by people of all ages.

THE GAME-PLAYING SOCIETY

Games we play can be classified according to the presence of three aspects: brawn (physical skill), brains (strategy), and breaks (chance). Games of physical skill are the most widespread. Anthropologist John Roberts studied fifty tribes picked from all over the world. Of these, forty-three had various games of brawn; only twenty had games of chance and nineteen, games of strategy.[7]

If you chose to observe the colorful and jubilant tribe of Americans in the summer of 1982, you could have viewed brawn games (which they call sports) such as the Sixteenth Annual World Pillow-Fighting Championships in Kenwood, California (where "contestants straddle a slippery pipe above a mud pit and sock each other with pillows until one or both topple") or the ninth annual KNBR Bathtub Regatta in San Leandro Bay Park, in Oakland, California (where "paddlers brave the currents for golden bathtub trophies and the coveted title of Fastest Tub of the West"). For strategy games, you could have visited Tupelo, Mississippi, for a national checkers tournament, St. Paul for chess, or New York and Los Angeles for Go; for games of chance, you could have found spinning roulette wheels in Las Vegas or Atlantic City.[8]

Games of brawn are the province of fans and physiologists. Games of chance fascinate gamblers and probability experts. Games of strategy, on which we are focusing exclusively, belong to everyone; while we all *live* such games, those who *think* about them, in abstract terms and symbols, pay homage to two brilliant men, a mathematician and an economist, both European emigrés who collaborated to found an entirely new field, game theory.

GAMES AND BEHAVIOR

Game theory's first full exposition came in *The Theory of Games and Economic Behavior* published in 1944. Its authors were a forty-one-year-old Budapest-born mathematician John von Neumann and a thirty-four-year-old economist Oskar Morgenstern. In 1928, while still in Europe, von Neumann had published an important paper on a basic game theory theorem. After his arrival in America in 1930, he made pioneering contributions to mathematics, economics, and theoretical physics. His collaborator, Oskar Morgenstern, later wrote that in games of strategy "each participant is striving for his greatest advantage in situations where the outcome depends not only on his actions alone, nor solely on those of nature, but also on those of other participants whose interests are sometimes opposed, sometimes parallel, to his own."[9] Since the actions of others may not be known with certainty, Morgenstern added, each player faces uncertainty. Rather than to *assume* rationality, game theory seeks to explore the meaning of "rational" and "irrational" in strategic conflicts. Problems of great philosophical complexity and beauty arise when a game player acts rationally, in an individualistic sense, only to find that he and other like-minded "rational" people are collectively worse off precisely because of their purposeful rationality.

Game theory takes as given only the "physical basis" of a social economy. Human beings adjust to that background, von Neumann and Morgenstern wrote, not by setting up one rigid system of apportionment, but rather by evolving a wide variety of alternatives, which may differ widely one from another. One objective of game theory is to deduce what the "established order of society" or "accepted standards of behavior" are likely to be.[10] The presence of "economic behavior" in the title of their book is not an afterthought; it is the ultimate purpose of the whole exercise.

WHEN IS A DOLLAR WORTH FIVE?

Later in this chapter, we shall stress and amplify upon the relation between game theory and standards of behavior. But first, let us analyze an actual economic game. Unlike the proverbial elephant, who is hard to define but easy to recognize if one saw it, games are both recognized and defined with ease. The following game has cousins in many contexts. Yale economist Martin Shubik calls it the *Dollar Auction*.[11] We all know how easy it is to turn five dollars' worth of purchasing power into only one dollars' worth. Forty years of inflation in America did that with ease. But despite our schemes and dreams, few of us ever discover how to make one dollar into five. Here is one way without ever leaving your favorite armchair.

DOLLAR AUCTION

An auctioneer offers to sell a dollar bill. Only one condition is set: both the highest bidder *and* second highest bidder must pay, though only the highest bidder gets the dollar. For instance, if Juan bids twenty-five cents and Maria, fifteen cents, the auctioneer gets forty cents, pays the dollar to Juan, and loses sixty cents. Maria loses her fifteen cents. Juan's profit is seventy-five cents.

There are two other rules: bids are in units of five cents; and if nobody bids for, say, one minute, the game ends.

Shubik recommends that the game be played with a large crowd, perhaps at a party. It is a "zero-sum" game because the sum of all profits and losses is zero. In the example, the losses of the auctioneer and Maria totaled seventy-five cents, precisely what Juan's profit was.

An interesting feature of the game, Shubik notes, is that it is generally possible to sell a dollar for considerably more than a dollar. "Payments between three and five dollars are not uncommon."[12] A coalition of all bidders, such that one person bids five cents and everyone else abstains from bidding, can pluck ninety-five cents from the auctioneer. The ninety-five cents can then be divided up among coalition members (in itself, no simple problem). The potential for players to band together makes this a so-called cooperative game. But many cooperative games are fiercely contentious, as the *Dollar Auction* usually is.

Shubik observes that bidding usually proceeds rapidly until the top two bids add up to just over a dollar.

A "look of realization" crosses the face of the participants, there is a pause and hesitation when one bid crosses the one-dollar threshold, and then follows a duel in which rivalry and self-preservation chase each other upward in a war of escalation. *Escalation,* in fact, is another good name for the game, Shubik suggests.

Why would anyone bid $1.05, or $5.00, for a tattered dollar bill? To win—to outbid the others and to emerge with a smaller loss than the nearest rival. By bidding $5.00, if it is the top bid, I lose $4.00; but a rival who offered nearly as much as I did loses almost a dollar more. Suppose my rivals think along the same lines. There is in theory no upper limit to the damage one bidder can inflict on another. If bidders are stubborn enough, a dollar bill—even a counterfeit one—could theoretically fetch the entire value of the gross national product. When we ourselves are involved in such a game, we call it a "bull market." When we watch others playing it, we call it a "speculative bubble."

DOLLARS AND MARKETS

Dollar Auction resembles the way all free markets work when forces of supply and demand are unhindered. Buyers have full information about products up for sale. They compete with one another just as sellers compete among themselves for the buyers' business. Anyone can enter the bidding, or drop out—generally, breaking into a market as a seller is much more expensive than leaving it through bankruptcy, an imbalance swindlers have been known to exploit.

But there is at least one major difference between auctioning a dollar and, for example, selling a dump truck. Only the dump truck buyer pays; the second highest bidder keeps his or her money and looks elsewhere. This important distinction lets us argue that in free competitive markets, when a seller and buyer strike a deal, both profit by it. Otherwise, one or both of them would have backed out. It follows, then, that unless one is exceedingly enamored with the economies of Albania or Byelorussia, one should support the price system, whose fundamental principle is that as long as something can be freely bought and sold, everyone is potentially better off, or at least as well off, compared with any other way of running things.

Suppose, though, that a well-heeled dump-truck collector shows up and offers three times the going market price. Dump-truck prices soar; and the article becomes more expensive for everyone. In one sense, all the other buyers become the "second bidders" of *Dollar Auction.* None of them is compelled to buy; but those who do will pay more than they would have, had there not been a self-seeking rival tugging up the price. Well, this is as it should be, economists may argue. When something gets scarcer because demand for it grows relative to the supply, for *whatever* reason, it *should* get more expensive.[13] But does this line of reasoning hold water?

In the past decade, depressed values of common shares made it cheaper to buy up productive assets (buildings, production lines, or whole plants) through takeovers—the purchase of some or all of a company's shares—rather than to buy or to build those assets directly. (A persuasive explanation for undervalued stocks, we shall argue, was the widespread irrationality of investors; see chapter 6.) In some of those takeovers—themselves non-zero-sum games with enormous sums at stake—corporate maneuvers made Machiavelli appear like a grade-school primer. One of the quieter, more modest takeovers took place in the health-care industry. Humana Inc. and American Medical International (A.M.I.) got into a bidding war over a "dollar," Brookwood Health Services Inc., based in Birmingham, Alabama. Humana offered $26.50 for each of Brookwood's 2.9 million shares, and Brookwood declined. A.M.I. then bid $40.00 through a tax-free exchange of stock (ours for yours), and Brookwood accepted. Humana then upped its bid to $42.00. A.M.I. countered with a $50.00 offer.[14]

Similar takeovers, some on a much grander scale, take place almost every day. Is it reasonable to claim that the final price was "appropriate" in terms of economic efficiency just because buyer and seller agreed? Shubik counsels us not to overgeneralize from *Dollar Auction* to other instances of escalation. Nonetheless, we surmise that these two apparitions of human frailty—takeover escalation and underpriced stocks—resonate against one another and, as in *Dollar Auction,* escalate the consequent social damage.

Bidding for a buck or for Brookwood can involve all of the values and emotions that glorify and debase human society—rivalry, cupidity, greed, sacrifice, honor, egoism, pride, self-esteem, and power. Qualities that make us human can make economic games played in large markets cruel and self-defeating. But even more serious problems arise when certain markets are missing. Several generations of economists have addressed this issue, including two recent Nobel laureates, Kenneth Arrow and James Tobin.

PEOPLE AND MARKETS

Every year on the 10th of December, the anniversary of Alfred Nobel's death, six prizes are awarded in Oslo and Stockholm. The most recent award, established in 1968 by the Central Bank of Sweden, is for economics. In conjunction with the ceremonies, recipients deliver public lectures in which they summarize their work and present their views of the world and its problems. The 1972 address of Kenneth Arrow, a specialist in microeconomics (behavior of individuals), and the 1981 address of James Tobin, a macroeconomist, shared an important basic principle. To understand that principle, let us define, or redefine, what economics is about, while introducing a slight but significant modification in the conventional textbook phrases:

Economics is the study of relationships among people, expressed as relationships among things, as they emerge from choices of constrained alternatives.

In market economies, relationships among people are concretized and quantified in market transactions where goods and services and assets are exchanged for money. The fundamental idea of which both Arrow and Tobin spoke is this:

If a full set of freely competitive markets for all goods and assets exists, and there is perfect costless information available to all, then prices—relations among things—bring both microeconomic and macroeconomic relations among people into harmony.[15]

The word "harmony" here is used in the sense that there is no business cycle, involuntary unemployment, or waste.

The organization of economic relations among people by means of the marketplace, known as the price system, begins to break down when some markets function poorly or are missing entirely. When this happens, economists say that there is "market failure." One case of market failure exists when a vital dignitary is not invited to the marketplace party. When markets dispose of our depletable resources, future generations are not present; they neither bid nor ask. Do we do them justice? Is solicitude for grandchildren a sufficiently powerful force? Does government act forcefully enough on behalf of the future, as its main or only advocate? It is sometimes said that the poor, the black, the handicapped, and the aged are weak constituencies. People who will live exclusively in the twenty-first century are the weakest constituency of all.[16]

Another type of market failure occurs with respect to uncertainty. No one can foretell the future. In some cases, past experience helps us compute the probability, or odds, that some event will occur; a market in that contingent event can then emerge. In January 1982, when the Russian satellite *Cosmos* was about to plunge to earth, Lloyd's of London made a market in insurance against death by spy satellite. Here, the risk was very small but at least roughly calculable. But in many cases, because potential damage is incalculable, or the odds are not known, or our imaginations are too limited, markets in contingent future events are missing. Here, too, there is market failure.

The third instance where market systems fail is, in our view, the most serious and worrisome of all. One crucial "market" is missing entirely—the market in which concern, thoughtfulness, and respect for others' well-being are traded and find full expression. The economy is riddled with circumstances in which one person's actions influence other people, for good or for ill, and where that influence is not adequately reflected in market prices. Here is an example. Motorbike motors are small and notoriously noisy. A teenager zipping home on his motorbike at 3 A.M. after a heavy date, through the streets of a large city, can be heard by an estimated 300,000 people. The cost to society of that motorcycle—disturbed slumber—is not reflected in the motorcycle's price tag or in the cost of the gasoline that fuels it. Littering, noise, and pollution are all examples of such missing markets; the harm the action induces is not part of the price of the product that causes such harm. All market systems are propelled by self-interest. In such systems, when prices do not fully reflect either the positive or negative consequences of economic behavior, and when people concerned with only their own self-interest fail to take those consequences into account voluntarily, the result is an economy that is inefficient, unjust, and uncaring; a society that is, in Solzhenitsyn's phrase, unworthy of its people.[17]

Economists have applied boundless ingenuity to the missing-market problem. Pollution? Sell rights to pollute in national markets; the highest bidders will be those to whom the environment is worth the most, as efficiency dictates, either for purposes of production or recreation.[18] Inflation? Sell rights to raise prices. The highest bidders (those for whom price rises are most worthwhile and thus presumably justified) win the rights; the supply of inflation is thus properly allocated. If the right amount of rights is issued, inflation sinks to zero.[19]

The fact that such markets strike us as somewhat bizarre suggests that societies find other ways to remedy market failure—generally, by slowly evolving habits, norms, rules, or conventions. David Lewis defines "conventions" as "regularities in behavior . . . agreed to by all members of a society and which specify behavior in specific recurrent situations."[20] Traffic lights are a social convention developed to regulate chaotic interactions at intersections. In some cities, they are universally obeyed (Moscow); in others, they are universally ignored (Beirut). Such conventions spring from the basic nature of people. How they arise and how well they do their jobs are legitimate, even primary, concerns of economics. A difficulty arises, though, when we try to use for this purpose market-oriented economic theories that stress relations among *things.* They turn out to be unsuitable. A framework is needed that emphasizes relations among human beings. Game theory fills this bill.[21]

For a century, economics advanced along a broad front by studying how *markets* were interconnected, the so-called general equilibrium approach pioneered by Leon Walras. These efforts continue, but we believe they are in part misdirected—like the person who seeks a dropped coin near a lamppost, rather than in the dark corner where it fell. Like other disciplines, economics sometimes paints its bull's-eyes around existing bullet holes in order to score high. We contend the best way to tackle interest-group economies is not through standard analysis of markets, though that can still be useful, but through analysis of people. Game theory is indispensable for this. It counsels us to ask: Who are the players? What are they after? What is the nature of the game? What are the possible strategies? Who gains and who loses? Who is likely to collude or collide? When games are repeated, what conventions emerge?

As with other branches of mathematics, game theory can be stratospherically abstract. But even its most rarefied versions beckon practitioners to look for real-world examples and applications. A major theoretical contribution to the theory of cooperative games arose when an Israeli mathematician, Michael Maschler, had a group of high school students play some games he devised.[22]

In a letter to *Science,* Wassily Leontief deplored economics' preoccupation with theorizing. He observed that about only 1 percent of all the articles published over the last decade in the *American Economic Review* was built on data the author himself had generated.[23] The solution is not to sentence theory to death, but rather to orient it more toward testable, people-based propositions.

THE GAME OF CAPITALISM, R.I.P.

There is one such proposition, which is subject to hot debate. Social institutions in Western economies that once encouraged entrepreneurship, risk taking, and innovation now stifle these qualities, so vital for growth and progress. To frame the issue somewhat differently: When does competitive drive tear the fabric of social cohesion, as it may in *Dollar Auction,* and when does it build and glorify? In the Industrial Revolution, entrepreneurs gambled their wealth on bringing new products and processes to market. The rules of the game then were clear and unpaternalistic. They were:

THE GAME OF CAPITALISM

Do you want to earn a dollar, or a million? Be our guest. Try. Raise your own capital and put it at risk. Whatever you make, you keep. If you lose all, expect no help or solace.

Only vestiges of this game remain today. Like paleontologists who reconstruct the entire *tyrannosaurus rex* from a femur or a tibia and a few ribs, we can envisage what the heyday of lone-wolf ventures was like from some modern games, such as those discussed in this book.

Part 1, comprising this chapter and the next, focuses on the individual. Chapter 2 discusses a "mixed-motive" game which arises in a wide variety of economic and social contexts. Known as *Prisoner's Dilemma,* it is a game in which individual self-interest and collective well-being collide head-on. Such games need cooperation and coordination, we contend; but the people we choose to play them—heads of unions, corporations, and government—are likely to be destructively competitive.

Families account for more than half of the nation's economic activity. Part 2 turns to economic games families play and shows how in the family context altruistic behavior pays even for egoists (chapter 3), and how cohesive, open firms resemble strong, open families in the manner in which they approach conflict and competition (chapter 4).

The "Colossus" roller coaster in Valencia, California, has a stomach-churning drop of 115 feet. Lately, our economy has taken to imitating it every few years. Part 3, dealing with small groups, interprets recessions and the business cycle, especially "long waves," as a result of an economic game played by different generations (chapter 5); it portrays inflation as a result of predatory games aimed at shifting economic burdens from one group to another (chapters 6 and 7) and explains why we hate inflation by interpreting it as a game where we have little influence on what we win or lose (chapter 8).

Calvin Coolidge said that the business of America is business. It is equally true that the business of business—and of labor and of government—is America. Part 4 is about economic games played by corporate interests and labor unions, with government as both player and referee. These games are dissected in chapter 9, whose title reveals their implications for America—three's a crowd. A way of reorganizing business-labor-government games, either through a social contract or incomes policy, was placed before leading corporate executives and labor leaders. Their reactions are reported in chapters 9 and 10.

From individuals, families, small groups, and large ones, we finally expand to the nation as a whole, the topic of part 5. Games nations play are the subject of chapter 11, particularly beggar-my-neighbor trade restrictions that tend to beggar ourselves as well. How our economic games and the people who play them should be changed is the subject of the concluding chapter.

ECONOMIES NEVER COLLAPSE

Even when economic games end badly, because they are played poorly or all too well, society survives; and economies, unlike buildings or bridges, do not suddenly collapse. There are two reasons for this. First, whereas bricks and boards break, human beings flex, bend, and bounce back. John Steinbeck described how hundreds of thousands of Okies fled the dust and drought of the Depression and migrated to California; as he correctly predicted, they came to own much of that state. Second, economies have much greater tolerances than bridges. In 1970, in Melbourne, Australia, engineers once attempted to remedy a 4½-inch discrepancy between the north and south halves of a new bridge they were building by weighting down the higher half; and the bridge tumbled down.[24] During the 1970s, economists experimented with floating exchange rates, Standard Drawing Rights, tax cuts, supply-side policies, and other devices. Damage was wrought, but there was no collapse.

When economies teeter, politicians frequently employ the metaphor of the social "safety net." As with collapsing bridges and crumbling buildings, the image of people leaping to safety is evoked. But the safety-net metaphor is misleading and inappropriate. People wind up needing rescue from joblessness, poverty, despondence, and dependency through poorly conceived and poorly executed macroeconomic policies. They do not voluntarily leap into social safety nets of welfare and unemployment insurance, they are pushed. No better social program was ever designed than policies which bring near-full employment; no better safety net exists than initiatives that successfully reduce unemployment. The best safety net is not to need one.

In the 1960s, economists believed they knew how to pilot the economy so that it neither soared nor dived, steering a steady course between the reefs of inflation and the shoals of unemployment. In the 1970s, we learned better. What went wrong? Why do old theories and policies seem obsolete?

In economics' heyday, John F. Kennedy and some of his intellectual friends liked to play the following game. Someone would provide an answer, and the aim of the game was to invent an appropriate question to match the answer. (Example: "So what, they kiss my robe too." "What did Joseph Stalin tell the Pope?")

Now the answer is: the game is up; the economy is down. What, then, is the right question? Is it: How to cut deficits, trim spending, reduce taxes? Or, how to set the growth of money? Or even, how to alter people's expectations in a way that avoids deplorable self-fulfilling prophecies like inflation? Each of these questions is associated with a group of economists who believes it is central. We contend there is an alternative. It is: In the economic games people play, how can social institutions be devised to make everyone ultimately a winner?

In a market system, the purpose of many of our social institutions is to encourage and facilitate competition. In a free society, it is argued, competition among people with energy and ability, anxious to better themselves both socially and financially, will ultimately prove a boon for society as a whole.

Is this view valid? Like many social and economic propositions, this one is illuminated by psychology—and, we shall argue, is shown to be doubtful. Herman Wouk once wrote that what matters is to live with honor, with dignity and without fear, in a way that best honors one's birth and one's intelligence.[25] The way competitive natures can come into sharp conflict with the universal goals of honor, dignity, and freedom from fear is the subject of the next chapter.

Does Survival of the Fittest Fit Us for Survival? Toward a Theory of Competition and Contention

"HE that wrestles with us," Edmund Burke observed, "strengthens our reserves and sharpens our skill. Our antagonist is our helper."[1] Herbert Spencer agreed. He coined the phrase "survival of the fittest" as a capsule description of Darwin's theory of evolution and applied the theory to the evolution of societies, and even of ideas.[2]

The economic paradigm of survival of the fittest is the spirited competition among people and firms operating in free markets. Just as nature selects the species best adapted to survive and reproduce, so markets select the most efficient producers, leaving those less worthy without customers or profits or the most valuable goods. What results, it is argued, is a tough, trim society that makes the most of its resources. In the human jungle, perhaps the race is not always to the swiftest, nor the battle to the strong—but, Damon Runyan said, that is the way to lay your dough.

The concept of Darwinian competition, when applied to human society, has won everything from fulsome praise (Henry Clay: "Of all human powers operating on the affairs of mankind, none is greater.") to bitter criticism (Friedrich Engels: "The most extreme expression of that war of all against all which dominates modern middle-class society."). In this chapter, we contend that competition is a far more complex and destructive type of behavior than economic theory claims. In many social contexts, coordination and cooperation are vital, we argue; but we pick for our leaders precisely those who spurn cooperation, even when freely offered. What results is a contentious, divisive society whose economic games are dominated by values inimical to our well-being and perhaps even to our very survival.

YOSSARIAN'S DILEMMA

The Scottish poet Robert Burns yearned for the power "the giftie gie us to see oursels as others see us!" It would, Burns wrote, "frae monie a blunder free us, an' foolish notion."[3] It may be a good thing that our self-perceptions are tinseled. Perhaps Burns ought to have asked instead for the power to see *others* as they really are. There is evidence that we do not and commit serious blunders as a consequence. Most of this evidence is based on how people behave in a type of game known as *Prisoner's Dilemma*.

Prisoner's Dilemma is a "mixed-motive" game, one in which there exists both opportunities for cooperation (mutual gain) and enticements of competition (gain at others' expense). Its name comes from the dilemma facing two lawbreakers who are arrested and separately questioned. If each remains silent, they are acquitted. If one turns state's evidence, he is lightly punished, while his accomplice gets a heavy sentence. But neither prisoner knows for sure what the other will do.

Some economic games embody only conflict, for example, zero-sum games, where contestants divide up a fixed sum and one player's gain is precisely equal to the other players' losses. Other games are devoid of conflict; all players gain or lose together. In most social contexts, both elements—conflict and cooperation—are present in varying degrees and mixtures. It is a matter of utmost importance to our economy and society how people relate to this mixed game structure, which ultimately turns upon how people relate to one another.

Mixed-motive games arise in a wide variety of places and situations. They are a major focus of interest in many disciplines other than psychology or economics. Biology analyzes the ecology of free resources—in Garrett Hardin's phrases, the "tragedy of the commons"—where individual rationality leads to overconsumption and premature depletion. Political science is concerned with "free-rider" problems, in which individuals enjoy public services but fail to pay their share of the cost. Regional science deals with "spillovers"—a context in which city governments provide benefits that spill over municipal borders and are enjoyed by the untaxèd. Legal scholars study the proper assignment of liability when one person gains at others' expense. Each discipline has its own assumptions, framework, language, and solutions. These differences sometimes obscure the fact that the basic underlying structure of the problem is identical.

Prisoner's dilemmas arise in a great many different contexts in society. In Joseph Heller's novel, *Catch-22*, Yossarian justifies his refusal to fly any more combat missions in the same way the "prisoner" justifies "squealing" on his accomplice.

"I don't want to fly milk runs. I don't want to be in the war any more."

"Would you like to see our country lose?" Major Major asked.

"We won't lose . . . Some people are getting killed and a lot more are making money and having fun. Let somebody else get killed."

"But suppose everybody on our side felt that way."

"Then I'd certainly be a damned fool to feel any other way. Wouldn't I?"[4]

A clerical error over a $7.50 bill once brought us the following letter from a collection agency: "We don't wish to jeopardize your credit standing, but the interests of the other customers who must bear the extra cost of your non-payment must come first." An unscrupulous deadbeat might be persuaded by the letter to continue to welch, reasoning like Yossarian, that (a) either other people bear costs rightly mine, in which case I profit, or else (b) other people welch, too, in which case I would be foolish not to do the same.

There are many economic situations in which the seemingly logical, rational behavior for an individual is to "let the other person do it." Hard, concentrated work? Let someone else do it. If he does, I exploit him. If he doesn't and I do, he is exploiting me. Inflation? Let others cut back on their spending. Unemployment? Let others step up their purchases. Taxes? Let others pay the full amount while I cheat.

The general structure of the "let the other person do it" dilemma is shown in figure 2.1. Suppose a group of individuals must each choose between "competitive" behavior—letting others work hard, fly milk runs, pay true income tax, while picking the diametric opposite oneself—or "cooperative" behavior—shouldering one's fair share of the burden. Competitive behavior dominates. Two fundamental human motives underlie the dilemma: greed for gain through exploiting others, and fear of loss through being exploited. Each motive alone is destructive. Together, they create a "let others do it" society in which not a single "other" does.

Everyone involved in a Prisoner's Dilemma conflict must develop an expectation about the likely responses of other people—whether they will act to exploit or to cooperate for mutual gain. In a society composed of well-meaning people, with good lines of communication among them, why should there be a dilemma at all? Evidence from social psychology points to a persistent error or bias in what people tend to expect from others, a bias that works against cooperation.

An important area of research in psychology is that of "attribution theory," which is concerned with "at-

	Others	
	Cooperate	Compete
Me Cooperate	Good Neighbors 2nd Best	They Exploit Me 4th Best
Me Compete	I Exploit Them 1st Best	Mutual Damage 3rd Best

Figure 2.1 Prisoner's Dilemma

This is a game in which what is rational for the individual and what is best for society collide head-on. Each player reasons: if others "cooperate," it is best for me to "compete," since that enables me to exploit them; if others "compete," it is best for me to "compete," to *avoid* being exploited. When everyone thinks this way, out of fear and greed, the outcome is next-to-worst. (The numbers show how the four outcomes are ranked by "me," from best [1st] to worst [4th].)

tempts of ordinary people to understand the causes and implications of the events they witness."[5] Some of the earliest work done revealed what Lee Ross and Craig Anderson term "the fundamental attribution error": in our attempts to understand why people behave as they do, we attribute far too much to disposition and human nature and far too little to the situation people are in.[6] In other words: observers tend to presume wrongly that people do what they *want* rather than what they *must*, against their disposition, because of the context of their behavior. For instance, advertising endorsements by athletes and movie stars are built on attribution error; even when people *know* that the endorsers have been well paid, that their words have been written by copywriters, and that the product may not even be used by the person supposedly praising it, it is still believed that Wilfred Beanpole would shrivel and die without his Flimzee basketball shoes.

BLIND EYE OF COMPETITORS

A striking instance of attribution error, one with important social and economic implications, was discovered by Harold Kelley and Anthony Stahelski.[7] They observed people playing a *Prisoner's Dilemma* game like the one in figure 2.1. Before doing this, they classified the subjects into two groups: "cooperators" who "will try to cooperate with the other player and will be concerned with my own score *and* the other player's score"; and "competitors" who "will work for myself, against the other player, and will be concerned *only* with my own score."[8] People were paired off in different combinations: cooperative versus cooperative, cooperative versus competitive, and competitive versus competitive. A series of games was played. Then play was interrupted, and subjects were asked for their judgments of their opponent's objectives. Kelley and Stahelski found:

1. Competitors wrongly assume all their opponents are also competitors, even when they play as cooperators.

2. Cooperators accurately label their opponents as competitors or cooperators.

Competitors tended to misjudge the goals their opponents had at the outset, when they were cooperative. Persistence of this misperception locks the game outcome into the "next-to-worst" cell for both players. Cooperators varied their behavior according to their opponents, making cooperative moves when playing with someone with similar goals, and more competitive goals when faced with a competitor.

This perception bias is a special case of the fundamental attribution error mentioned earlier. Competitors play "compete" moves time after time, observe that their opponents begin to do the same, and attribute this result not to the *structure* of the game (which makes a "cooperate" response to "compete" moves a heavy loser) but in fact to the *disposition* of the player, perceiving the latter to be disposed to competitiveness. This expectation frustrates a possible joint shift to "cooperate." Kelley and Stahelski call this theory the "triangle hypothesis" (see figure 2.2). Replication of their experiments in different countries—the United States, Belgium, France, and the Netherlands—suggests that the phenomenon it describes is global.

THE CONTENTIOUS SOCIETY

The triangle hypothesis is useful for building a theory of why our society has become increasingly factious and contentious.

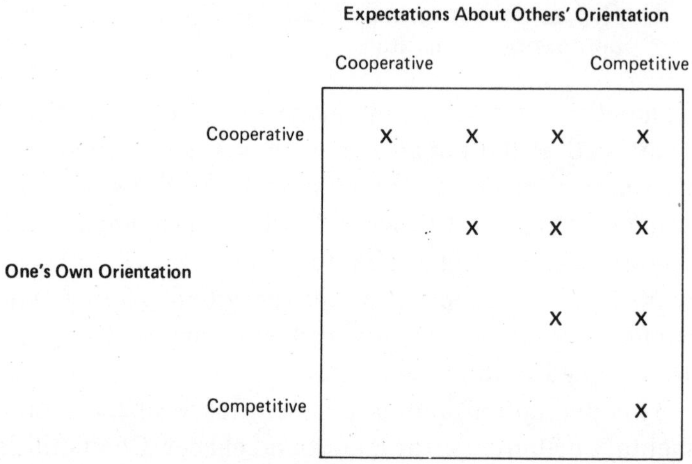

Expectations About Others' Orientation

	Cooperative			Competitive
Cooperative	X	X	X	X
		X	X	X
			X	X
Competitive				X

One's Own Orientation

Figure 2.2 The Triangle Hypothesis
Cooperative people see others as they are: cooperative or competitive. Competitive people see others as competitive, whatever their behavior or true orientation.

Every organization has within its folds a wide variety of human beings, ranging from those who are fiercely competitive to those who are benevolently cooperative. Those most likely to rise to the top of an organization—a union, corporation, or even government—are those who are most competitive. In the battle for control, they consistently exploit the cooperative behavior of their peers. Group choice is known to be riskier than individual behavior; when groups choose leaders, they are thus more likely to pick ruthless competitors who profess extreme policies that promise both large risk and large gain. Neville Chamberlain was a cooperator; note his fate. His replacement, Winston Churchill, was a competitor. In unions, competitive leaders with militant demands appeal to union members more than moderate cooperative types. In corporations, c.e.o. [chief executive officer] is spelled c-o-m-p-e-t-e. In politics, especially in the U.S. presidential race, only tough competitors last out the long grind from the Maine straw poll and the New Hampshire primary to the first Tuesday in November.

An example of competitiveness is a recent takeover of a large bakery company, after what *Business Week* termed "one of the bitterest proxy fights in recent history."[9] The successful competitor was a thirty-three-year-old former commodities trader without experience in the industry, who incurred a personal debt of $5 million in order to gain control of the $500 million company by paying an interest bill which, by his account, was "twice his annual salary." His business plans for the company were not much different from those of the incumbent he ousted. Is this an example of free enterprise, of what Andrew Carnegie called the "survival of the fittest in every department" or of Henry Ford, the "keen cutting edge of business?" Or is it what the World Council of Churches termed "the embodiment of primeval selfishness?" In a world where otherwise qualified people are unwilling or unable to incur $5 million in a personal debt, the burly herd may get the firm.

In general, the fact that society consistently selects those who are most competitive and places them at the head of its institutions has negative implications for our long-run well-being. The fittest—those seeking cooperation and compromise—do not survive. The least fit, those who persist in competitive behavior, dominate. The result: needless prolonged strikes, wasteful profusion of brands and products, and even international strife where none is called for. According to Edmund

Phelps's catalogue, you get unsafe factories and unsafe products, bad debts, discrimination, gouging, extortion, and short-weighing.[10] Churchill was a great boon in his time, but the free world is not currently at war.

If it is true that divisive, polarized societies are weaker than cohesive, purposeful ones, then by Herbert Spencer's Darwinian logic, such societies should eventually disappear. We may well be observing such a process now unfolding on a global scale, as Mancur Olson has so persuasively shown.[11] Olson reasoned that the older a nation grows, the more socially destructive opportunities arise for one group to gain at the expense of another—and the more people there are who are eager to take advantage of these opportunities. In the very long run, such societies may vanish, but extinction is not a remedy with much appeal for those doomed to it.

EGOISTS, OR ALTRUISTS?

According to the economic theory of the "invisible hand," a collection of self-centered competitors striving for personal gain generates infinitely more wealth than a group of soft-hearted altruists each concerned with others' welfare. Not all economists believe that theory is appropriate for the twentieth century. Nobel laureate Kenneth Arrow said, "every commercial transaction has within itself an element of trust. . . . it can be plausibly argued that much of the economic backwardness in the world can be explained by the lack of mutual confidence."[12]

Does Survival of the Fittest Fit Us for Survival?

How, then, can society transform itself? The process of fostering trust is a difficult one. Psychologist Morton Deutsch, who has made detailed studies of altruism and cooperation, argues that "competitive and cooperative processes . . . tend to be self-confirming, so that the experience of cooperation will induce a benign spiral of increasing cooperation, while competition will induce a vicious spiral of intensifying competition."[13] We now seem stuck in the latter spiral. Economists regard people's tastes, desires, and perceptions as sacrosanct; but, perhaps we should consider investing resources to alter people's orientations from competitive to cooperative[14]—or, alternately, revise our social contract (see chapter 12).

Up to this point, we have tried to show the negative side of competition and competitiveness in largely abstract terms. We now turn to a more concrete expression of competition's negative by-products: economic games where rivalry among the players can make all of them worse off, and where cooperation could make all of them better off. Take, for instance, the game in figure 2.3, which we call *Winning Isn't the Main Thing*. On the face of it, this is a game with a total absence of conflict. The dominant (best in every case) strategy is "cooperate." If people act rationally and choose their dominant strategy, everyone gets his first best outcome. But suppose that for players, "winning" means to get more *relative to other players.* Such players, on the presumption that everyone else continues to play "cooperate," will pick "compete" to exploit others and gain a relative advantage. When everyone acts this way, everyone gets his worst possible outcome. In the long run, society may reform itself; but in the long run, we are all dead. With everyone choosing "compete," the game becomes *After You, Garçon* (see chapter 4); each person wants the other to be first to switch to "cooperate." Stubborn players, who believe winning isn't the main thing but the *only* thing, may remain stuck in the rut of intransigence for a very long time.

But isn't it possible that the desires of altruists and cooperators may also collide, with negative consequences for society? Indeed, there is even an altruist's dilemma, similar to *Prisoner's Dilemma.* Suppose that on a crowded commuter train, someone gets off and a seat becomes vacant. Two altruists offer it to each

		Others	
		Cooperate	Compete
Me	Cooperate	Best for All	3rd Best for Me 2nd Best for Others
	Compete	2nd Best for me 3rd Best for Others	Worst for All

Figure 2.3 Winning Isn't the Main Thing

This game is ostensibly devoid of conflict; the dominant strategy for everyone is to "cooperate." However, when players seek to maximize the *gap* between their payoff and that of others, they may be tempted to switch to "compete." The result: the worst of all outcomes, when everyone believes that winning isn't the main thing but the *only* thing.

other—two *stubborn* altruists. If neither sits down, they are both worse off than if one gives in.

Altruism and cooperation can at times be complicated; if not properly coordinated, the results can be unfavorable, as O. Henry shows in his famous short story, "The Gift of the Magi."

GIFT OF THE MAGI

Jim and Della each want to buy the other a special Christmas present. Della has only $1.87, 60¢ of which in pennies. Jim is flat broke.

Della cuts off her beautiful long hair and sells it (unbeknownst to Jim) to buy a new chain for Jim's proudest possession, a watch.

Jim sells his watch to buy Della fancy combs for her long hair.

They exchange presents on Christmas Day, with ironic results.

The question is: Which society would you prefer, one made up of Jims and Dellas or one comprised wholly of those who act and play like all-pro center linebackers, both on and off the field? In which society are messes less pernicious or easier to untangle?

BE NICE, BE FORGIVING

Recently, political scientist Robert Axelrod organized an unusual tournament.[15] The game was *Prisoner's Dilemma*. The fourteen entrants were computer programs designed to select "compete" or "cooperate" moves; 200

41

rounds were played. The payoff matrix awarded three points for mutual cooperation and one point for mutual defection; and when one program played "cooperate" and the other "compete," the cooperator got zero and the defector got five points. The winning program was Anatol Rapoport's TIT FOR TAT, which averaged 504 points (perpetual cooperation yields a score of $200 \times 3 = 600$; perpetual competition yields $200 \times 1 = 200$). TIT FOR TAT begins with "cooperate" and thereafter copies what the opponent has done on the previous move. TIT FOR TAT believes that once spurned, twice wary. Cooperative behavior meets cooperation; competitive behavior is greeted by the same.

According to Axelrod, a single property distinguishes high-scoring programs: the top eight, which scored 472 or above, were "nice," meaning that none of them was the first to defect (play "compete" when the opponent plays "cooperate"). None of the bottom six was "nice." "It is remarkable," Axelrod concludes, "that a single property would so clearly separate the successful rules from the unsuccessful ones. At least in this tournament, it paid to be nice."[16] The property that largely accounted for the ranking of the top eight was "forgiveness"—the extent to which a defection by the opponent is forgiven, or punished. TIT FOR TAT punishes defection, but only once, thus preventing vindictive "lock-ins" on competitive moves.

In society, competitive people play TAT NOW AND FOREVER and are unlikely to be either "nice" or "forgiving." Both their own scores and those of their opponents are likely to be low. When one player locks on "compete," an opponent who may be cooperative and who plays TIT FOR TAT also locks on "compete." An outside observer watching the game would not be able to tell the players apart. Moreover, when many players are involved, the presence of just one die-hard competitor can in some cases lock society into near-to-worst results. The tournament revealed "subtle reasons for the individual pragmatist to be nice, forgiving, and optimistic," Axelrod concluded.[17] It is an open question why social norms deviate significantly and substantially from these qualities.

BENIGN ERRORS

Not all misperceptions of others' intentions or game structures are malignant. Some are benign, or even positively benevolent. Arthur Stein uses the Cuban missile crisis as an example. The Russians put missiles in Cuba on the assumption that the United States would capitulate, but they were prepared to withdraw them, he notes, if the United States was ready to launch an air strike. This is a version of a game known as *Chicken,* or *Brinkmanship,* where each side prefers to capitulate rather than to engage in mutual destruction but would rather bluff the other side into capitulation first (see chapter 11). If we assume that the United States was not in fact prepared to go to war, the ultimate Russian misperception that America *was* so prepared led to withdrawal of the missiles. In this case, Stein argues, "deception facilitates the avoidance of conflict rather than exacerbates the possibility of its occurrence." The Soviet misperception facilitated de-escalation.[18] While misperceptions may be benign, counting on them for society's survival itself is a kind of misperception. If and when players begin seeing misperceived games and opponents as they really are, the consequences could be unpleasant, or worse.

CONCLUSION

We have argued that in modern society, survival of the fittest is not always the most fitting for our survival. We place our fate in the hands of those who perceive the world like football coaches. In this century, Edmund Burke's maxim needs shortening; those who wrestle with us—shouldn't. And the setting in which the presence of cooperation and altruism or their absence is most strongly felt is that of the family. Members of families, too, play economic games whose outcomes are complex and fascinating. We now turn to this topic.

PART II

Families

What is one's country but one's family on a large scale?

Horace Walpole

CHAPTER 3

The Nation as Household: Games Families Play

WHAT IS A FAMILY? Carson McCullers's nine-letter definition is "the we of me." Every individual in society has attributes unique to himself—the "me" part. Within the bounds of habit, custom, and law, these personal characteristics reveal themselves in the economic games that people play. At the same time, every member of society has links and allegiances with other people, ranging from family ties through memberships in professional organizations, unions, service clubs, and religious groups up to fealty to the nation itself. These bonds are the "we" part.

Like ripples in a pond, our group allegiances begin close to the center, in the family setting, and extend in widening circles until they embrace our national borders.[1] The theme of this book is the tension between the "we" and the "me" as expressed and resolved in commonplace economic games played by small, medium, and large numbers of players.

More than any other social institution, the family is best suited for revealing the causes and nature of the "we" versus "me" tension for at least three reasons.

First, families are microcosms for whole nations, as Walpole said two centuries ago.[2] Many games played within families have the same inner structure as games played by business, labor, and government. Gregory Bateson used the phrase "the infinite dance of shifting coalitions" to describe unstable families,[3] but it could equally apply to a great many other games played in wider frameworks.

Family researchers David Kantor and William Lehr invented the term "psychopolitics of family life" to describe the relation between the interior person (the psyche) and the politics of family interaction.[4] The psychopolitics of family life is similar to the intrigues of corporate life or the political economy of interest groups. Political philosophers like Hobbes, Locke, and Rousseau wrote about how individuals give up some of their rights to the state as part of a social contract. Family therapists such as Jay Haley, Lynn Hoffman, Virginia Satir, Don Jackson, and Gregory Bateson have closely studied how individual family members concede certain rights as part of a family social contract, or in some cases, refuse to do so. There is a good deal of similarity between family and polity.

Second, families are "schools" where people are socialized and first learn how to get along with others. How people learn to adjust and adapt to one another from childhood within the family circle has a decisive effect on how well these same people will later relate to their spouses, friends, neighbors, and peers in later life, in offices, factories, and boardrooms.

Finally, families are literally firms that produce tangible and spiritual goods and services and distribute them among family members. Family games generate happiness or misery and divide them up among the players. How smoothly and fairly this is done has a direct bearing on our national wealth and well-being.

This chapter will explore the three faces of the family—as metaphor, school, and firm—as expressed in economic games. We shall show that the same factors that make families strong make whole nations strong. Then in the next chapter, we will reverse the family-as-firm metaphor and ask how our understanding of successful, healthy families can help us build successful, healthy firms.

FAMILY COMES FIRST

Statistics showing the alleged breakup of family life are plentiful.

- Between 1960 and 1980, divorce rates more than doubled.[5]
- One household in five has only one person in it.[6]
- Of marriages that take place in this decade between a third and a half will end in divorce.[7] A similar fraction of remarriages will also be dissolved.[8]

Some interpret these statistics as proving that the role of the family in our lives has become increasingly less important, or even that the family is now becoming obsolete. Increased willingness to dissolve marriages and disrupt family life, or even give it up altogether, must be conclusive evidence that the importance of families to people has sunk to a low level.

Contrary to these and the above statistics, however, is evidence showing that to a large majority of people, family life is as important as ever—perhaps even more so. Polls taken during the 1970s—the decade when divorce rates may have peaked—show that egoistic goals such as "a fulfilling career," "opportunity to develop as an individual," and "making a lot of money" trailed far behind "a happy family life" as the "most important life goal."[9] A 1982 Gallup poll asked people to rate a series of items according to their importance. Respondents gave scores to each item ranging from 0 (extremely unimportant) to 10 (extremely important). "Having a good family life" topped the poll, with 82 percent of the respondents scoring it a 10 or a 9. "Being in good physical health" (81 percent), "personal happiness or satisfaction" (77 percent), and "having a high income" (37 percent) trailed behind. The primacy of a "good family life" held across most age, race, and sex cross-sections.[10]

But what generates happy family life? What is its most important ingredient? Research by family therapists suggests it is "intimacy."

Every economy needs inputs—labor, capital, energy, and raw materials—to combine to produce goods and services, and their value is measured in the gross national product. "Intimacy" is one "product" every society needs which escapes the national accounts entirely.[11] Judging from the poll results just cited, the quantities of intimacy that society produces may be as crucial to our happiness and security as the $3 trillion of output the economy produces each year. The task of the family, one that no other institution can fulfill, is to provide "an orderly access to intimacy," Lynn Hoffman has noted.[12] People still clearly recognize that the family's production and distribution of intimacy is as critically important to their well-being today as it was in the past. The family is our social envelope, as one researcher put it, as important for individual survival as amniotic fluid is to the unborn child.[13]

Paradoxically, a major reason for the breakdown of so many families is *not* because family life is considered of no importance by its members, but because family life becomes *excessively* important. With one American in five changing residence at least across a county line every year,[14] with the mindless impersonality of the assembly line or office, and with the decline in organized religion, the family bond has become for many people the sole source of solace, friendship, support, and love. No wonder some families break apart under this weight. Marriage was never intended to carry that heavy a load unaided, William Ouchi wrote, and indeed it cannot.[15] God sets the solitary in families, the Psalmist wrote.[16] But perhaps He did not intend families as our sole line of defense against loneliness and isolation.

Family life is far from obsolete. To the contrary—like the strongest of a team of draft horses, it is pulling more than its fair share of the strains of modern life. Since from families and their games we can learn much about how larger, more impersonal groups can improve their access to intimacy, family games can show society how conflict among members of small and large groups can best be resolved. "The family is one system that transcends the limits of a single person," Lynn Hoffman wrote, "yet is small and clearly bounded enough to serve as a researchable unit."[17]

CLOSE LINES . . . OR FAR

The family that plays together, stays together—or, flies apart, depending upon the games it plays, how it plays them, and who sets and enforces the rules. Observers of families have found it useful to watch how families, both happy and troubled ones, play simple games like the *Train Game,* described below, and *Clothesline.* The latter is an unusual game devised by Virginia Satir,[18] and like *Dollar Auction,* described in chapter 1, and the *Nuts Game,* described later on, you can try it for yourself.

CLOTHESLINE

This game is meant for members of a family of, say, five. Each player needs four twenty-foot lengths of clothesline. A player ties each length of line to his waist with a shorter piece of rope, then hands the end to another player who then ties it to *his* waist. After exchanging rope ends and tying them, each person should be fastened to every other person by two twenty-foot ropes.

Do the following experiments:

1. Thirty feet away, the phone rings. The eldest child answers it.

2. Mother smells something burning on the stove and moves to turn it off.

3. Two children begin to wrestle.

4. Think of an important event about to occur in the family, or an everyday situation that causes problems. Act it out with the ropes still fastened.

People do not run around all day fastened to each other with ropes, Virginia Satir notes. The links among us are fashioned of love, care, duty, and comfort—less visible, but certainly more significant than ties made of sisal and hemp. One purpose of *Clothesline* is to improve communication. Players are asked to say what they feel while entangled. The objective is to teach family members how to engage in "straight, clear and full communication" when they are entangled and intertwined by conflicting interests, desires, and goals, rather than by clotheslines.[19] Family therapists strongly emphasize the crucial role of communication among family members, a result that transfers directly to communication within corporations, as the research and development games in the next chapter show.

Clothesline contains some instructive mathematics. Two players need only two lines. Three players need six (3 × 2). In general, N players need $(N)(N-1)$ lines. This is because each of the N players requires one line to fasten to $(N-1)$ other persons. When N is a large number, the total number of lines required is very close to the square of N. This implies a kind of Newton's law of interpersonal relations. Newton proved that the pull of gravity exerted by a body varies directly with the mass of that body. The law of interpersonal relations says that for a group of people, the potential number of links among the members varies directly with the square of the number of people in the group.

In other words, the potential ties between an individual and other people grow much faster than the size of the group. This law can work to the group's advantage when it is used constructively to generate intimacy, or to its disadvantage when each person tugs on his ropes irregardless of how many others are made to stumble and fall.

Newton also proved that the pull of gravity varies inversely with the square of the distance between two bodies. Generally, the larger the group, the greater the average physical or mental distance among its members. The question then arises, as the size of a group increases: Does not the *distance* effect (the increasing impersonality of interpersonal ties) overwhelm or offset the *numbers* effect (which expands the total number of such ties)? We suggest it does not. Stanley Milgram once conducted a "small-world" experiment. He asked people in the Midwest to pass envelopes on to people assigned as "targets" in New England. Only people whom those in the Midwest knew personally could be used as links. Milgram's results showed that linking Kansas farmers with Massachusetts clergymen required a remarkably small number of intermediaries.[20] Interactions among people weaken far less with "distance" than does the pull of gravity between planets. As a result, a family, firm, or entire nation that believes or pretends it is playing *Do Your Own Thing,* when it is in fact playing *Clothesline,* will end up tangled in a

Gordian knot that not even Alexander the Great's
sword could unravel.

CLOSELY WATCHED TRAINS

Whereas in *Clothesline,* frictions among family members are incidental to the performance of individual
tasks (being mainly a game of coordination), in many
family games, clashes arise out of direct conflicts of interest. This is demonstrated by the *Train Game,* Robert
Ravich's game designed to be played by married couples. (A similar, though more complex, game was devised by Morton Deutsch to study conflict and cooperation among persons not tied by marriage or blood.[21]) He
used it to identify three distinct patterns of relations between two people. This game is directly applicable to
economic games and leads to an interesting, pointed
conclusion.[22]

TRAIN GAME

Two players each have toy trains going in opposite directions. One section of track is passable for only one train at
a time. There is an alternate route, which is longer. Neither
person can see the other's side of the board. Each player can
lower a gate that blocks the opponent's access to the short,
direct route. Train wrecks can, and do, occur.

The payoff is determined by how long it takes *both* players
to get their trains to their destination.

Ravich found three distinct patterns:

- Competitive: each player, to gain the most for himself, tries to inflict maximum damage on the opponent
- Dominant-submissive or solo altruism: one spouse habitually lets the other take the short route while taking the longer one for himself
- Cooperative: both players take polite turns in using the direct route

Competitive players got predictably low scores in comparison to altruistic or cooperative ones; in games and in life, head-on collisions are expensive.

Ravich discovered, somewhat surprisingly, that marriages of competitive players were not more rancorous or less stable than marriages of cooperative or altruistic players. Many games are not primarily an end toward achieving some goal or prize, but rather are a means of facilitating communication among the players. Ravich suggests that people who are competitors may get low scores, but they are at least in direct contact with their counterparts. On the other hand, ritualized submission or "first you-then me" patterns of playing the *Train Game* often reflected ways couples used for avoiding communication with one another. For firms, as for families, poor internal communications can be very destructive, as we try to show in chapter 4.

EARTH AS A NUT BOWL

In the previous chapter, we used *Prisoner's Dilemma* as a common game that has elements of both cooperation and competition. One version of *Prisoner's Dilemma* is psychologist Julian Edney's *Nuts Game.* This game has not, to our knowledge, been used in a family setting. It is, however, appropriate for examining the efficacy of selfish and selfless behavior in economic games that families—and society as a whole—play.[23]

NUTS GAME

Three or more players sit around a shallow open bowl containing ten hardwood nuts. After the timed game begins, each player can take nuts from the bowl, at any time and in any quantity. The goal is to get as many nuts as possible. After each 10-second interval, the number of nuts in the bowl is automatically doubled from an outside source. The game continues for a preset period, or until the bowl is emptied by the players.

The bowl symbolizes a resource pool, and the nuts, the resources themselves. (The nuts are given value by the subjects exchanging them for money or credit.) Each nut that is taken depletes future resources. Edney reported that "approximately 65 per cent of groups never in practice reach the first replenishment stage because they exhaust the pool by taking all the nuts out in the first few moments of the game."[24] As with *Prisoner's Dilemma,* the narrowly viewed, individually rational strategy is to grab fast and first, both to keep from being left with nothing if others do, and to exploit others if they do not; when all do this, the game comes to an abrupt end, and the cupboard of the future is left bare.

We surmise that families—especially strong, well-integrated ones—play the *Nuts Game* more successfully than strangers or even acquaintances. The reason is that for family well-being, altruism is functional and efficient. We shall shortly make use of the *Nuts Game* to explain why this is true.

GAME TYPES AND PEOPLE TYPES

The *Train Game,* the *Nuts Game,* and perhaps, in a limited sense, even *Clothesline* all exemplify a broad class of economic games known as "non-zero-sum." Unlike zero-sum games, where the sum of players' gains and losses always equals zero, these games have a small or large positive increment that accrues to players provided they can cooperate, or at least refrain from destructive competition.

In the previous chapter, we suggested that competitively-oriented people tend to rise to the top of organizations like corporations, unions and government, and that when such people play non-zero-sum economic games, the result may be mutual destruction, with society as a whole a loser. There are, however, many kinds of economic games, including some where fierce rivalry is socially profitable. Professional sports—now a major economic industry—is an example. Close, hard-fought games between motivated teams boost spectator attendance and enjoyment. But even in sports, game structures are mixed; inter-team rivalry and competition are functional, but effective team play by definition requires close intra-team cooperation among players.

At any given moment, a great many kinds of economic games are in progress being played by an equally large number of different types of players. The question we turn to now is: Can anything be said about the efficiency of particular *types* of players—competitive, cooperative, or altruistic—in producing collective well-being, *irregardless* of the nature of the economic games in progress?

In the economic games we play, all of us act at various times in three different ways, depending on the game context, the prize, and our partners and opponents: as *fierce competitors* out to achieve more than other people, even if this means getting less in absolute terms for all players; as *cooperative egoists* concerned only with our own winnings, but reasonably so, and willing to join with others if there are chances for mutual gain; and as *altruists* whose own personal welfare is improved when other people are made better off. It is probably possible, at considerable cost and effort, to sort people according to which of the three types they predominantly fit. This leads to an interesting speculative question: If three equally endowed societies were set up, each inhabited by a single type of person—competitor, egoist, or altruist—and if sufficient time were allowed to pass to permit each society to develop its own norms and institutions and to settle into a pattern of daily existence, which society would ultimately be wealthier, healthier, and more stable?

In the real world, every society is made up of all three types of people, as well as of people who defy categorization or embody all three types. This is fortunate. A totally homogeneous society would likely be boring, rigid, and stagnant. Still, one can try to identify which *tendency* of the three contributes most toward a well-functioning society. Since a three-society horse race is impractical to organize, even conceptually, it is possible to adopt an alternate approach—to treat the family as a microcosm of society and to study interactions among family members who are competitors, egoists, or altruists.

Within the family setting, presence of at least a minimal amount of altruism appears to be crucial. If it is present, it acts as a kind of catalyst that alters the behavior of egoists toward benevolence and thoughtfulness toward others. If it is absent, it leads to economic games that degenerate into rancor and malevolence.

And in the next section, we provide a relatively rare instance in which economic reasoning has been applied to the psychology of behavior that exhibits care and concern for other people's well-being.

THE ECONOMICS OF LOVE

A growing number of economists are becoming convinced that the models and methods of psychology must be enlisted if we are to understand fully economic phenomena. Conversely, a small number of economists have adapted economic tools and theories to illuminate social and behavioral issues. Foremost among these is Gary Becker of the University of Chicago. He has used the basic economic model of interdependent individuals whose happiness depends on how much they spend, save, study, and work, within the limits of their resources and abilities, to analyze noneconomic decisions about marriage, divorce, and family size. Lately, he has turned his attention to the family and enunciated and proved a theorem about family behavior that has important implications for other social groups.[25] His theorem states:

> Within the family, the presence of an altruist who can deal out material rewards or penalties has the effect of making all other family members *behave* altruistically toward one another, no matter how selfish or "rotten" they are.

Becker calls this interpretation of family behavior the "Rotten Kid" theorem,[26] and it stands in sharp contrast to economics' "survival of the fittest" theorem. The latter theorem holds that the cupidity and egoism of self-interested individuals, minimally constrained by bonds of law and custom, work to create the wealthiest of societies, if not the most just. However, Becker still affirms survival of the fittest for competing *firms*. It was Adam Smith who enunciated that view first and best in 1776: "it is not from the benevolence of the butcher, the brewer, or the baker, that we expect our dinner, but from their regard to their own self-interest."[27]

To illustrate the theorem, suppose we arrange for a family—a father, mother, and two children—to play the *Nuts Game*. Family therapy theorists take into account the important point that families, unlike groups of strangers, have both a past and a future as well as a present. Mutual trust developed over the past and mutual dependence likely to stretch far into the future work to moderate narrowly egoistic behavior in symbolic games within families. Indeed, family ties and history tend to convert every game into what game theo-

61

Reach Out and Touch Someone

Plato drew a distinction between the moral rightness of a deed, determined only by the act itself, and whether the deed was "good" or "bad" determined also by the motive of the person doing it. The behavioral definition of altruism is acting to help others. Most of us would agree that altruistic behavior is right. Suppose we act altruistically purely because it gives us pleasure. Is this not just another form of selfishness, Platonically right, but bad? Is not a *true* altruist someone who, paradoxically, helps others though he suffers in doing so?

While philosophers debate the issue, advertising agencies act upon it. One of the most brilliant and successful advertising campaigns is Bell Telephone's "Reach Out and Touch Someone" theme, designed to encourage long-distance calls and built on the message that altruism is fun. Here is how one of its architects, Fred McClafferty, explained it:

> I suppose there's a small element of guilt in some of our advertising, but we try to keep it pretty light. . . . What we try to do is keep the obligation level very light, and, of course, artistic, and relate it to an upbeat, positive theme. I think this was especially true in the way the creative people handled the . . . concept of mutual reward—meaning that a long-distance phone call should be rewarding both to the person called *and* to the person who makes the call. I think this was something of a stride forward in our philosophy, because up to then our advertising had generally implied that the reward factor was obtained mainly by the person called. You should call your mother because *she'll* feel good. What we hadn't really considered until the [advertising] task force called our attention to it was that by calling your mother *you'll* feel good also. So,

> armed with this knowledge of mutual reward, we've been able to introduce an element of obligation into our new campaign, but with a definitely positive side to it: *you* gain and *she* gains. I think it's one of the reasons our commercials have such a happy tone to them.[28]

rists call supergames—played repeatedly forever—and metagames—where players pick strategies in full knowledge of what other players intend to do.[29]

Let family members begin drawing nuts from the bowl. As Edney reported, the sanctions of nature work to limit excessive egoism. By the rules of the *Nuts Game*, the number of nuts in the bowl is doubled every so often. "If I take one nut *now*, I may deprive myself of two nuts available *later.*" In this sense in the *Nuts Game*, each player plays not only against other players but also against *himself.* Ability to defer gratification acts as the internal arbiter; with nature doubling its riches from time to time, the powers of two are the game's constitution.

This "now-or-later" game, however, is usually overwhelmed by the overlapping game of "them-or-me." A nut foregone now may *not* necessarily generate two nuts later, if someone else takes that nut first. Underlying "them-or-me" is mutual trust or suspicion. If distrust dominates, even the explosive profit of exponential growth—ten doublings yield over a thousand nuts from an initial pair, twenty doublings yield over a million—is unable to overcome short-run greed. As a result, the bowl may quickly be emptied.

Now, suppose one of the players—the head of the family—is an altruist, defined as someone who seeks "to produce, maintain or improve the physical or psychological welfare and integrity of other persons."[30] Suppose also that the *Nuts Game* is played in two stages: (1) the members draw nuts from the bowl and place them in a common pool—the household income; and (2) the family head distributes that income among the members according to a known formula.

Note that the players' incentives to grab nuts from the bowl before the others do is now sharply reduced; "your loss" is no longer "my gain" but "my loss" as well when the bowl is depleted.

For long periods of history, families functioned in this manner, with the family head controlling autocratically the family's production of goods and services and their allocation among family members. In many societies, this is still true. But in order for the family "Nuts Game" to be played fairly and well, it is not necessary to have a totalitarian structure. Let each family member do exactly as he or she wishes in the *Nuts Game*—snatch all the nuts, even grab nuts other people have saved up—and suppose everyone in the family is selfish and thoughtless, except for the head who is an altruist. Suppose also that the head has on hand a stock of nuts which he or she uses to act upon altruistic feelings by bestowing them on other family members. After a round of the *Nuts Game,* one or more family members may be left empty-handed, either through theft or because someone else grabbed faster. The loss of this "poor" member will be a felt loss for the altruistic head, who will then act to redistribute nuts away from those with a lot and toward those with a few—a redistribution favorable to the well-being of altruist and recipient alike, and unfavorable to the egoist, who loses.

The Nation as Household: Games Families Play

In the simplest possible case, let the head of the family frequently redistribute nut wealth so that each family member has exactly one-fourth of the total stock. This rule severely restrains egoistic behavior since it is taxed at rates varying from 75 percent (for grabbing from the bowl) to 100 percent (for taking nuts from other people's piles). Because of the altruist's redistributions, selfish actions that damage total family "income" also harm the egoist who does the actions. One-quarter of a small amount of nuts is inferior to one-quarter of a large amount, even to an egoist. Purely out of self-interest, then, egoists will refrain from such acts and will behave *as if* they sought the well-being of others as well as of themselves. They will not grab excessively nor filch.

In a sense, nature reinforces self-restraint by replenishing the nut resources. We know, however, that a reinforcement remote in time is far weaker than an immediate, palpable reward. The altruistic family head therefore assists nature greatly by reinforcing restraint and punishing greed, at once.

Paradoxically, the principle regarded as a paragon of unworkable, utopian socialism—everyone receives according to need, everyone gives according to ability—turns out to be not only fair but also efficient within the family framework, despite the fact that smashing the link between work and pay supposedly is fatal for efficiency.

For the "Rotten Kid" theorem to work, it is not necessary to assume "socialism." Let all the family members keep all the nuts they take. Suppose now that the family head supplements each person's income with gifts of nuts from his stock. Let one player deplete the bowl by snatching the last three nuts, thus depriving the family of six nuts in the next round. The altruistic head will spread this net loss of family income among the members by reducing his contribution to the egoist by *more* than the three nuts he snatched. The reason is this: by snatching, the egoist has made the family poorer. The altruist wants everyone to share this misfortune and will act to ensure that everyone, *including the egoist,* ends up with fewer than would have been the case had the three nuts been left in the bowl. Crime, the egoist learns, doesn't pay.

In Professor Becker's example, the question is posed: "Would a selfish Tom raise his income by $1,000 if his action would also lower the income of his sister Jane by $1,500" even if nobody in the family knew the source of Jane's misfortune?[31] The answer is no! Tom's action reduces the family income by $500. Therefore, the "consumption" of *both* Jane and Tom, relative to what it was before the misfortune, must, in the eyes of an altruist, be reduced in order to spread the misery evenly. The family head will reduce his subsidy to Tom by more than $1,000 (assuming it exceeded that amount in the first place) while increasing his contribution to Jane by somewhat less than $1,500. Tom will swallow his ego; to do otherwise doesn't pay. Becker's corollary to the "Rotten Kid" theorem is, "Each beneficiary, no matter how envious of other beneficiaries or of his benefactor, would maximize the family income of the benefactor, and hence would help those envied."[32] Both altruist and egoists can gain.

This symbiosis between altruism and egoism is *possible* and represents one path toward mutual cooperation, but it is also fragile. If the family head is not altruistic enough, it may still pay for egoists to reduce family income for their own gain. If the family head is *too* altruistic, egoists may exploit it and act to gain at his or her expense. Family therapists also note the imbalance in a situation where the health of a family rests on the sacrifices of one person (even though those sacrifices may ultimately be profitable for the person making them).

As with any ecological system, balance is vitally important to the health of the family. Ecologist Barry Commoner has set out four principles governing such systems. The last of these is the principle of economic scarcity, "there is no free lunch."[33] The balance of family life works toward, in D. H. Robertson's phrase, "the full but thrifty utilization of that scarce resource Love—which we [economists] know just as well as anybody else to be the most precious thing in the world."[34]

WHAT'S IN IT FOR ME?

A major difficulty in applying economic models like Becker's to family processes is this—in an economic transaction, goods and money change hands in a specified ratio and the deal is presumed to benefit both parties, otherwise it would not take place. In the kind of "social" exchange that takes place within families, one person may help, or harm, another without any immediate *quid pro quo;* the nature of the reciprocation may be unclear, left to some future date, and confined to some vague sort of expectation.

Becker's "Rotten Kid" theorem is based on an altruist making economic transfers. The theorem is much less precise when *social* exchanges alone take place. In the next chapter, we suggest that internally healthy corporations resemble well-functioning families in that altruistic behavior predominates. In firms, as in families, social as well as economic exchanges take place. In interpersonal relations—as opposed to work for pay—social exchange dominates. For altruistic behavior to pay off, it must be reciprocated. This requires a high degree of mutual trust among family members, or corporate employees. When such trust is lacking, as it may be in a collection of corporate or familial egoists, neither a social contract of forbearance nor an altruistic father or chief executive officer may be sufficient.

There is a Chinese saying that the root of the kingdom is in the state; the root of the state is in the family; and the root of the family is in the person of its head. Becker's theorem revolves around the crucial role of the family head. But for it to work, there need not exist in the family an actual altruist head with sweeping powers of redistribution. It is sufficient for family members, however egoistic, to construct an agreement, or social contract, which imposes sanctions upon destructively selfish behavior and awards compensation to persons injured by it. Why would a group of egoists ever devise such a contract, let alone maintain it? Simply because to do so is in their own self-interest. An effective technique used by family therapists is to bring families toward an implicit sort of social contract, a task which is often extremely difficult. This difficulty is magnified manyfold when a whole nation is involved; nonetheless, for nations and families alike, the structure of the problem and its possible solution are quite similar.

An economic system that is both highly equitable and highly efficient—due to harmonious relations among people—is the kibbutz. Albert Einstein, an expert on the most basic of relationships—matter, energy, space, and time—once visited an Israeli kibbutz, the first one in fact, Deganya. "What is the relationship here between men and women?" he asked. "Every man has just one woman," his host replied defensively. No, Einstein explained quickly; what he meant was the *mathematical* relationship, the *ratio* of men to women.[35] What is relevant, however, is the *social* relationships within the kibbutz. The presence of a system for equitably allocating resources among members—with major decisions taken collectively at marathon Saturday-night meetings—leads everybody to work to maximize kibbutz income, even those concerned only with their own personal well-being.

FAMILIES ARE PEOPLE MAKERS

The role of altruism in society has preoccupied geneticists and biologists, as well as psychologists and economists. According to the law of natural selection, a gorilla, an amoeba, a human being, or—in the view of sociobiologists, even a single gene—increases its chances of survival, the more single-mindedly self-serving its behavior. Why altruism is not eliminated by natural selection has been called the central problem of sociobiology.[36]

A response of the social scientist is that environments, as well as genes, are hereditary, and that nature selects the fittest *groups,* not just the toughest individual members of a species. Communities and families with strong internal bonds of love and affection will compete successfully with groups without such bonds. Though many biologists reject the idea of natural selection of groups,[37] the course of history is doubtless nothing if not the natural selection of nations over time. What works for the smallest social unit, the family, can by projection work for the largest, the state.

We have long since slowed the biological process of natural selection, by nurturing the weak, infirm, and troubled. The very emotions of sympathy and love that help the "unfit" survive and negate Darwinian selection, however, ensure a more important type of survival—that of society as a whole. Surely in the clash between muscular genes and fellow-feeling social norms, the latter will have the upper hand.

At the turn of the nineteenth century, French biologist Jean de Lamarck put forth his second law: all the changes that occur in individuals after they are born are preserved by reproduction to the new individuals which arise.[38] We now know otherwise; geneticists have shown that acquired (biological) characteristics, of the kind of which Lamarck spoke, cannot be inherited. At the same time, through studying human behavior, we have learned in this century that there is a social ecology version of Lamarck's second law: acquired *social* characteristics *are* very often socially inherited. One of the most important mechanisms for acquiring and later transmitting social values is the family, as a school for learning interpersonal relations and for socialization.

"The little world of childhood with its familiar surroundings is a model of the greater world," Carl Jung remarked. "The more intensively the family has stamped its character upon the child, the more [the child] will tend to feel and see its earlier miniature world again in the bigger world of adult life."[39]

"You, the adults, are the *people makers*" is Virginia Satir's striking phrase. "The family is the 'factory' where this kind of (feeling, loving, creative, productive) person is made."[40]

But families, like factories, are subject to mishaps and breakdowns. A leading type of disorder in families is schizophrenia, whose chief symptom is detachment from reality. An important theory about the cause of schizophrenia in families—the "double bind"—turns out to have allegorical implications for society as a whole.

CHOOSE YOUR CHAINS

Q. What is worse than a single Prisoner's Dilemma bind?
A. Two of them—a double bind.

Satirist Dan Greenburg, in his book *How to Be a Jewish Mother,* offers the following formula: "Give your son Marvin two sport shirts as a present. The first time he wears one of them, look at him sadly and say in your Basic Tone of Voice: 'The other one you didn't like?' "[41] This two-shirt dilemma is a "damned if you do damned if you don't" bind. Even in contexts less amusing than the one Greenburg invented, it is usually not pathological, because the bind does not encompass all contexts—for Marvin, only shirts are involved—and because the person can at will step out of it (for example, Marvin: "I'm saving it for weekends, Mom").

There are situations, however, in which we *believe*

we have freedom of choice, and that belief turns out to be illusory. This is the basis of a theory of schizophrenia developed by Gregory Bateson and known as the "double bind."[42] Bateson's theory emphasizes the family context within which personality disorders arise. A simple way to describe it is in terms of two separate *Prisoner's Dilemma* matrices.

In a single *Prisoner's Dilemma*, an individual player is torn between the fear of being exploited and the desire for mutual cooperation. Despite this dilemma, he has the freedom to choose between "cooperate" and "compete," although "cooperate" may open him to being exploited by his competitor. Since, however, most family games are repeated many times (supergames), there is the hope that the competitor will see the light and switch to "cooperate." When a player picks "cooperate," that choice ensures that the mutually destructive compete-compete outcome will not occur; in addition, the exploitative compete-cooperate is foresworn by the player. The fact that a player is able to eliminate totally these two outcomes, and, in particular, forego the role of "exploiter," confers a certain amount of freedom and dignity.

Suppose, however, that instead of facing a *single Prisoner's Dilemma,* a player faces *two* of them, Dilemma A and Dilemma B. Dilemma B is a kind of converse, mirror image of Dilemma A; what cooperative behavior produces in Dilemma A, competitive behavior produces in Dilemma B, and vice versa. Suppose also that the player's opponent chooses not only some strategy within a given game context, but also decides *which* of the two games, A and B, are in fact going to be played—*after* the first player has decided on his strategy. This is a double bind. The first player cannot now avoid being made to act as an "exploiter"—which is precisely what the second player wants—every single time the game is played.

This situation, an invention of the devil, sounds contrived. Bateson's original double-bind article, however, offers a more down-to-earth example.[43] A tired mother is bothered by a child. Instead of telling the child to go away, the mother tells the child to go to bed because he needs his sleep. In this way, she tries to cover up her annoyance with the child by expressing concern for his needs. The child may either agree to go to bed, or refuse. If he refuses, the mother interprets it as challenging her concern for his needs. She sees the refusal as "unloving" (Dilemma A) and becomes angry. If he agrees and goes to bed, the mother interprets his readiness to leave her without argument as rejection or withdrawal—again, as "unloving"—and shuns the child (Dilemma B). So, what appeared initially to the child as freedom of choice—submit or rebel—turns out to be no choice at all. The only way out of a double bind is to leave the field (not an option for children), to behave erratically and randomly, or to become exceedingly cautious about commitment to *any* choice or behavior. The latter two behaviors are pathological.

Double-bind games are not confined solely to pathological family contexts. In double-bind social games, players act as if they were independent and free to choose, but in fact can neither affect the game's outcome nor escape the confining structure and rules. The rules of the game, A. W. Watts observed, "confer independence and take it away at the same time, without revealing the contradiction."[44]

THE ILLUSION OF ALTERNATIVES

The essence of the double bind is not, however, help-lessness—the complete absence of choice—but rather the "illusion of alternatives," in Weakland and Jackson's phrase.[45] Knowledge without power is discomfiting, but knowledge with the *illusion* of power is downright self-destructive.

"One aspect of being an American that receives attention from the public press," Weakland and Jackson write, "is the freedom to do what one wants and to tell the other fellow to 'go to hell.' Americans, by reputation, are their own bosses and resent being told what to do."[46]

But much of this freedom is illusory. Some of our "freedoms" are single binds: freedoms to congest, pollute, deplete, and disrupt, since others act likewise. Other freedoms are more complex, double binds, in which bureaucratic mechanisms allow us the Henry Ford Model-T choice syndrome: customers could pick any color they wished, provided it was black.

The coexistence of free enterprise and a tangled bureaucracy to ensure that it stays free is the ultimate double bind. In his essay, "The Market As Prison," political scientist Charles Lindblom argues that "market systems imprison policy," as business enterprise punishes reform that works against its narrowly-defined interests. But policy also imprisons the market.[47] Two examples are antitrust laws and the diffuse ownership of corporate stock. In the 1970s, the three largest U.S. auto companies began research on antipollution devices. When they began to pool their cooperative efforts, the Department of Justice sued them, thus ensuring the free-

74

dom of wasteful redundancy. Property rights are cherished in a market system. For many big companies, right of ownership is split among thousands of individual stockholders; when everyone owns the company, no one does, leaving management free to impose its will on those who are "free" to own stock.

Some writers have suggested that despite their names, competitive market economies are in fact built on altruism. In *Wealth and Poverty,* George Gilder asserts that the essence of capitalism is giving, and he approvingly quotes Richard Posner: "Because the individual cannot prosper in a market economy without understanding, and appealing to the wants and needs of others, and because the cultivation of altruism promotes the effective operation of markets, the market economy also fosters empathy and benevolence, yet without destroying individuality."[48] Gilder refers to potlatch, the custom of gift giving in many societies: "Competitions in giving are contests of altruism . . . the contest of gifts leads to an expansion of human sympathies. The circle of giving (the profits of the economy) will grow as long as the gifts are consistently valued more by the receivers than by the givers."[49] The *motives* behind the Kwakiutl's potlatch or General Motors' dividends, wages, and retained earnings, however, may be less benevolent than Gilder believes. The anthropologist Lévi-Strauss observed that a major function of gift giving is "to surpass a rival in generosity, to crush him if possible under future obligations which it is hoped he cannot meet, thus taking from him privileges, titles, rank, authority and prestige."[50] If the gratitude of labor recipients is a measure of business's benefaction, labor leaders' pronouncements in chapters 9 and 10 do not jibe with Gilder's version of munificent altruistic capitalism.

CONCLUSION

The United States is not a small homogeneous family. It cannot operate like a family that harmoniously synchronizes the use of the shower or the family station wagon, the leather armchair or the computer. Yet the same features that help families run smoothly can also help economies. "We cannot allow our institutions to become so unfeeling and unthinking," William Ouchi writes, "that they make work and social intercourse unbearable for all of us most of the time."[51] Just as strong families do, "we must find those organizational innovations which can permit a balance between freedom and integration which go beyond our current interpretation of individualism."[52]

The concept of a social contract is one such innovation that merits careful thought. Such a contract comprises agreement on the rules governing our economic games and explicit "rules about rules"—how the rules of the game are to be decided. In succeeding chapters we will expand on the possible advantages of a social contract and ways of constructing it.

CHAPTER 4

Successful Corporations:
It's All in the Family

IN the previous chapter, we viewed the family as a sort of microcosm of the corporation, whose function is to generate both conventional and psychic income and to distribute them to its "workers." We observed the key role played by an altruistic family head, or alternately, by some type of social contract. Points of similarity were noted between the way families divide up tasks and riches and the way firms and corporations perform these functions. This chapter applies our knowledge of family life to help answer the question: What makes a corporation successful, stable, and profitable?

In contrast with the standard economic cliché that posits a "big trade-off" (inverse relationship) between equality and efficiency—more equality is achieved only at the expense of less efficiency, and greater efficiency is gained only by sacrificing equality—existence of norms or mechanisms to ensure fairness, harmony and communication also make the family more *efficient* at producing income. Does this result hold for corporations as well? Is the corporation-as-family metaphor purely theoretical, or does it have practical applications as well? This chapter addresses these questions. What would happen, we wonder, if the president of an ailing company chose to turn to a family therapist, instead of a management consultant, for help and advice?

CORPORATE THERAPY

The chief executive officer of a billion-dollar corporation reaches his desk before 7:00 A.M. Its gleaming mahogany surface is marred only by a pen-and-pencil holder and a low stack of papers. He glances briefly at the reports—knowing their contents all too well—and swivels his chair to look bleakly out over the hazy Manhattan skyline. The figures show an operating loss for the fourth straight quarter. Sales are steady, but forecasts suggest they will weaken toward the end of the year. There is labor unrest in three plants in the Midwest, even though a new wage agreement was signed just last month. Marketing is upset about the new designs that the research department submitted. The sharp young vice-president so skilled at investing cash, even for a weekend, is resigning to join an investment bank. Interest rates appear to be edging upward again. And the promising new division he set up last year is not living up to expectations. Bleak.

The chief executive officer reaches for the intercom

button. "Jennifer, find out the name of the best family therapist in town. Get me an appointment as soon as possible!" A case of corporate pressures straining the executive's family life? Such cases are common. In our little story, however, the corporate head intends to seek help for his *corporate* family.

Firms, like families, face constant stress, challenges, and disruptions originating both inside the organization and outside it. Rivalries among corporate divisions for manpower, money, and authority strain the corporate fabric. Challenges from new or improved products and processes developed by other companies endanger profits and market shares.

Every firm has its own distinctive style in dealing with internal and external stress. So does every family. Family therapists David Kantor and William Lehr used the methods of anthropology to study the family tribe by implanting "participant observers" to live in families and note their behavior and conversation. They discerned three distinctive family types: open, closed, and random. After explaining the special features of each, we shall suggest that the most successful corporations, which William Ouchi labels "Type Z," resemble open families.

FINGERPRINTING THE FAMILY

The mountains? Or the seashore? The legendary battle over where the family will spend its annual vacation will help us illustrate Kantor and Lehr's three family types.[1]

In the open family system, order and change result from "the interaction of relatively stable evolving family structures." A "group consensus" is worked out and carefully preserved, maintaining a balance between collective cohesion and individual freedom. Each member is encouraged "to feel a personal responsibility toward each of the other members as individuals, and toward the family group as a whole." An open family will make its holiday plans by an open and possibly lengthy discussion in which all family members take part and freely express their preferences. Information and opinions are exchanged. Some family members may change their minds once or twice. Gradually a consensus emerges—the seashore. Some opposition remains; last-ditch efforts at persuading the majority are made, and finally all agree. The family will spend its three weeks splashing in the Pacific.

In contrast, closed families are run by "those in authority"—by one or both parents. The closed family "tries to be certain of where it is going and when it will get there." There is "family-wide discipline—a set of disciplinary measures to which the entire family is subject. . . . Members are expected to expend energy directly toward specific targets without deviating away from them toward others." When ubiquitous family guidelines impinge on one or more members, the family reacts to the crises by suppressing the individual, or at times, by splitting. Only rarely is the family budget of time, space, and energy altered. Parents may choose a vacation site in the mountains. Their objective is to vacation where opportunities for climbing and hiking will help maintain or even increase the family members' physical fitness—a goal toward which they all work all year round by jogging and participating in swimming programs. For the ten-day stay in the Rockies, a daily schedule is decided upon. There may be some discussion within the family, but it is perfunctory and the issue is never really in doubt.

The third type of family system is the random one. Here, families experiment with "unstable" structures as reference points for order and for change. Members "attach, detach, commit, and shift their energies at will." The random family "has a knack for spontaneously generating effects, for locating energy very quickly, for readily expending it in the direction of a particular target and diverting it just as readily. . . ." In this type of family system, crisis is routine. The life plan is spontaneous, based on a credo of "doing what one wants to do when one wants to do it." Membership is nonobligatory. There is a conviction that "if a family centers itself in some nonvoluntary or coercive way, it is not centered genuinely or properly." Members maintain relations with one another and with targets "strictly on the basis of personal choice." As a result, when family members' choices contradict or clash, one member may end up losing his or her freedom so that the other can exercise his or hers.[2] A random family may leave its vacation plans unsettled until the last minute. Almost by default, it decides to head toward the mountains. Then someone notes in a newspaper that the *Mona Lisa* is being exhibited in a New York museum. Plans are altered at once, and the family heads to New York with a vague notion of staying between a couple of days and a week in a motel, with friends, or with an aunt who may have just returned from France, or is still there. One of the children opts out and asks to go instead to summer camp with a friend. On the way to New York, an unspoiled and uncrowded campground is found in the Appalachians. The family decides to remain there for its vacation, with an older teenager choosing to persist and take a bus on his own to New York.

Kantor and Lehr assert that there are "flaws inherent in each typal design," with none of the three "ideal or perfect."[3] They observe that most families reveal behaviors common to two or three types, depending on the situation and context.

It strikes us that companies, too, can be "fingerprinted" and classified by the style of their management as open, closed, or random. Unlike Kantor and Lehr, we come out openly for open companies, which, we suggest, embody many of the positive, constructive, and stable features common to William Ouchi's Type Z companies.

THE FAMILY FIRM, FROM A TO Z

William Ouchi has studied a group of American companies, all of them profitable and successful, whose internal structures and value resemble those in typical successful Japanese companies. He called these firms—which include IBM, Procter & Gamble, Eastman Kodak, Hewlett-Packard, and the U.S. military—Type Z and contrasted them with Type A (A for American) firms.[4]

Type Z companies encourage lifetime employment (versus short-term employment in Type A firms), diverse nonspecialized career paths (versus high specialization in Type A), collective decision making and responsibility (versus individual in Type A), and broad wholistic concern. In many ways, they resemble Kantor and Lehr's open families:

- "The open (family) system's power regulations are marked by laterality [room to move and to change]. Members are encouraged to exercise their talents."[5]

  "Career paths in Type Z companies display much of the 'wandering' around across functions and offices that typifies the Japanese firm."[6]

- "In the open family system, order and change are expected to result from the interaction of relatively stable evolving family structures."[7]

  "When operating changes are involved, Type Z organizations tend to be unusually adaptive. . . . Decisions are shaped by serious attention to questions of whether or not this decision is suitable, whether it 'fits' the company."[8]

- "Each member [of the open family] is free to establish his own movements toward other members or targets, as long as he stays within the guidelines established by family consensus. . . . Members are much freer [than in closed families] to determine when, in what order, for how long and at what speed they will do things."[9]

  "[In Type Z firms] each individual is also effectively told to do just what that person wants. . . . The socialization of all to a common goal is so complete . . . that individuals will naturally seek to do that which is in the common good."[10]

- "The open family develops, maintains and projects a standard that requires a consensus for organizing the total space in which the family lives. . . . No design can become a family centering design until each member has consented to its adoption."[11]

  "[Type Z firms] are intimate associations of people engaged in economic activity but tied together through

> a variety of bonds. . . . Z organizations have achieved
> a high state of consistency in their internal structure."[12]

What is it that equips open Type Z firms best for adaptation to change, willingness to undertake risky, long-term investments, and the fostering of a loyal, skilled work force with low rates of turnover?

Consider a closed firm where division or branch success is measured strictly by profitability. A request from one branch to another to borrow staff may be denied, or inferior people may be dispatched, even though such a transfer may be of great benefit to the firm as a whole. Even if Division B gains much more than Division A loses, Division A may veto the whole idea. This type of organization, Ouchi notes, yields "low coordination, low productivity, and high frustration."[13] It is strongly reminiscent of the family that lacks an altruistic head, or some form of social-contract consensus.

Contrast this type of firm with Type Z companies built on the precept that if "most of the top managers agree on what the company ought to be trying to do and how it ought to go about that set of tasks, then they will be able to rely on their mutual trust and goodwill to reach decisions far superior to anything that a formal system of control [i.e. closed family system] could provide."[14] A high degree of mutual trust exists among workers in Type Z companies. "Trust underscores the belief that goals correspond, that neither person is out to harm the other," Ouchi writes. "This feature, perhaps more than any other, accounts for the high levels of commitment, of loyalty, and of productivity in Japanese firms and in Type Z organizations,"[15] and, he might have added, in open families. Thus just as the internal structure of a family has much to do with how the family will deal with external stresses, so do internal relations within the firm strongly influence how the firm responds to outside pressures—including relatively minor ones arising in day-to-day decision making.

R & D: THEME AND VARIATIONS

Nature has two different kinds of events that it strews before our intellect for thought and consideration—the humdrum and the colossal. One of science's most problematic biases is its preoccupation with the colossal—in economics, depressions, hyperinflation, and stock market crashes; and in psychology, schizophrenic families, for example. For firms as for families, we may well learn much more about firms from commonplace details of day-to-day life than from rare, dramatic conflicts. The commonplace is a check on the dramatic, Kantor and Lehr argue, a warning and testament that conflict and argument are not all or even perhaps most of what a family may be about.[16] This is equally true for firms.

Two common games that families play daily are *First to Shower* and *Take Out the Trash*. In *First to Shower*, the most alacritous wins; players compete to be first. In *Take Out the Trash*, indolence triumphs; players battle to be last. (As all parents learn, children often treat *all* games, including *First to Shower*, as *Take Out the Trash*.) For many companies, one of the most important everyday tasks is the arrangement of human and material resources in order to invent and innovate new products and services. With the family games as our models, we now turn to some research and development (R&D) games.

The following game context is faced repeatedly by business executives, generally for high stakes.

R & D

A company, and its competitors, face a difficult choice: "take the plunge" and invest large amounts of money to develop a new product or process, or "play it safe" and wait for others to take the risk and then enter the market after it has been proven profitable.

This game may be perceived in two ways: as *Quick Draw* (the corporate version of *First to Shower*) or as *After You, Garçon* (parallel to *Take Out the Trash*).

QUICK DRAW

Company executives reason: If I go ahead and innovate while my competitors play it safe, I stand to make big profits. If I play it safe while they take the plunge, I save R & D spending but lose out on big profits. If we all play it safe, things stay as they are. If we all take the plunge, the market may be too small for all of us and there may be big losses, at least initially (see figure 4.1).

In this game, the company does not have a dominant strategy, that is, one that works out best no matter what the competitors do. What the company does depends crucially on what it *thinks* or perceives its competitors will do. If the expectation is that competitors will take the plunge, the best bet for the company is to play it safe and avoid big losses. If the company thinks its competi-

Successful Corporations: It's All in the Family

		Competitors	
		Take the Plunge	Play It Safe
Company	Take the Plunge	Big Loss	Big Profit
	Play It Safe	Small Profit	Break Even

QUICK DRAW

		Competitors	
		Take the Plunge	Play It Safe
Company	Take the Plunge	Big Loss	Small Profit
	Play It Safe	Big Profit	Break Even

AFTER YOU, GARÇON

Figure 4.1 R & D Games

In the game of *Quick Draw,* the first player to take the plunge profits. When both do so, however, both lose. It pays to take the plunge only if you think the other players won't.

In contrast, in the game of *After You, Garçon,* it pays to let the rival players take the plunge first. Garçon takes the risks, while you take the gravy.

NOTE: Losses or profits in the two matrices refer to those of the "company"—the player who picks the row.

---

tors will play it safe, the right move is to take the plunge, thus earning big profits. As in the Old West, you draw on your opponent when you think you are faster. When both gunfighters err and draw simultaneously, they wind up in Boot Hill. For example, in the early days of main-frame computers, several large corporations "drew" simultaneously—and ended up burying their computer divisions under heavy losses.

MINNETONKA, GOLIATH, AND SOFTSOAP

A real-world example of *Quick Draw* is the saga of Minnetonka, Goliath, and Softsoap. In 1980, a small Minnesota-based company named Minnetonka Inc. in-

87

troduced a new product, Softsoap—liquid soap dispensed from a squirt gun by a touch of the finger. Consumers liked it. They found it was clean, did not mess up soap dishes, did not shrink to infuriating slivers, and you didn't slip on it in the shower or bathtub.

While Goliath—giant rivals like Procter & Gamble (despite being a Type Z company), Armour-Dial, Lever Bros., and Colgate-Palmolive—played safe, Minnetonka sold $35 million worth of Softsoap in the first year. It then chose to plunge ahead and spend close to that amount ($30 million) on advertising and promotion alone in 1981—half of it devoted to distributing 200 million coupons. Minnetonka general manager Wallace Marx said, "This is high-stakes poker. It's going to cost a lot to get in and a lot to stay in." A competing company's executive commented early in 1981, "You can never be sure about trying to change consumer habits. I'm not ready to jump on the bandwagon yet."[17]

In *Quick Draw*, the price of error is very high. Large, closed Type A corporations may be run by executives less eager to make big profits (at big risk) than to avoid large losses. Such firms fit the definition of a conservative: someone who looks both ways before crossing a one-way street. They tend to perceive the R & D game quite differently, not as *Quick Draw* at all but as:

AFTER YOU, GARÇON

In contrast to *Quick Draw*, big profits are seen to accrue not to the first to "take the plunge" but to the last. Alacrity implies making costly errors and incurring big expenses that other firms benefit from. If the company thinks its competitors will take the plunge, its best strategy is to play it safe and wait (see figure 4.1).

Successful Corporations: It's All in the Family

In *After You, Garçon,* there is again no dominant, best-in-every-case strategy. A cautious innovator who wants to minimize his losses will play it safe. The worst he can do then is break even. When all game players reason that way, everyone plays it safe. (Note that "play it safe" is a so-called minimax strategy—the choice that minimizes the largest possible loss—for both *After You, Garçon* and for *Quick Draw.*) Cautious Type A firms with a sharp eye on quarterly profit statements are likely to perceive R & D games as *After You, Garçon,* even when this is inaccurate. The best time to deal with procrastination, they reason, is tomorrow, and they make their moves accordingly.

Misperception of R & D games is closely related to what Harvard Professors Robert Hayes and William Abernathy have called "managerial myopia." In their widely quoted article on this subject, they cite a symptomatic line of reasoning.

Why risk money on new businesses when good, profitable low-risk opportunities are on every side? It's much more difficult to come up with a synthetic meat product than a lemon-lime cake mix because you know exactly what that return is going to be. A synthetic steak is going to take a lot longer, require a much bigger investment, and the risk of failure will be greater.[18]

The reasoning here is, let someone else pioneer new technologies, change consumer preferences, develop new markets, and risk his neck. Once he has broken untilled soil, we can farm it at our ease. The difficulty with *After You, Garçon* is that Garçon may be thinking, "after you, Fred"—in which case neither Garçon, Fred, nor anyone else may innovate so much as an improved paper bag for a very long time.

Worst of all is that companies may think they are playing *After you, Garçon* when in fact the game is *Quick Draw,* and foreign companies know this. Garçon may turn out to be Japanese, West German, or French. He may build a better compact car, video recorder, microcomputer, or digital watch. When this happens, all that is left is to blame the government, fate, history, or unions, and then to bid for big bailout loans.

Neither *Quick Draw* nor *After You, Garçon* are zero-sum games. In both there is potential for conflict—my gain is your loss—side by side with the promise of cooperation—we both gain. The vital difference is: in *Quick Draw,* the early bird gets the profits. In *After You, Garçon,* the early bird gets the worm.

Economist Dale Mortensen has studied a version of *Quick Draw* which he calls "the innovation race." In his model, a large number of competitors try to be first to make a specific discovery. The chance that some *one* of them will make the discovery depends on the total sum of all their R & D efforts. Once a discovery is made, the inventor (through patents) receives its full value; the others get nothing. In this model, excessive amounts will be spent on R & D, well beyond what is socially efficient. The reason is that in the absence of coordination and cooperation among the players, all but the successful inventor will incur large capital losses.[19] Apparently, waste can result from too many players perceiving the R & D game as *Quick Draw,* just as decay results when too many see the game as *After You, Garçon.*

Semiconductors are a good example. The president

of Control Data Corp. estimates that companies spent $1 billion "to make a product that somebody else is making anyway."[20] The mixture of *Quick Draw* and *After You, Garçon,* in its most pernicious and wasteful manifestation, is a market economy where consumers stand bewildered in front of thirty shelf-yards of potato, corn, wheat, and banana and plantain chips while producers eagerly awaiting new 256K RAM semiconductor chips face a bare cupboard. If a choice must be made between the two evils of wasteful proliferation of new types of semiconductor chips and the absence or scarcity of them, we ought to pick the waste of duplication. There is, however, no need to choose, as Japan's Ministry of International Trade and Industry (MITI) has shown.

THE NOT-SO-SECRET LIFE OF MITI

Geneticists emphasize the importance of diversity in maintaining a strong gene pool. Diversity is equally important in maintaining the strong fabric of society; variety is the staff of life not just its spice. For instance, while the open family, Type Z company may be best suited for innovating, a business environment composed *solely* of Type Z firms could well turn out to be extremely inefficient—unless the collection of Type Z firms itself became a big, cooperative, open family.

Innovation is said to be Japan's second religion after Shinto. How do dynamic open-family firms in Japan avoid trampling one another in *Quick Draw?* To improve coordination, and forestall waste and redundancy, some sort of cooperative venture is indicated. This is precisely the role of Japan's MITI, whose role in some ways resembles that of the altruistic family head who keeps aggressive, competitive siblings from filching cookies from one another. A major function of MITI is to facilitate communication among firms trying to achieve a common or similar goal.

During the 1950s and 1960s, MITI acted like the father figure in a closed family. It had the power to dole out licenses to deal in foreign exchange. Since no company could import or export without trading in dollars, marks, and francs, MITI had the all-embracing power to set what, when, and how companies could produce. This power was taken away at the end of 1980.[21] MITI's new role became that of the coordinator in an open family. It continues to provide money for high-technology research, along with other ministries, and offers no-interest loans to private industry. But its still powerful influence now derives more from persuasion, suggestion, and consensus rather than from legally binding directives. The influential MITI document *Vision of Industry in the Eighties,* published in March 1980, is a good example. More than 10,000 people took part in drawing up this White Paper, which builds an industrial strategy for the rest of this decade. Only about twenty-five pages in length, the White Paper concludes that Japan had to double the share of its already high GNP devoted to Research and Development.[22] With broad national participation from all parts of society in drawing up this plan, it may well succeed, whereas a handed-down-from-above decree might likely fail.

Japan recently announced a decade-long program,

costing billions of dollars, to develop fifth-generation computers embodying artificial intelligence with MITI playing a key role. Such computers would be able to think and solve problems on their own—and perhaps even read, understand, and criticize this book. To achieve this goal, the Institute for New-Generation Computer Technology was set up. It employs forty top scientists from all walks of industry. The institute brings to mind a not dissimilar structure set up in America, with success—the Manhattan Project. Every two weeks, the researchers returns to their companies to update their employers on new discoveries and their potential applications.

It is sometimes claimed that the Japanese are not a competitive people. This is false. As individuals, groups, and corporations, the Japanese are exceedingly competitive. They have, however, found ways of *channeling* and directing this competition. Their competitive energies find expression in ways that avoid the waste of duplication and mutual destruction, but instead work toward attainment of mutually-agreeable goals.

OPEN FAMILIES, OPEN LINES

Like open families, Type Z companies spend what appears to be enormously wasteful amounts of time and energy on pure palaver and debate. Among spirited free-thinking individuals, working through to consensus is not done quickly or easily.

This chapter, for instance, and the preceding one are

together approximately the length of the MITI White Paper. But it took 9,998 fewer people to produce them. Is this book therefore more efficient? Not at all; this type of "economic" calculation is erroneous. Consensus is built on communication. Communication, in turn, takes time and resources. Expenditures on communication, in firms as well as in families, are among our most productive investments. As John Milton wrote in "Paradise Lost": good, the more it is communicated, the more abundant it grows.

Internal lines of communication are to firms what supply lines are to armies at war—vulnerable, crucial, invaluable when working, and disastrous when cut. Family therapist Virginia Satir wrote that "once a human being has arrived on this earth, *communication is the largest single factor determining what kinds of relationships he makes with others and what happens to him in the world about him.* How he manages his survival, how he develops intimacy, how productive he is, how he makes sense, how he connects with his own divinity—all are largely dependent on his communication skills."[23] Development of such skills within large companies is as important as it is within the family setting.

Some large companies *purposely* break lines of communication—between innovators and researchers, and their corporate headquarters. "Companies such as IBM, General Motors and Xerox, in which innovation is critical, typically segregate their researchers and those who come up with new product ideas," William Ouchi observes, "sometimes locating them on the opposite end of the continent from headquarters in order to shield them from the sometimes oppressive corporate culture."[24] Families, indeed society as a whole, also treat deviance by isolating it—though the objective is to keep society from becoming deviant rather than to keep "deviant" researchers from becoming socialized. In families such isolation can create what Lynn Hoffman called a "deviance-amplifying process"—a feedback loop where isolation amplifies deviance, which aggravates isolation and so on. The same process can occur in companies. Ouchi adds, "What happens (in companies that isolate innovators) . . . is that those scientists indeed become deviant from the main-line culture, develop lots of different ideas, and then discover that the headquarters decision-makers reject their ideas as being too deviant."[25] This, despite the fact that the three companies mentioned in this context are regarded as Type Z.

The importance of intra-firm communication within innovative companies is affirmed in a study of 116 innovations by Sowder and Chakrabarti. A majority of the innovations failed. The highest failure rate occurs when the idea comes from top management—an outcome that is itself an indictment of closed corporate structures. Most researchers have a limited understanding of business, a weakness marketing experts can spot. Innovations succeed most often when researchers and marketing people communicate and agree. An account of the study concluded: "The most successful innovators are companies in which (Research and Development) efforts are thoroughly integrated with the rest of the business. That requires two-way communication between commercial departments and R & D staff. . . . You cannot hive off R & D to a separate compartment and expect it to work."[26] Clearly, deviance-amplifying structures are no more profitable for corporations than they are for families, or for that matter for society itself.

META-THOUGHT

One of the prime features of a healthy family is its ability to reorganize—to change its structure, lines of communication, mechanisms of production and distribution, and the rules of its games—when challenges arise that make change vital. This is equally true of the corporate family, and indeed of our society and economy as a whole. Caught up in our economic games, we frequently find it difficult to perceive the need for sweeping change even when the situation is critical.

Within families, a precondition for change is "meta-communication"—the ability to discuss not only specific games and rules themselves, but broad types of games and rules and ways to implement them. Meta-communication requires that we step outside of specific frameworks and view them from many possible angles. The assumption that the nature of our corporations and the economic system within which they work are immutable is an enemy of this type of thought.

A familiar puzzle asks us to join nine dots, arranged in a square, with four straight lines without lifting pen from paper. People usually confine their lines to the small square the dots form, even though the problem as stated imposes no such constraint. As a result, we fail. Only when we allow our lines to leap beyond the perimeters of the nine-dot square is a solution possible.

Once this leap of thought occurs, the problem is simple; but remarkably few people make it on their own.

America is in need of change, both in the economic games people play and in the way they think about those games and the rules that govern them. In this section, we have argued that the non-zero-sum games individuals, families, and firms play require interpersonal relationships different from the one-dimensional competitive ethic on which the free-market system is based. The following section, which deals with economic games played by small groups, extends this claim to the specific context of inflation, unemployment, and the business cycle.

PART III

Small Groups

"A slow sort of country!" said the Queen. "Now, *here,* you see, it takes all the running you can do, to keep in the same place. If you want to get somewhere else, you must run at least twice as fast as that!"

Lewis Carroll

Kondratieff's Revenge: Does a Third Wave Make a Permanent?

IN MAY 1982, we attended a gathering of investors in New York City. A successful commodities broker from Chicago came up to us and asked if we knew anything about a defunct economist named Nikolai Dmitrievich Kondratieff. Why was the name of an obscure Russian, dead for fifty years, suddenly on the lips and minds of Americans preoccupied with their financial statements, and in the pages of *Business Week* and the *New York Times?*[1] Was it because he has claimed that we are subject to regular, recurrent cycles of boom and bust, with each cycle spanning two generations? If so, did we begin another "bust" period in the 1970s? How did Kondratieff's ghost take revenge in 1972? What is it in human nature that spawns such long cycles? And do three full long waves of economic activity lead us to believe such waves are a permanent phenomenon?

This chapter leads off our analysis of the dismal U.S. and world economies over the past decade by addressing the question: Is there order and regularity in the ebb and flow of market economies? Our search for plausible answers leads us to ponder two types of games: the marketplace for votes and the battlefield of ideas. There are, we shall argue, ways in which Western economies behave as they did a century ago; at the same time, the world has in our time undergone a sweeping revolution in how people *perceive* their relations with one another. These changed perceptions, superimposed on old familiar business cycles, help explain why conventional economic theory has, along with the economy, sagged badly, and why economic recovery and the recovery of economics are so closely intertwined.

In this chapter, we are going to discuss the mysteries of the business cycle—ways that economic history seems to repeat itself. The remaining chapters of this section focus on the backwards economy—ways it does not.

ENTER WORLD STAGFLATION

The great inflation of 1973–83 did not begin with the contrived scarcity of oil and energy. It began with a very real shortage of wheat and feed grains. A series of agricultural failures, and a particularly unsuccessful harvest, brought Soviet grain buyers to New York in

1972 and 1973 with especially fat order books. They dickered with several large, secretive and competitive American grain exporters. When the size of the Russian appetite became apparent and the total American commitment to export food and feed grains was added up, wheat prices soared—*after* the deals were signed and sealed. The price of a bushel of U.S. No. 1 hard red winter wheat was $2.83 in the second quarter of 1973, about double its level in 1970. It rose about 40 percent in the third quarter of that year and by early 1974 had doubled to $5.67.[2] Victors in this game were the Soviet buyers and consumers, and perhaps American farmers who later enjoyed higher prices. Losers were American consumers. Through a domino effect, higher wheat prices pushed up meat prices, which in turn pushed up prices of other foods. This inflation in food prices preceded the quadrupling of crude oil prices in 1974 and aggravated its impact.

From 1963–72, inflation in Western industrial economies averaged about 4 percent. From 1973, annual inflation was from three to seven percentage points higher (see table 5.1). Nor did this inflation buy us growth. For the same countries, GNP grew close to 5 percent a year, on average, during 1963–72. Following the strong 1976 recovery from the deep 1973–75 recession, growth of GNP was lower each year than in the preceding one and sagged downward to less than 1 percent in 1982.[3]

If the world economy is thought of as a freight train, the American economy is the engine tugging a string of boxcars up toward recovery, or down toward depression. For a time, after World War II, it seemed as if the United States had, with Keynes's help, straightened some of the wrinkles in the rail. Periods of expansion

TABLE 5.1
Inflation and Growth in the Industrial Countries

		Average								
	1963–72	1973	1974	1975	1976	1977	1978	1979	1980	1981	1982
Annual Percent Change in GNP, Inflation-Corrected	4.7	6.2	0.6	−0.5	4.9	4.0	4.0	3.6	1.3	1.2	0.8
Annual Percent Change in GNP Deflator*	4.2	7.4	11.7	11.1	7.6	7.7	7.5	7.9	8.9	8.4	7.6

SOURCE: "Occasional Paper No. 9," *World Economic Outlook* (Washington, D.C.: International Monetary Fund, 1982), p. 143.
NOTE: Since 1973, GNP has grown more slowly (except for 1976) than it did during the period 1963–72. At the same time, inflation has been at least three percentage points higher.
*Inflation measured as the rate of increase in a weighted average of GNP-component prices.

lasted longer than before the war, recessions were shorter and shallower. Growth exceeded its long-term trend. Unemployment rarely topped 7 percent and at times dipped under 4 percent. During 1948–67, consumer prices rose on average just over 1.5 percent yearly.[4]

During the 1970s, something happened to transform a placid trunk line into a roller coaster. The decade began quietly enough with a mild recession that ended early in 1971 with a rapid recovery. Then came the grain-price and oil-price shocks of 1973 and a deep world recession during late 1973 through 1974. Inflation accelerated, growth slowed, and productivity weakened (see the game of *Hot Potato,* in chapter 6). Another brief, sharp slump occurred in the spring of 1980—the credit-card-debacle recession.[5]

A terrifying downward plunge of the roller coaster began in early 1981. High interest rates plummeted the American economy into recession. The rest of the world followed; Europe soon learned it could not maintain expansionary, low interest rates while America had steadfastly unprecedentedly high rates. A weak recovery in late 1981 was snuffed out; the economy pitched downward again in 1982. Unemployment counts climbed to 12 million; the rate of unemployment—10.8 percent at the close of 1982—touched end-of-the-Depression heights. Among young blacks, half were jobless.

Moreover, there appears little reason for great optimism. Reagan administration projections forecast a slow fall in unemployment from 10.7 percent in 1983 down to 6.6 percent in 1988, provided growth runs at 4 percent annually.[6] In other words, America can hope for a rate of unemployment equal to that of a recession year—1961—on condition that growth is restored to its historically rapid pace of 1947–67. So far, the feisty 1983–84 economic recovery has not invalidated these relatively bleak projections for joblessness.

What went wrong? As with many questions in economics, there is an overly simple, wrong answer and an overly complex, correct one. The simple answer is that the Reagan administration chose to wring inflation out of the economy—perhaps mistakenly believing that that was the wish of the voters, as Eisenhower had believed a generation earlier—by stringent fiscal and monetary measures that if necessary would cause recession and unemployment. The complex answer is that our economy has undergone a fundamental, behavioral change making it utterly different from its structure and pace in 1970, 1960, and 1920. The nature of this change, creating what we call the "wrong-way" economy, is discussed in depth in the following chapter.

Twice in two years, in 1980 and 1981, monetary authorities lowered interest rates abruptly, only to shoot them up again. The third time interest rates came down was in August 1982, an event perhaps not unrelated to approaching congressional elections. Though the drop in interest rates seemed to have little effect, it may have kept things from getting much worse. The much maligned "political business cycle" may for once have done us all a good turn.

Why did the United States and world economies stumble so badly? There are no simple answers. One explanation is that the sources of economic instability in the 1970s were not fundamentally different from those of the preceding two centuries. To explore that view, we proceed in this chapter to explore two behavioral theories of economic cycles: four-year political fluctuations stemming from pre-election spending, inflation, and postelection austerity; and fifty-year "generational" cycles in which each generation, like decrepit generals, fights the current economic war by wrongly assuming it duplicates the previous one. We turn first to the political business cycle, whose existence is easier to demonstrate than its much longer, shadowy cousin, the Kondratieff wave.

STAYING IN POWER

With governments exerting direct control over a big chunk of the national income and indirect influence over another large part, the path to understanding economics runs through the province of politics. Few, if any, economic events recur as dependably as Halley's comet (with the possible happy exception of payday for those who have jobs and the unhappy April 15 tax filing date). Such is not the case with politics. In America, an absolutely reliable political ritual takes place the first Tuesday of each November: elections. In years divided evenly by four, presidents are elected; in even years, congressional elections are held.

A simple theory linking economy and polity is this: "Incumbent politicians desire re-election and they believe that a booming pre-election economy will help to achieve it."[7] If this theory holds true, we should expect to find evidence—in democratic countries—of

STAYING IN POWER

There are two groups of players: voters and incumbent politicians. Before tugging the handle of the voting machine, voters ask: What has the party in power done for me lately? Anticipating this question, the incumbents push buttons and pull levers at their disposal (printing presses and check-writing machines) to ensure the answer will be favorable: jobs, cheap credit, cars, houses, and higher incomes.

It may well be hard to tell if this game is real or perceived. If enough people *think* impending elections mean a boom, the wave of optimism and spending may be enough to generate the anticipated result, without the incumbent party lifting a finger. Evidence suggests, however, that experienced politicians help such "bootstrap" effects along, just to be safe.

Incumbent parties have in recent years been a major casualty of economists' inability to understand the national economy and hence of government's ineffectual attempts to control it. Between 1976 and 1981, there were seven national elections held in the large democracies of North America and northwest Europe.[8] The parties in power lost six of them. Apparently, voters do not bear long-standing grudges. A careful study by Yale's Ray Fair concluded that for American presidential elections, "voters do not consider the past performance of the non-incumbent party and with respect to the incumbent party consider only the events within the year of the election."[9] There were a lot of bad years between 1976 and 1981.

To generate a political business cycle, it is not necessary for everybody to favor governments that spend freely before elections. It is sufficient that significantly more people are favorably swayed by preelection boomlets than are deterred or dismayed by them. According to Professor Edward Tufte, this is almost universally the case; he found evidence of "electoral-economic cycles" in twenty-seven democracies.[10] William Nordhaus found that for three countries— Germany, New Zealand, and the United States— "the coincidence of business and political cycles is very marked."[11]

While the evidence for election cycles is strictly circumstantial, it is more than enough to convict.

- Between 1961 and 1978, there was a close relation between annual return on stocks and the number of years before or after presidential elections: two years prior to elections, 21.7 percent; one year, 15 percent; the year immediately following an election, 3.6 percent; and two years after, −15.2 percent. A strategy that involved buying stock the last day of October two years prior to a presidential election, and selling it the last day of October preceding the election, would have returned a profit of 5.4 percent on investment (compared with, for example, 2 percent a year on a straight buy-and-hold strategy).[12]
- Despite the vaunted, alleged independence of the Federal Reserve System, since 1960, the money supply has expanded faster during the two years preceding a presidential election than during the two years following one (with a single exception).[13]

Congressional elections follow similar laws of motion. James Tobin attributed Republican defeats in 1932, 1954, 1958, 1960, and 1970 to recessions.[14]

What are the economic implications of election-year

spending? There are at least two: one favorable, the other negative. A distressing implication is that countries with the enviable habit of picking their leaders in free elections may not have sufficient time to properly administer stiff doses of economic medicine. However austere a government's policy, it may have but two years in which to get the job done. If setting our economic house in order takes four years, the job may *never* get done; in other words, what is economically desirable may not be politically feasible. The inflationary bias of elections, piled on top of the inflationary bias of a generation traumatized by the Depression, may send prices soaring. Indeed, in America, it did. A second implication, which is more hopeful, is that governments that believe severe deflation and unemployment is the right way to houseclean a weak, sluggish economy either reverse themselves when elections loom or are deposed by the voters if they refuse.[15] The iron-willed deflation of Mrs. Thatcher has made this proposition shaky, however; and the actions of the Reagan administration in this election year of 1984 will provide it with an important test.

FIGHTING THE LAST WAR

A politician thinks of the next election, and a statesman thinks of the next generation. Perhaps it is a matter of degree; for statesmen also think about elections, and politicians about generations. The generation politicians tend to consider is not the unborn one of the future but the aging current one to which they belong. Our emotions, knowledge, and perceptions are powerfully influenced by experiences in youth. Even societies that do not venerate age tend to reserve positions of authority for the older and wiser. Is society, then, directed by those who see the world not as it is or will be but as it *was?* In eras of rapid change, this can result in much mischief. We may look upon this phenomenon as a kind of recurring game, where one generation inherits power, authority—and gigantic messes—from the previous one.

In this game, there appears to be conflict between nature (the economic environment) and each generation in turn. In fact, despite the orderly transfer of power, conflict arises between a ruling generation and its predecessor, muffled by the veil of time.

GENERATIONS GAME

From birth until their mid-twenties, people learn and acquire experience. During this phase, the previous generation controls and runs the economy, while events shape and influence the perceptions and personalities of the young. When people are in their mid-to-late fifties, the ruling generation begins a smooth orderly transition of power, handing the reins over to the younger generation, who proceed to run things its way.

This game is stylized and contrived. In reality, new cohorts are born every year. A gradual changing of the guard occurs every year rather than every generation. Still, history does provide us with signposts, and society with ambiences, that enable us to identify certain generations and label them as "lost," "beat," "Depression-raised," "postwar," and so on. The abstraction of the *Generations Game* may be more helpful than misleading.

Inherently contentious and divisive, the *Generations Game* may in fact generate bitter conflict and a long-wave business cycle. Suppose Generation No. 1 suffers from the Chinese curse, "may you live in interesting times," and it grows and matures in a period of boom and inflation. On assuming power, this generation bases its policies on its past experience. These policies will likely be anti-inflationary: balanced budgets, tight money, and high interest rates. If severe enough, such policies can turn boom into bust (deflation). If there already exists a weak cycle, with the boom petering out, Generation No. 1's policies will aggravate it, increasing its amplitude and deepening the recession or depression. And as Generation No. 1 sows, so shall Generation No. 2—in its live-and-learn stage—reap. Generation No. 1 retires after about twenty-seven years. Generation No. 2 takes over and immediately changes course. Traumatized by years of unemployment and stagnation, budget deficits soar, money growth catapults, and interest rates plummet—bust becomes boom, and so on. A fifty-four-year-long business cycle is completed. It was a long wave of precisely this length that the Russian economist Kondratieff claimed to have detected, though he did not attribute its cause to the *Generations Game.*

This account may seem fanciful, especially for periods of history when central governments were small and weak and could not destabilize society with "stabilization" policies because economists had not yet invented them. But many economists believe it is an accurate description of the post–World War II inflation.

THE ENEMY:
INFLATION OR UNEMPLOYMENT?

The Brookings Institution economist Walter Salant believes in a generational cycle. "The society that emerged from World War II had been traumatized by the Great Depression of the 1930's," Salant writes. "... the Depression experience made the public and the government more sensitive to economic distress than either had ever been before the Depression."[16] When World War II ended, there was a widespread expectation that demobilization and the abrupt drop in public spending would cause recession or depression. Public policies were shaped with this fear lurking in people's minds. Workers and businessmen came to believe that the authorities would not tolerate sharp downswings, and their expectations were fulfilled; a legislative oath to this effect was sworn, in the Employment Act of 1946. As a result, prices and wages were free to climb but were constrained from falling. "Greater confidence by firms and workers that severe setbacks will be avoided has led to an inertial tendency in United States wage and price behavior," concluded Robert J. Gordon.[17] As the late Arthur M. Okun summarized, "when an economy is made depression-proof and deflation-proof, private expectations and then conventions become asymmetrical, introducing an inflationary bias into the system."[18]

Is it then the case that "the foundation of the current stagflation problem is in large part the success in coping with a major earlier problem"?[19] Marx himself could not have devised a more delectable dialectic. Have we now, after having learned to despise inflation, veered sharply, and disastrously, to excessive deflation, led by a conservative American president? We address this question in the next chapter.

John Maynard Keynes ended his book *The General Theory of Employment, Interest and Money* by claiming that "in the field of economic and political philosophy, there are not so many who are influenced by new theories after they are twenty-five or thirty years of age, so that the ideas which civil servants and politicians and even agitators apply to current events are not likely to be the newest."[20] An old idea that pervaded the thoughts of civil servants, politicians, and perhaps even agitators during the 1960s and 1970s was one due to Keynes himself: large amounts of public spending—and if need be, big deficits—are needed to bolster insufficient private demand. Though Keynes's *General Theory* was published in 1936, it came too late to dig the world out of the Depression. Many years stretch between the propagation of an idea and its assimilation and application. By the time Keynes's proposition came into its own, private demand was no longer insufficient. By then, however, the political and social popularity of large-scale public spending was well entrenched and unencumbered with ifs and buts. Ironically, by showing the world how to force back the rising tide of unemployment, Keynes unintentionally helped fan the fires of inflation. He did not live to forestall this, nor could he have foreseen it when he wrote the last phrase of his *General Theory:* "... soon or late, it is ideas, not vested interests, which are dangerous for good or evil."[21] If Keynes's ideas eventually became a force for evil— through runaway budget deficits, as we shall explain in chapter 7—it was through their misguided, mistaken interpretation by practitioners, and not as a consequence of Keynes's theory itself.

THE KEYNES' MUTINY

With increasing frequency, pronouncements of the death or obsolescence of Keynesian economics are heard. Nothing could be further from the truth. Keynes proposed; cabinets and legislatures disposed. And what Keynes proposed remains valid. It is what people *did* with his models and proposals that sadly distorted them. For this, human nature is to blame—not Keynes.

The revolution Keynes inspired in the way we think about economics can best be explained by analyzing a game we call *The Keynes' Mutiny* (see figure 5.1). Until Keynes came along, economists felt for the most part that national economies would achieve full employment without government interference (despite fourteen major depressions in the United States alone after 1800). This optimistic view was premised on the idea that every dollar of income sooner or later is ploughed back as a dollar of spending, thus making it impossible for aggregate supply to get out of whack with aggregate demand. Keynes rebelled, pointing out that this was not necessarily so. What families held back, through saving, became resources available for firms' capital formation together with firms' own retained profits. Nothing in the world guaranteed that millions of individual decisions by families and firms would lead us to the promised land of full employment, Keynes argued. Families spend according to their means and the standard of living they want. Firms spend in line with the prospects for profit and the cost of capital. The links between families and firms—interest rates paid on savings and wages—may be too tenuous, sluggish, or insensitive to counteract either inadequate, or excess, demand.

		Firms	
		Save	Spend
Families	Save	Depression	Stable Growth
	Spend	Stable Growth	Inflation

Figure 5.1 The Keynes' Mutiny
In this game of coordination, when both families and firms spend, the result is excess demand and inflation. When both families and firms save, there is deficient demand and depression. Only when families save while firms spend, or vice versa, is there stable growth.

In *The Keynes' Mutiny*, two players, families and firms each decide whether to emphasize saving or spending. Their joint decisions determine total aggregate demand. The savings of families provides the resources for the (investment) spending of firms. If firms spend heavily while families save, aggregate demand is just right relative to the economy's capability of satisfying it. High investment spending by firms offsets low private consumption of families. Similarly, if families spend heavily while firms save, again the economy is neither too hot nor too cold; high consumption counterbalances low investment. In both these cases, the economy trods a smooth path.

If *both* firms and families choose to save, too much is held back from the stream of income. Depression results with no intrinsic force arising to dispel it. If *both* firms and families choose to spend, too little is held back from the income stream. Aggregate demand overwhelms supply, and prices rise as a result (inflation).

If firms and families each made decisions by flipping a fair coin, without coordinating their plans with one another, we would have stable growth half the time, depression a quarter of the time, and inflation a quarter of the time. Such a result would be far better than what we have experienced for the last two centuries. The reason we have not had stability for one year in two, even after the *General Theory,* is this: families and firms are made up of people; they are us. People's emotions tend to move in concert, either toward open-pursed optimism or tight-fisted pessimism. Hence there are alternate periods of boom and bust. This kind of game is known as a "coordination problem."[22] It arrives at a happy end usually when players realize their common interest and work out rules for cooperating—for example, taking turns. The role Keynes envisaged for government was not that of a nursery school teacher trying to keep unruly firms and families in line, but that of a balancer injecting, or withdrawing, aggregate demand as the situation demanded. Keynes himself called it a game. "The game of hazard which [the individual enterpriser] plays is furnished with many zeros, so that the players *as a whole* will lose if they have the energy and hope to deal all the cards."[23] Note the dire consequences that occur when *The Keynes' Mutiny* is superimposed on the *Generations Game*. A spend-spend outcome coupled with antidepression deficit spending is inflationary. A save-save outcome along with anti-inflation budget cuts is highly deflationary—a possible explanation of the recession, or depression, of 1979–83.

It was this severe downturn in the economy that rekindled interest in long-wave business cycles and led many people to ask whether we were not in for a recurrence of the depressions of 1873 and 1929, which seem to recur every half-century. In this context, it was inevitable that the name of Nikolai Dmitrievich Kondratieff would emerge from obscurity, along with fears of a fourth wave.

THE FOURTH WAVE

For those who feast on her mysteries, history offers two sorts of entrées—random events and regular recurring phenomena. The task of science is to find out which is which; we are not told in advance. Human nature much prefers reason, order, and system to chaos and entropy; the efforts of thinkers to discern patterns in what appears as disorder will therefore last as long as the human race itself.

We have had good success in fathoming the systematic laws of the physical world. For instance, a recurring event of one type—a plague epidemic—sent Newton from crowded London to his farm to mull over another event. He promulgated a new, and important, law of gravity. Newton's friend Edmund Halley used the new law to discover another regularity; he claimed that three comets that had appeared at seventy-five-year intervals were in fact the same one. Halley passed the acid test of a claim for regularity: successful prediction. He forecast that the comet would reappear in 1758, and when it did, it was named after him (long after he had died). Since then, Halley's comet has reappeared twice and will again in 1986; there is no longer any doubt about its recurrence.

In ferreting out regularities with respect to people, and the societies and economies they fashion, we have been less successful. We still do not know for certain whether there are forces that make economies expand and contract at regular, *predictable* intervals, nor do we understand the nature of such forces.[24] Unproven theories abound. One such theory was devised by Joseph Schumpeter. Building on the work of others, the very learned Schumpeter—who had read almost everything written in economics, in several languages—suggested that there were several sets of concentric cycles. There were, he argued, short forty-month Kitchin cycles (named after the economist who first analyzed them) nested within longer nine-to-ten-year cycles (named after Juglar), in turn set within the fifty-four-year "long cycles" that Kondratieff described.[25] These last cycles he labeled "Kondratieff cycles," after the Russian economist whose 1925 paper in German first speculated about them.[26] Schumpeter felt the key to economic fluctuations was patterns of scientific discovery and innovation. His "wheels-within-wheels" theory seems to resemble, from the vantage point of 1984, the fantastic epicycles that astronomers invented to preserve the Ptolemaic "sun-around-the-earth" theory in the face of increasingly dissonant observations. New data and theories have since sprung up; for example, Simon Kuznets's fifteen-to-twenty-year "intermediate" cycles. But when the industrial economies of the West weakened in the 1970s, interest in Kondratieff's theories was rekindled, as the long-wave "comet" appeared dimly on the horizon for a persuasive fourth time, and right on time.

KONDRATIEFF WAVES

About Nikolai Dmitrievich Kondratieff we know very little. He was born in 1892 and was clever enough to become, at age twenty-five, deputy minister of food under Kerensky. "I arrived at the hypothesis concerning the existence of long waves in the years 1919–21," he wrote later. It was at that time that he set up his Business Conditions Institute in Moscow, where he wrote several works on business cycles. In his 1925 paper (later trans-

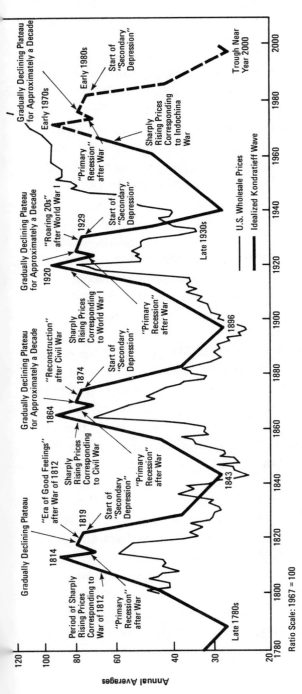

Figure 5.2 Nikolai Kondratieff's Long Waves

After painstakingly compiling thirty-six different sets of data on prices, interest rates, production, and so forth, the Russian economist Nikolai Dmitrievich Kondratieff (1892–1931) thought he detected what he called "long waves" in the capitalist economies: boom-bust cycles lasting forty-seven to sixty years. Kondratieff wrote his "long wave" paper in 1925; he dated the trough of the third wave as "probably" 1914–20. A worldwide depression began in 1930, the year Kondratieff was arrested by Stalin. In 1931, he was sent to Siberia where he died. Some economists believe the 1979–83 world recession completes a fourth Kondratieff wave.

SOURCE: Walt Whitman Rostow, *Why the Poor Get Richer and the Rich Slow Down: Essays in the Marshallian Long Period*, p. 53. University of Texas Press, Austin. Copyright © 1980. Reprinted by permission of the publisher.

lated and published in America in 1935, appropriately enough, in the depths of the Depression), Kondratieff reports on his study of thirty-six different variables and their cyclical behavior over time. "There is," he claims, "reason to assume the existence of long wages of an average length of about 50 years in the capitalistic economy."[27] He notes "three great cycles" in the movement of the price level, the last of which was only half completed (see figure 5.2). He makes no sweeping claims, only that "the existence of long waves of cyclical character is very probable."[28] Nor would he speculate about *why* there were long waves. ". . . we had no intention of laying the foundations for an appropriate theory of long waves," he concluded; although in a later paper, never translated, he suggested reinvestment cycles might be a root cause.[29]

Kondratieff drew up the first five-year plan for agriculture. He pleaded for realistic targets and expressed skepticism about comprehensive planning, arguing against overburdening farmers. Not long after Stalin assumed power, Kondratieff was arrested and forced to appear as witness at a "show" trial. Never tried himself, he was sent to Siberia in 1931, where he is presumed to have died.[30]

Some phenomena are hard to study because they are short-lived. Physicists study nuclear particles so fleeting that a trillion trillion of them can be born and die, consecutively, in fewer than two seconds. Other phenomena are difficult to grasp because they last so long relative to the human life span of threescore and ten. Existing data allowed Kondratieff to identify only two full "long waves" and half of a third, even though he delved into history as far back as 1790. Had he survived

Stalin and Gulag, it is not impossible that he would be alive today; if so, he would be ninety-two years old. Kondratieff was an undeviating Marxist. He was convinced that "long waves arise out of causes which are inherent in the essence of the capitalist economy."[31] He would be highly amused to learn that the onset of the economic decline that marked the peak of the fourth Kondratieff wave began not on account of a capitalist weakness, but because of a perennial *socialist* shortcoming: the inefficiency of Soviet agriculture, the very topic on which Kondratieff's prophetic warnings landed him in Gulag rather than in grandeur. We might well call the stagflation of the 1970s Kondratieff's Revenge or Kondratieff's Vindication.

CONCLUSION

Arthur James Balfour once wrote, "Our whole political machinery presupposes a people so fundamentally at one that they can safely afford to bicker."[32] Whether or not you can afford something depends on its price relative to your means. Political and generational cycles, and Keynesian bouts of inflation and unemployment, arise from recurring patterns of human behavior—familiar economic games that are played repeatedly at fixed intervals. The bickering these games entail imposes upon us intolerable costs—downswings in economic activity that repeat themselves every two, four, or even fifty-four years. We can ill afford them.

Kondratieff spoke of long waves as a failing of capitalism. But in our most recent economic crisis, for the fourth wave, the economic doldrums touched the planned economies of the East as well as the market economies of the West. Divided by ideology, East and West had at least one thing in common during the decade of the 1970s, especially toward its end—hard times. Kondratieff's Revenge was late, but even-handed.

Backward Runs the Economics: Predatory Games in the Indexed Society

SHORT, medium, and long waves of business activity washed over the world economy after World War II just as they had done prior to the war and prior to Keynes (though some evidence suggests a trend in modern times toward shorter, shallower cycles[1]). An observer might well comment, "Plus ça change ..." But in the past decade, long-standing economic relationships began to reverse themselves. Policies once thought to be *de*flationary—tight money, high interest rates, and high taxes—came to be regarded as *in*flationary. Economic barometers like unemployment and common-stock prices that once responded positively to higher inflation reacted negatively.

Picture the gearshift of your car. Suppose that one day you got into your car, turned on the ignition, moved the gearshift to Drive, stepped on the gas, and began zipping along at 30 m.p.h.—in reverse. Suppose all cars behaved this way. Until people got the hang of the new, topsy-turvy world, chaos would reign. That is precisely what happened to the economy in the 1970s. To paraphrase Wolcott Gibbs's parody of *Time* magazine: backwards runs the economics until reels the mind.

Why has the economy mutated? What created the "wrong-way" economy? Why would an observer decide that, after all, *"ce n'est pas la même chose"*? And how can things be set right again? The answer lies, we claim in this and the following chapter, in understanding the predatory games played by an indexed society—a society in which prices, and hence people, are inextricably linked to one another both through market forces and legal contracts, with the consumer price index acting as a starter's pistol. Some of an indexed society's favorite games are described below. What created those games, and how they conspire to produce a wrong-way economy, are the subjects of chapter 7.

ECONOMY SOARS, SPUTTERS, AND REVERSES

In the 1920s and 1930s, two events in aviation history occurred that served to prefigure and symbolize post–World War II economic history. In May 1927, a twenty-five-year-old pilot flew from Roosevelt Field in Long Island, New York, to Paris in just over thirty-three hours—a distance of 3,600 miles and the first time it had been done. On landing, he climbed out of his cockpit and announced poetically, "Well, here we are." The pilot was, of course, Charles Lindbergh. His feat prompted people to think of "their old best dreams," as Scott Fitzgerald wrote.

Thick fog covered Bennett Airfield, near New York, in the early dawn hours one Sunday in 1938 as a battered Curtis Robin J-6 monoplane lumbered slowly into the air. The aircraft had no radio or beam finder. The pilot's view was blocked by extra gas tanks needed to reach his declared destination, California. Making a sweeping turn over Jamaica Bay, the plane headed east out over the Atlantic, instead of west to California, as ground crew watched in disbelief. A day later, the pilot broke through the fog over Dublin and landed at Baldonnel Airport. He said he was surprised to see grass roofs and cobblestones instead of New Mexican deserts and told authorities he had flown 3,000 miles in the wrong direction because of fog and a broken compass. The pilot was Douglas Corrigan, henceforth nicknamed "Wrong-way." His flight was celebrated in fun and laughter by a world weary of economic depression and leary of impending war.[2]

The flights of Lindbergh and Corrigan serve as parables. For nearly a decade, through the 1930s, the limping market economies of the West had been weighed down by unemployment and stagnation. Then Hitler unleashed the dogs of war. Spending on arms and armies injected huge amounts of purchasing power. Production and employment soared. At the war's end, despite experts' predictions of a return to depression, America and Europe took off on a flight of growth that, like Lindbergh's, was of unusual length, speed, and smoothness. Two decades of such growth led experts to believe that the secret of piloting a modern industrial economy had been cracked.

Then, a minor error was committed. President Lyndon Johnson chose both margarine and munitions, refusing to raise taxes to finance the Vietnam war spending.[3] The sparks of inflation were later fanned by the Soviet grain purchases mentioned before, OPEC, and consequently an ingrained belief that inflation had become permanent. In the economic games people played, that belief turned into a self-fulfilling prophecy. The result was an economy whose causal arrows, like Corrigan, began heading in the wrong direction.

WRONG-WAY ECONOMY

Here are just a few of the "wrong" directions that baffled us in the Corrigan economy of the 1970s.[4]

- With budget deficits, the more red ink the government spills, the more it stimulates the economy, we once thought. Now, rumors of soaring deficits depress the stock market and spread gloom. Red ink has become black news.
- Budget deficits sooner or later become printed money. More money, we used to think, means *lower* interest rates. By the law of supply and demand, an increase in the supply of money should lower its price (the interest rate). Now, it is believed that deficits,

faster money growth, or both work to *raise* interest rates.

- Presidents Kennedy and Johnson sought tax cuts to stimulate *spending.* President Reagan sought them—to boost *saving.*
- Inflation and unemployment marched in opposite directions in the 1960s. In the 1970s, they walked hand in hand, a phenomenon we came to know as stagflation.
- Common stocks once were a refuge from inflation. In the 1970s, they became a trap.
- High interest rates and high taxes were once thought to be *de*flationary, restraining demand by making borrowing more expensive and by leaving less disposable income in the pockets of consumers. Now, raising interest rates and taxes is thought by some to work to raise prices (namely, *in*flationary) by increasing costs of production, increases which are quickly reflected in market prices.

What unites these reverse causalities is this. Underlying each is an attempt by an economic game player—wage earner, supplier of capital, manager, owner of a business, and bureaucrat—to raise the price he or she *charges* for an owned or controlled resource or good. The price is raised for one of two reasons: (a) to help the game player's after-tax money income catch up with the prices he or she *pays;* or (b) to boost the game player's money income *in advance of* anticipated price increases. What may begin as a series of defensive moves of the first type, rapidly evolves into a norm of offensive moves of the second type. When this happens, an indexed society stops behaving like Lindbergh's *Spirit of St. Louis* and begins to behave like Corrigan's creaky J-6. To understand this metamorphosis, let us see how the economic game society plays evolved and changed.

ZENO AND THE INFLATION TURTLE

A Greek philosopher named Zeno in the fifth century B.C. loved to invent paradoxes. His best-known one bears his name. Suppose, Zeno said, a fleet runner chases a tortoise, cutting the gap between them in half every so often. Even if the runner is Sebastian Coe or Carl Lewis, he will never enjoy turtle soup. Half the distance always remains between them, if only a hair's breadth or a micrometer.*

What happens when a group of Zeno's—workers, businessmen, and importers—chase an inflation tortoise, or, more accurately, an inflation hare? The object of the chase is to keep money income from trailing behind prices. In the following three games that we portray, the chase becomes increasingly more futile and successively more disastrous for society. We begin with that pet phrase of economists, "assume that . . ." in all three games the contestants and the initial situation are the same.

- There are three groups of players: laborers, bakers, and importers.
- Laborers get $10.00 an hour, and each bakes twenty

*The solution to the paradox is the mathematical idea of convergence to a limit. The runner of course does catch the tortoise, and by using the formula for the sum of a geometric series, $1 + \frac{1}{2} + \frac{1}{4} \ldots$, you can compute when and where.

loaves an hour. If we ignore the cost of flour and water, bread therefore costs 50¢ a loaf to produce.

- Bakers use a 100 percent markup and charge $1.00 a loaf.
- Importers buy water from a neighboring country for $1.00 a gallon and sell it for the same price (for now, we ignore their profit).
- People live on bread and water alone.

This example is, of course, in the great tradition of otherworld theorizing. We find it useful for understanding real aspects of this world. One of the laborers, by coincidence named Zeno and good at figures, invents what he calls the consumer price index (CPI), or cost of living index. It is a weighted average of the price of bread and the price of water. Zeno's life is made easy by the fact that everyone in society spends precisely half his income on bread and half on water. The CPI is therefore:

$$100 \ (\tfrac{1}{2} \times \$1.00 + \tfrac{1}{2} \times \$1.00) = 100$$

Zeno multiplies by 100 to clean out decimals, which he dislikes.

In each of the following three games, we start proceedings by introducing what economists call an external shock: in this case, the Organization of Water Exporting Countries (O.W.E.C.) raises the price of water by 20 percent. Here is how Zeno and his friends react in the games: the *Spirit of 1776,* the *Dispirit of 1956,* and the *Despair of 1976.*

SPIRIT OF 1776

People—workers, bakers, and importers—all believe inflation is transient; no one has the power to do anything about it—nor would anyone do anything if he could.

After water rises in price by 20 percent to $1.20, Zeno is asked to recalculate the CPI and quickly complies. He gets the following:

$$100 \ (½ \times \$1.00 + ½ \times \$1.20) = 110$$

His announcement to the press is: consumer prices have risen by 10 percent.

Nothing happens to wages (still $10.00 an hour), the price of bread (still $1.00), or future water prices. For the rest of his life, Zeno hands the press photocopies of his earlier announcement, because his CPI stays at 110.

What has happened is this: society's real income has gone down by 10 percent because exactly one-half of peoples' shopping baskets have become more costly by 20 percent, while wages and profits have stayed the same. O.W.E.C. benefits by the exact amount that Zeno and his compatriots lose. After the initial 10 percent price rise, no further inflation occurs. (O.W.E.C. may repeat the exercise from time to time, but the results are the same.)

The *Spirit of 1776* is built on the premise that people do not react to increases in the prices they pay by trying to raise the prices they themselves charge. There are several reasons why this may be true. People may be unaware that the prices they pay have risen, especially if the increases are small and infrequent, below some threshold level. Even if they are aware of inflation, they may feel powerless to charge more for their labor or capital because buyers will not agree to pay more, or because competition among wage earners and suppliers of capital makes such increases risky or impossible. This type of "learned helplessness" contributes to stable prices, though it may be a most unpleasant feeling.

Predatory Games in the Indexed Society

Psychological aspects of learned helplessness, as both a result of inflation and as an explanation of why we dislike it so much, are examined in chapter 8.

If price rises persist, the game changes. People begin to behave differently.

DISPIRIT OF 1956

People no longer believe inflation is transient and evanescent. They are aware of it, and this awareness is expressed in changes in behavior.

Unions exist, and they work to raise wages. Management too acts to raise prices. Labor contracts begin to include cost-of-living allowance (COLA) clauses that boost wages by part or all of the rise in consumer prices.

Suppose that Zeno and his fellow workers seek, and get, wage increases equal to the full rise in the CPI. Bakers, in turn, raise the price of bread by the same percentage as the increase in wages.

In this indexed society linked to the CPI, will not inflation go on forever, once it gets started? The answer, surprisingly, is no—because it is not quite a fully indexed society.

Assume again that water prices rise by 20 percent. Zeno's calculation of the CPI is:

$$100 \ (½ \times \$1.00 + ½ \times \$1.20) = 110$$

Half of the shopping basket Zeno and his friends buy has risen in price by 20 percent; half (bread) costs what it always did. The overall cost of the shopping basket has thus risen by 10 percent. In the *Spirit of 1776,* that would end the game. Workers and bakers would take a 10 percent cut in their real incomes; while their *money*

133

incomes stay the same, the prices they pay rise by 10 percent. But in the *Dispirit of 1956,* Zeno invokes the COLA clause, a pause that refreshes. Wages thereupon rise 10 percent, to $11.00 an hour. Bread once cost fifty cents a loaf; now an hour's labor costs $11.00 and yields twenty loaves, so the cost per loaf is now $11.00/20 = $0.55. Since bakers' costs have risen by 10 percent (from fifty to fifty-five cents), they raise the price of bread by 10 percent, too, to $1.10 ($0.55 × 2).

Since bread has risen in price, Zeno has to recalculate the CPI:

$$100 \ (½ \times \$1.10 + ½ \times \$1.20) = 115$$

He announces a further five-point rise (roughly, 5 percent) in the CPI. Wages must be increased again, by this percentage, and as a result, bread too gets more expensive. The CPI in the next round is:

$$100 \ (½ \times \$1.15 + ½ \times \$1.20) = 117.5$$

Despite his aversion to decimals, Zeno resists the temptation to round off upwards and keeps the .5 instead of making it 118.

The game goes on. Further rounds of wage and price increases are:

$$100 \ (½ \times \$1.175 + ½ \times \$1.20) = 118.75$$

$$100 \ (½ \times \$1.185 + ½ \times \$1.20) = 119.375$$

And so on.

You may by now have guessed that the CPI is closing

in on the 120 level, cutting the distance between itself and 120 by half in each round, just like Zeno and the turtle. The CPI catches the tortoise when wages reach $12.00 an hour (a total increase of 20 percent), bread prices reach $1.20 (a total increase of 20 percent), and the new CPI is:

$$100 \ (\frac{1}{2} \times \$1.20 + \frac{1}{2} \times \$1.20) = 120$$

In this game, where wages and domestic (that is, locally-produced) goods prices are all indexed (tied to the CPI), an initial X percent rise in *anything* causes an eventual X percent rise in *everything.* Then, inflation grinds to a halt.

A much more dramatic game than this one could have been constructed. In principle, even if initially only one-half of 1 percent of the consumer's basket rises in price by X percent, eventually the whole basket increases in price by X percent. This can be proved by working through the *Dispirit of 1956* with Zeno and his friends spending 99.5 percent of their income on bread and only 0.5 percent on water. (Be sure you have plenty of paper. The CPI again closes in on 120, but it takes many more rounds than before. This could make the price of paper more expensive.)

Why label this game the *Dispirit of 1956?* People seem better off than in the *Spirit of 1776.* There, they lost 10 percent in real income (recall that wages stayed at $10.00 an hour while the CPI rose by 10 percent). Here, wages, bakers' profits, and the CPI also rise by 20 percent; so isn't everyone back to where he was initially, in real terms, thanks to indexing?

The answer is: yes and no. One price is *not* tied to

the CPI: the price of water. Suppose water is paid for in dollars. O.W.E.C. watches its initial 20 percent price rise get eaten away as it is paid in inflated dollars whose purchasing power (the inverse of the CPI) is sinking. Zeno cannot control the price of water. But he and his friends *can* influence the "value" of dollars (what a dollar can buy). In the end, the effective price of water is what it was to begin with: $1.20 in inflated dollars that buy 20 percent less than they did earlier—in real terms, $1.00. Zeno, the workers, and the bakers got back their initial 10 percent loss in real income because of inflation. Is not, then, inflation the good wind that blows no ill and, eventually, stops blowing altogether when it has done its job?

The problem is that O.W.E.C. and importers are in the game, too. They resent watching their initial gains expropriated by inflation, which erodes the value of the dollar by 20 percent and cancels their 20 percent price increase. When *they* act, the game again changes.

DESPAIR OF 1976

Every price, including that of water, is indexed (linked to the CPI).

Zeno's first-round computation looks the same as in the previous games:

$$100 \ (\tfrac{1}{2} \times \$1.00 + \tfrac{1}{2} \times \$1.20) = 110$$

As in the *Dispirit of 1956,* wages and bread prices consequently rise 10 percent. This time, however, so does the price of water, as O.W.E.C. and the importers fight to keep pace with inflation just like laborers and bakers do. Water rises to $1.32, and Zeno's new CPI figure is:

$$100 \ (\tfrac{1}{2} \times \$1.10 + \tfrac{1}{2} \times \$1.32) = 121$$

He announces to the press that, once again, consumer prices jumped 10 percent. Wages are now $11.00, bread costs $1.10, and the dollar is worth 20 percent less than it was before water got more costly. But the game is not over. The next round sees wages rise a further 10 percent, as do bread prices and water prices:

$$100 \ (\tfrac{1}{2} \times \$1.21 + \tfrac{1}{2} \times \$1.45) = 133$$

Again, the CPI has risen 10 percent. In fact, Zeno is beginning to see the handwriting on the wall. It will, he sees, *keep on* rising 10 percent each round, forever. Workers and bakers lost 10 percent of their income to O.W.E.C. in round one. In later rounds, they tried to get it back as they did in 1956. But this time, it didn't work because water prices kept jumping ahead, too. Unless something drastic happens, Zeno will chase the inflation tortoise forever and never catch it. When society is fully indexed, an initial price rise in anything generates *eternal* price rises in everything.

Things could in fact get much worse. The *Despair of 1976* could turn into a variation of *Quick Draw*. Zeno and the bakers might try to get the jump on O.W.E.C., and on one another, by raising wages and bread prices by 20 percent. If O.W.E.C. responds by raising water prices by 30 percent, the result is an escalation game not unlike the *Dollar Auction*. Here, the CPI does not rise by 20 percent each round, it increases by a growing percentage. If things get sufficiently out of hand, as they have from time to time in history, the *rate* at which inflation accelerates may itself accelerate. Latin American inflation is an example of this.

In the indexed society playing the *Despair of 1976,* what becomes increasingly more frustrating to everyone is this:

The end result of the *Despair of 1976* is no different from that of the *Spirit of 1776.* In both games, wage earners and entrepreneurs end up with 10 percent less in real income.

The *Spirit of 1776* ends after one round. The *Despair of 1976* goes on endlessly and futilely. In the game itself, everyone may hang on to his relative position. But *stopping* the game—for example, by imposing a draconic recession accompanied by high unemployment—may involve enormous costs such that nearly everyone may lose. In this sense, the *Despair of 1976* is a non-zero-sum game.

Economist Robert J. Gordon recently studied fourteen historical episodes across nine countries, including the United States, in which inflation was halted.[5] These are his main findings.

- In only four of the fourteen episodes was inflation slowed markedly through demand-restraint policies, *"with only a 'minor' loss in output."* They were: the United States, 1920–22; France, 1963–66; Japan, 1976–80; and Italy, 1963–68.[6]
- No such episode has occurred in the United States since 1922.
- There are no other examples of successful "low-cost" episodes of stopping inflation in other countries.

A fifteenth episode occurred in 1982, when the American consumer price index rose by less than 4 percent after three straight years (1979, 1980, and 1981) of double-digit inflation. (Inflation was extinguished so abruptly, in fact, that in December 1982 the CPI *fell* by 0.3 percent.) Wholesale prices rose 3.5 percent in 1982, the smallest increase in a decade. A heavy price was paid for this success, however. Unemployment reached post-Depression record levels of over 10 percent, or 12 million jobless. America plunged into a long, deep recession and dragged other industrial countries with her. Because of this world recession, inflation tumbled in Europe too. In 1982, Britain had the smallest increase in consumer prices for thirteen years—5.4 percent—but paid for it with 12 percent unemployment. In Common Market countries, there were 21 million jobless at the end of 1982, with unemployment rates topping 17 percent in Belgium and 14 percent in Ireland.

In an indexed society, inflation can be stopped. But many people wonder whether it is worth the price, and whether there is not a better way than smothering inflation with unemployment. The surprisingly vigorous economic recovery in 1983–84 blunted the cutting edge of the question very little.

SNAP, OLD MAID, HOT POTATO, AND MUSICAL CHAIRS

The *Despair of 1976* is often played in wonderfully sophisticated variations, the most common being *Hot Potato*. The *real* game of *Hot Potato* has the following rules:

HOT POTATO

"You will need: at least eight players, about 15 minutes' playing time, a piano or record player, and potatoes.

All the children get down on the floor on their hands and knees. All but one are given a potato which they hold in their right hands. When the music starts the potatoes are passed around to the left and are kept going until the music stops. The player who doesn't have a potato when the music stops is eliminated from the game. The game ends when only one child is left."[7]

The *economic* game of *Hot Potato* has two slight but significant rule changes—there are many potatoes, and nobody ever leaves the game. (Inflation may be unpleasant, but unlike unemployment, it is not generally a cause of suicide.) It works in the following way. Some external power—OPEC, fate, or nature—conspires to make us poorer by making us give up more of our resources for a barrel of crude oil, by making both us and our resources relatively less productive, or by inventing Japan. Our total real output falls, or possibly grows slower than what we have been accustomed to. Initially, a burden-potato lands in someone's lap—for example, that of the oil companies, who have to pay more for crude oil to their suppliers. Defying the laws of physics, they raise prices faster than the speed of light—anything moving faster than light in theory goes backward in time (or at least in science fiction)—and shift the potato to consumers. As wage earners, consumers seek and get higher wages, thus moving the burden onto the shoulders of their employers; they in turn raise their prices, making some of the burden land on the government, which finds the things it buys more costly; thereupon the government boosts spending, runs deficits, prints money, and causes the burden to move back to consumers, who get more wage increases; after this interest rates rise as banks try to keep pace, making credit more costly and causing investors to cut back; this shifts part of the burden to future generations, who have a lot of trouble reacting since they do not yet exist. The game gets endlessly complex and even the most astute keen-eyed observer quickly loses sight of the potato, which often is sliced into french fries and spread around only to reemerge whole every once in a while. In the heat of the game, sometimes we forget that there *is* a potato. But it is certainly there—and no amount of indexing, burden shifting, or price hiking can make it go away.

The copyright on predatory games played by an indexed society rightfully belongs to John Maynard Keynes, whose vision of economics, we have argued, has been prematurely labeled obsolete by many people largely because it was misunderstood. In his *General Theory* he writes:

> This battle of wits . . . is, so to speak, a game of Snap, of Old Maid, of Musical Chairs—a pastime in which he is victor who says Snap neither too soon nor too late, who passes the Old Maid to his neighbor before the game is over, who secures a chair for himself when the music stops. These games can be played with zest and enjoyment, though all the players know that it is the Old Maid which is circulating, or that when the music stops some of the players will find themselves unseated.[8]

Here Keynes is referring to games of financial investment. But in a series of memos written during the early years of World War II, as economic advisor to the British Treasury, Keynes describes the *Despair of 1976* and *Hot Potato* in explicit terms. He begins with his notion of the "gap"—the difference between what government, firms, and families want to spend, and what is available for them to purchase, a gap created by the needs of war.

Keynes estimates the size of the gap in 1941 to be about 10 percent of the existing standard of living (measured by private consumption). "How can it be filled?" he asks in a memo on budget policy written on February 17, 1941.[9] Not by inflation, as in 1917. "It is impossible," he writes, "to effect a [price] rise which is sufficiently steep to restore equilibrium. . . . Today about half of total wages are tied to the cost of living by a formula and rise automatically after the briefest interval. Thus this traditional outlet is denied to us. Probably a good thing. . . ."[10] To Keynes, the indexed society of 1941 would rationally choose from the outset not to play *Hot Potato* at all. Were he alive, he might be amused or angry to see the indexed society of 1973–82 play it with zest.

In a later memo, Keynes returns to the theme of "filling the gap"—a metaphor responsible for an amusing David Low cartoon in the *Evening Standard,* showing Chancellor of the Exchequer Sir Kingsley Wood searching under his desk for gap fillers, while a Western Union boy is putting out the call for Maynard Keynes.[11] Keynes notes five ways to do this: higher taxes, higher savings, price controls, drawing down inventories, and higher prices. He rejects the last method in a description of a game identical to the *Despair of 1976:*

suppose an average [initial] rise of 10 percent [in prices] . . . The rise in prices will increase the incomes of the lucky vendors of the goods. Some part of this increase they will pay away in increased taxes . . . , some part they may save, but some part they may spend in an endeavour to maintain an increase in their own personal consumption; with the result of a further rise in prices at the second round. Moreover the initial rise in prices may cause higher wages and therefore higher incomes to wage earners, also with the result of a further rise in prices. Thus an initial 'gap' of no more than 10 percent may lead, sooner or later, to an unlimited rise in prices. That is the stupidity of this method of meeting the problem.[12]

In the post-Keynesian era, a sixth, politically appealing way is employed to "fill" the gap between what we want to spend and what we are able to produce: promises, proclamations, and palliatives. This creates a new gap: credibility. Society must dispose of both the Keynesian and credibility gaps.

STOCKS AS INFLATION HEDGES: HEDGE YOUR BETS

We end this chapter, as we began it, by pondering the wrong-way economy. One of the most important and controversial mutations in the 1970s occurred in the relation between common stock prices and inflation, a change highly relevant to the millions of Americans who hold shares.

The first two paragraphs in a February 24, 1951, *Business Week* article began: "There's basic soundness in Wall Street's current sales slogan: 'Protect yourself from inflation, buy common stocks,' " and "History has proved many times that you can hedge against inflation in the stock market—in practice, as well as in theory."[13] The theory was simple. Inflation generates profits. Profits generate dividends and the expectation of more. Dividends hike stock prices. For two decades, the theory worked. Between 1946 and 1967, the New York Stock Exchange composite stock index rose by more than 500 percent, while consumer prices climbed only 74 percent.

During the period 1968–73, doubts arose. Some experts began to hedge their claims about the merits of common stocks as an inflation hedge. The ensuing decade left no doubt; stock price averages were basically the same in August 1982 as they were in 1973, even though consumer prices doubled. Just to keep up with inflation, the Dow-Jones industrial average should have topped 1,800 in the summer of 1982. Instead it dangled between 900 and 1,000. Throughout this period, rumors of worse inflation drove stock prices *down,* and hopes of less inflation drove them *up.*

Why? What changed? There are several explanations. One belongs to Leo Tolstoy, who said that history would be a very fine thing if only it were true. A study by Glenn Johnson, Frank Reilly, and Ralph Smith trimmed somewhat the stocks-as-inflation-hedge gospel. They found that during the 1949–51 inflation, twenty-two of the thirty Dow-Jones industrial stocks surpassed a benchmark rate of return (8.2 percent); but during the 1955–57 price spurt, only ten of the thirty stocks qualified as inflation hedges, and during 1965–67, only *two* stocks made it.[14] Moreover, they found that taking all three inflationary periods together, not even *one* of the thirty Dow-Jones industrials was an unfailing benchmark beater, and only six of the thirty consistently matched inflation.

Nonetheless, there is little doubt, as Professor Charles Nelson notes, that "if one had surveyed academic and nonacademic students of the stock market in the year 1968 . . . one would have found wide agreement with the proposition that rates of return on common stocks move directly with the rate of inflation."[15] Since 1973, the causal arrow has reversed itself, both in theory and in reality. A mere whisper of worse inflation drives stock prices down.

Three explanations for this have been advanced. Professor Eugene Fama's theory, couched in technical language, is this:

> The negative relations between stock returns and inflation are proxying for positive relations between stock returns and real variables which are more fundamental determinants of equity values. The negative stock return-inflation relations are induced by negative relations between inflation and real activity which in turn are explained by a combination of money demand theory and the quantity theory of money.[16]

In rough translation: inflation is bad for the economy. A bad economy is bad for common stocks. This raises a key question: *Why* was the inflation of the 1970s bad for the economy (stagflation), when the inflation of the 1950s and, partly, the 1960s was rather good for it? We grapple with this question in the next chapter.

A second theory comes from Martin Feldstein, chairman of the Council of Economic Advisors. He blames high taxes imposed on profits. This occurred, he argues, when inflationary, paper profits were taxed, even when real profits were negative or zero. He singles out in particular the use of historic cost depreciation, which understates true costs in times of rising prices and levies taxes on artificial (inflation-induced) capital gains.[17]

Both Fama and Feldstein find rational, objective reasons for putting inflation and stock prices at opposite ends of a seesaw. Most economists hold the belief that investors are rational and markets are efficient. One economist who does not is Franco Modigliani of M.I.T. In a controversial article, he and his associate Richard A. Cohn claim that "because of inflation-induced errors, investors have systematically undervalued the stock market by 50 per cent."[18] Rationally valued, they claim, the Standard & Poor 500 should have been at 200 at the end of 1977, instead of at 100. This disavowal of investor rationality was for some the equivalent of an ayatollah preaching apostasy.

Modigliani and Cohn blame inflation too, which, they say, causes investors to undervalue future profits and dividends. Here is why. The sound procedure for valuing a financial asset is to figure out what real future profits (*net* of inflation—in, for example, constant 1984 prices) will be, and then to compute what the present value of those future profits are now. (For instance, the present value of $100 received in 1989 at 15 percent interest is $50 now; that is because $50 invested at 15 percent interest would be worth $100 after five years.) The correct rate of interest for present-value calculations is the *real* rate—the market interest rate minus the rate of inflation. But, say Modigliani and Cohn, while investors net inflation out of their estimates of future dividends, they use market interest rates in their present-value calculations. When market interest rates are very high, as they were in the late 1970s, this makes future dividends, however high they might be, seem unattractive. "Our empirical results imply that each percentage point of inflation typically reduces market value by a staggering 13 percent," they write, "relative to what it would be if valued rationally."[19]

In mid-August 1982, we asked Professor Modigliani if he thought investors would ever wise up. Yes, he responded, if interest rates come down. The resulting bull market would be rapid, not gradual.[20] They did, and it was. As congressional elections loomed, Federal Reserve authorities threw their full weight, and height, against interest rates. Federal funds rates dropped abruptly; and interest rate pundits predicted they would keep falling. On August 17, the Dow-Jones industrials rose thirty points. The bull market was to send the Dow-Jones to over 1,100.

Investing is, of course, a game, complex, precarious, and at times perverse. Investing in a market laden with irrational investors is fraught with paradox and peril. A smart investor who had correctly valued stocks in the early 1970s and bought heavily would have lost his shirt—inspiring, predictably, Professor Modigliani's quip, "If you're so smart, why aren't you poor?"[21] And Keynes once likened professional investing to "those newspaper competitions in which the competitors have to pick out the six prettiest faces from a hundred photographs," with the prize going to the competitor whose choice is closest to the average choice of all competitors.[22] This suggests the game of *Beauty Queen*.

147

BEAUTY QUEEN

There is only one rule: winners are those who pick the favorite, as judged by all, in secret ballot.

This is not a case, Keynes notes, of choosing which you think is prettiest, or even which you think *others* think is prettiest. We are, he says, at the third degree where "we devote our intelligences" to guessing what average opinion expects average opinion to be. There are those who practice the "fourth, fifth and higher degrees."[23] *Beauty Queen* investing is hard enough in an environment of rational investors. In an irrational, wrong-way world, it is even more precarious.

History, poet Paul Valéry said, is the science of things that never repeat themselves. Burton Malkiel has suggested that common stocks will regain their lusters as a good inflation hedge for the 1980s, not because prices will soar (capital gains) but because dividends will be generous relative to stock prices (income).[24] Will the *Beauty Queen* guessers pick them?

CHAPTER 7

To Fight Inflation, Raise Prices: The Backward Economy Dissected

TWO newspaper headlines serve as classic examples of the new wrong-way economy and introduce a discussion of what caused it to mutate. The *International Herald Tribune,* November 21, 1979, featured "ISRAEL DRASTICALLY RAISES PRICES TO FIGHT INFLATION." Raise prices—to fight inflation? And the *International Herald-Tribune,* October 10, 1982, juxtaposed side by side, "JOBLESSNESS IN U.S. PASSES 10 PERCENT" and "NYSE EXTENDS RECORD ADVANCE." The same day that unemployment in America was announced at double-digit figures, the first time since 1940, the New York Stock Exchange rose strongly for a third consecutive day, on rumors of lower interest rates.

As defendants are wont to mutter to tough judges, we

149

can explain. In Israel, the government heavily subsidizes basic foodstuffs. By cutting the subsidies, and thus raising their prices, the finance minister hoped to trim his budget deficit, and consequently, cut inflation. The logic was that deficit shekels cause more inflation than one-time price rises. (Parenthetically: it failed. Israel's 133 percent inflation in 1980 topped its own record and, for that year, the world's.)

In America, the hero/villain was interest rates. High interest rates had driven the economy into recession and led to record unemployment. When these rates dropped in the summer and fall of 1982, common stocks became more attractive; money shifted from bonds to stocks, either for simple reasons (bonds paid less) or the complex Modigliani-Cohn rationale (lower interest helped investors correct their undervalued perception of stocks). Hence, there was the concomitance of rising stocks and peak unemployment. For particular cases of backward causality, it is not hard to find an explanation. But is there a more general way to interpret the mutated economy and why it changed?

WAGES, DEFICITS

A persuasive theory has been proposed by Nobel laureate Sir W. Arthur Lewis.[1] He compares the inflation of 1899–1913 with that of 1950–79. His study shows how a history of our past can reveal the tribulations of the present.

The Backward Economy Dissected

Professor Lewis detects two new elements in the anatomy of modern inflation. One is the rapid way in which money wages—and indeed, all incomes—now adjust to rises in the cost of living. A second is the peacetime profligacy of governments, which print money to support their deficits and cite Keynes to justify it.

In 1776, Adam Smith could note that "the wages of labour do not in Great Britain fluctuate with the price of provisions. . . . In many places, the money price of labour remains uniformly the same sometimes for half a century altogether."[2] At the turn of this century, money wages began a secular increase. But, as Lewis notes, this rise did not become correlated with the cost of living until 1939.

The consequence of this relatively recent marriage of wages and consumer prices is this—"*any* increase in costs in any part of the system is liable to 'enter' into wages, and thereby to be transmitted to all other prices."[3] In the unindexed society of 1899–1913, if one commodity became more expensive and people went on buying it as before, they would have less money to spend on other things, and the price of those things would fall correspondingly. This offsetting effect could not prevent inflation, but it meant price rises were mild and did not build up a head of steam. Recall that in the *Spirit of 1776*, the game lasted but one round. In the indexed economy of 1950–84, if one commodity becomes more expensive and people keep buying it as before, they demand higher wages as compensation to enable them to buy as much of everything as they did before the price rise (see the *Despair of 1976*, p. 136). In this

151

way, a rise in prices in one sector of the economy—grain or energy—can quickly spread into a general inflation.

Oil prices are an example. Some economists deny that the quadrupling of crude oil prices in 1974–78 was an important factor in the inflation of the 1970s. In the United States, only about one dollar in every forty of the national product goes to energy. A 300 percent rise in one-fortieth of the nation's shopping basket amounts to 7.5 percent general inflation $(300 \times 1/40)$ spread over five years—about 1.5 percent a year, which is only a small fraction of the actual rise in the CPI. But, as Lewis explains, "what makes a price rise in an important commodity sector potentially explosive is that it triggers a chase by other prices,"[4] as we observed in *Hot Potato.*

When wages and prices rise, the money value of spending and output increases in step. A larger quantity of money is therefore demanded to facilitate this expanded money sum of transactions. If the government refused to provide this extra money, would not the *Despair of 1976,* or *Hot Potato,* soon grind to a crashing halt? Possibly not. A constant amount of money can support a greater amount of spending when each cash dollar or deposit dollar changes hands more frequently—that is, through a rise in the so-called velocity of money. One trillion dollars that change hands ten times a year, on an average, provide the same effective money supply as two trillion dollars that change hands only five times a year. While governments can control the supply of money, they cannot directly determine how quickly people will choose to get rid of it.

Appeal to this argument, however, is quite unnecessary. The model of Keynes legitimized budget deficits

to counteract unemployment; but the italics were soon
forgotten and dropped. Government, Lewis observes,
once given the power to unbalance the budget, uses that
power "to emancipate itself from other fiscal controls
. . . most governments, though not all, simply misuse
their power to add to the money supply."[5]

Keynes's budget dictum is symmetrical, calling for
deficits during recession and surpluses during inflation.
But as James Buchanan and Richard Wagner note,
"democratic political pressures are likely to generate an
assymetrical application of the Keynesian prescriptions. . . . The Keynesian destruction of the balanced
budget constraint is likely to produce a bias toward
budget deficits, monetary expansion, and public sector
growth. Politicians naturally want to spend and avoid
taxing. The elimination of the balanced-budget constraint enables politicians to give fuller expression to
these quite natural sentiments."[6] Like the one-eyed Ho-
ratio Nelson at the Battle of Copenhagen, governments
persistently turn their eye—the blind one—on the signal
of inflation and excessive spending. It is therefore the
combination of the indexed society and the red-ink society that is so inflationary. Wage dollars turn localized
price rises into general ones, and deficit dollars "vali-
date" the extra wage dollars.

"In most countries," Lewis contends, "the man in the
street or in the village would be better off if his government were not permitted to print money or to borrow
from the banks, whether by tradition or by law."[7] In
1982, the Reagan administration proposed to Congress
a constitutional amendment (the twenty-seventh) that
would require federal governments to balance their
budgets. Support fell far short of the required majority.

If asking the cat to guard the cream is silly, then requiring her to padlock the dairy is, regretfully, even sillier.

Debasement of the currency through deficits may have grown in *scale* since 1939, but it has not changed in *nature* for two centuries. "Princes and sovereign states have frequently fancied that they had a temporary interest to diminish the quantity of pure metal contained in their coins," Adam Smith observed sardonically, "but they seldom have fancied that they had any to augment it."[8] The enormous growth in the scale of post-1974 deficit financing is apparent in figure 7.1, which charts aggregate budget deficits in eleven major countries, including the United States, since 1960. Total deficits in the 1970s were several times larger than those in the 1960s. The American budget deficit in 1982–83 likely approached the 1980 combined deficits of all eleven countries.

The importance of these huge deficits is twofold: they supplied money that fueled cost-push inflation, and they represent governments' energetic efforts to pass the "hot potato" on to others, just like the other players. (Games in which the government is a disastrously effective player are analyzed in chapter 9.) The result is the most notorious economic game of all time, without which our book would be sadly lacking, *Keeping Ahead of the Joneses* (merely keeping up with the Joneses, in an indexed society, is of no use at all).

In an indexed society, wages, costs, and prices can be inextricably linked to one another without a single COLA clause or legal provision. Market forces will do the job, if people anticipate inflation and have the wits and power to alter the prices they charge appropriately. One type of market indexation is competitive wage in-

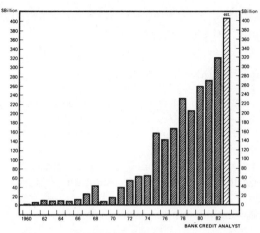

Figure 7.1 Aggregate Budget Deficits in Eleven Major Countries (Australia, Canada, France, Germany, Italy, Japan, the Netherlands, Spain, Sweden, the U.K., and the U.S.), including Federal Agency Debt.

SOURCE: BCA Publications Ltd., 3463 Peel Street, Montreal, Canada H3A 1W7. © BCA Publications Ltd. 1983.

---

creases, where individuals, families, small and large groups, professions, whole unions, and union confederations all try to keep pace with, or get a bit ahead of, competitors.* Few of us escape this game in the course of our working lives, or, get much fun out of it.

In at least one way, economic games and stand-up comedy are similar—in both, timing is everything. When, for example, Smith fights to keep ahead of, or

*An elaboration of the import of such market indexation, when it is perfect and complete, is the main contribution of the "rational expectations" theory. According to this approach, with perfect market indexation, the government is powerless to cause unemployment. But the army of 12 million unemployed in 1982 bears witness that misguided policy can create both inflation and unemployment, sometimes together.

to keep from falling behind, Jones, we observe the game of Keeping Ahead of the Joneses.[9]

KEEPING AHEAD OF THE JONESES

Smith and Jones each work for the same employer; both are on two-year contracts. Jones's contract expires at the start of even-numbered years; Smith's, at the start of odd-numbered years.

On January 1, 1984, Jones earns 10 percent more than Smith. Smith smarts for a year, then on January 1, 1985, he demands a 20 percent raise to get ahead of Jones. Jones responds a year later in the same way.

An astute sports reporter patient enough to follow the game for six years would have the following scorecard.

	Jones	Smith	Comment
1984	$10,000	$11,000	Smith makes more money than Jones
1985	$12,000	$11,000	Jones gets 20 percent raise, pulls ahead
1986	$12,000	$13,200	Smith gets 20 percent raise, pulls ahead
1987	$14,400	$13,200	Jones gets 20 percent raise, pulls ahead
1988	$14,400	$15,840	. . . and so on
1989	$17,280	$15,840	

His account of the game is horribly dull, despite the bottomless barrel of synonyms that is part of his craft: Smith edged ahead in 1984, but Jones equalized and forged ahead in 1985. Then Smith squeezed ahead in 1986, and again, Jones spurted forward in 1987. Smith responded by bursting ahead in 1988, Jones stepped up the pace and sprang into the lead. . . .

The irony of this game is that on average, over a 2-, 4-, or 2N-year period, where N is any positive whole number, Smith and Jones earn exactly the same. In this sense, *Keeping Ahead of the Joneses* is just another variation of the *Despair of 1976*. Nonetheless, for eternity, Jones and Smith take turns as Sisyphus pushing the rock up the hill or watching it tumble down again. They alternately worry about their counterpart pulling ahead or about trying to pull ahead themselves.

INDEXATION: HERE AND ABROAD

How do you call a halt to such futile games when they embrace most parts of society? How in fact do you "de-index" society?

Ideally—by not permitting indexation from the outset. The year 1948 was a watershed point for students of indexation. Struggling with postwar reconstruction and traumatized by hyperinflation of the 1920s, the Federal Republic of Germany enacted legislation, in its 1948 *Wahrungsreform,* which forbade linking payments to the consumer price index. The ban was not absolute, exceptions were made, and the 1948 clause was modified in 1964; but the "clause 3" principle that the value of an obligation should be always expressed in nominal, money value and not in real "purchasing-power" terms has been largely retained.[10] It may not be coincidental that among the major industrial nations, West Germany had the smallest rise in inflation during 1974–80, compared with 1971–73.[11]

On May 25, 1948, the United States chose to adopt indexation rather than to ban it. General Motors (GM) and the United Auto Workers (UAW) signed a new contract calling for quarterly adjustment in workers' wages to reflect movements in the consumer price index.[12] This was far from the first indexed wage contract. The late Phillip Taft found that wage rates in the iron industry were linked to iron prices in the early 1870s.[13] But the UAW-GM contract set off a trend. It is now estimated that in the United States, some 65 million people have a substantial part of their incomes linked to consumer prices; and 60 percent of workers under large contracts (those covering 1,000 or more workers) are now covered by COLA clauses.[14]

Curiously, while indexation has long been important in U.S. labor markets, it has been banned from capital markets, more or less by accident. Even though economists with widely divergent views such as James Tobin (Keynesian) and Milton Friedman (monetarist) support the creation of a "purchasing power bond" (whose principal and interest are linked to the CPI), no such bond exists. The reason, it has been suggested, is the "gold clause" Joint Congressional Resolution of June 5, 1933, which took the United States off the gold standard and banned provisions that called for payment in, or linked to, gold. The second sentence of the gold clause states that "every obligation, heretofore or hereafter incurred, ... shall be discharged upon payment, dollar for dollar, in any coin or currency . . .which is legal tender."[15] If literally construed, this clause can be, and has in fact been, used to invalidate legal agreements whose principal is indexed. A few years ago, in 1977, the gold clause was abolished by Congress. But there has been no rush either by government or private firms to issue indexed bonds. One explanation is that corporations are leery of contingent liabilities—debts whose amounts are not fixed but vary with, for instance, future inflation. Similar reasoning—though ethical, not profit-oriented—underlies a ruling by Maimonides, who stated that an indexed debt was contrary to Jewish law because "a man cannot obligate himself to something whose measure is uncertain."[16]

Despite the gold clause, being indexed is like being pregnant: either you are, or you aren't. In Israel, indexation is nearly universal; all wage contracts are linked to the CPI, with linkage payments made quarterly, as are bond principal and interest, savings deposits, mortgages, television licenses, income tax debts, and even tax brackets. It is commonly said that indexation has insulated people from inflation, but at the same time has protected inflation from people (that is, from popular protest) and aggravated it.[17] Modern technology does its part in linking costs and prices to one another with minimal delay. The Israeli food conglomerate Tnuva has its fifteen discount supermarkets linked electronically with its central computer, so that prices can be adjusted every morning.

There are signs that indexation may begin to buckle if assaulted by severe economic recession and unemployment. In 1981, the United Rubber Workers agreed to defer indexation payments in their contracts (though they asked for them back in 1982), as did the United Auto Workers in 1982.[18] But one important arena of indexation, apart from labor contracts, shows no signs of weakening: linkage of government expenditures to prices. According to one estimate, only one-quarter of federal government expenditures is "discretionary," while the other three-quarters are linked to inflation in one manner or another.[19] People may propose, and Congress can dispose, if it wishes, with indexation; political forces make such an event, however, improbable. Keynes may have unwittingly legitimized deficits; indexed spending perpetuates them.

The road to indexation is smooth and paved; the path back from it is strewn with rocks and thorns. The game of *Keeping Ahead of the Joneses* suggests why; but the game of *Happy New Year* comprises one type of social contract that a right-thinking society might construct to help get its timing right and set matters straight.

INFLATION ENDS ON JANUARY 1

If inflation ends not with a whimper but with a costly bang, if people are unhappy about seeing the purchasing power of their currency eaten away, if the shaky dollar induces managerial myopia (unwillingness to invest in the future), uncertainty, and "helplessness" (see following chapter), if the doubtful dollar makes markets unstable and inefficient—we ought to put a stop to the indexed society and discard its predatory games, *Despair of 1776, Hot Potato,* and *Keeping Ahead of the Joneses.* Why not just announce the game is over? If nobody gains from it, that should be comparatively easy. It turns out, however, to be extraordinarily difficult.

Buried within the indexed society is the basic paradox discussed in chapter 2 as the *Prisoner's Dilemma*— if only one player gets higher wages or charges higher prices, while all other costs and prices stay the same, that player benefits. What is rational for one individual is rational for all individuals. But when *everyone* behaves in this way, *everyone* loses. Conversely, if only one player *refrains* from raising his wages or prices while everyone else inflates, that player is exploited and loses out. What is rational for an individual (inflating), then, turns out to be irrational for all individuals as a group.

How can the paradox be resolved? Chapter 12 proposes drawing up a revised social contract. For now, we offer a simpler solution proposed once in a letter to the *Economist*. A version of it exists in Japan. We call it the game of *Happy New Year*.

HAPPY NEW YEAR

Wages and prices may be changed only once a year, on January 1. All labor contracts expire precisely at midnight on December 31. On January 1, all wages are increased by Z percent, where Z is *any* number workers might choose. By law, all prices are automatically and simultaneously raised by Z percent at once (or, for the sophisticated, by Z percent minus the average rise in productivity).

How many years of this would it take, we wonder, for Z (and inflation) to shrink almost to nothing?

FLOAT THE DOLLAR, SINK BUDGET BALANCE

Thus far in this chapter, we have been preoccupied mainly with ballooning budget deficits and soaring money wages. There is a third aspect of the backward economy that contributed its share to our post-1973 troubles: the shift from fixed to floating exchange rates that took place rather dramatically in March 1973. Faced with utter chaos in world foreign exchange markets, heads of the world's main central banks met hurriedly in March 1973 and decided to close those markets, recalling Roosevelt's bank holiday on March 6, 1933, exactly forty years earlier. When exchange markets were reopened, the world had a new, hastily patched-together monetary system based on floating exchange rates. The transition from fixed to floating rates, which aggravated inflation, deserves some explication.

Under fixed exchange rates, the central bank—the official bank responsible for controlling a country's currency and its relation to other currencies—sets the price of its currency in terms of other currencies and commits itself to maintaining that price. Under floating exchange rates, forces of supply and demand set the price of foreign exchange in free, competitive markets on a daily basis. (Fixed rates are never truly fixed, because Central Banks change them from time to time, nor are floating rates truly free to float since Central Banks intervene at times to shove the rate up or down; see chapter 11.)

Economists in general love floating exchange rates. The reason is simple. When free markets are allowed to work, the forces of supply and demand should work to bring the external value of every currency to its appropriate "market-clearing" level. Impersonal markets work better, it is claimed, than imperfect bureaucrats. There is a major problem, however, related not to the economics of exchange rates but to the politics and psychology of government budgets. Once, when governments overspent and inflated the domestic economy, thereby debauching the currency, they had to spend scarce foreign exchange to support the (fixed) price of their currency in terms of other currencies, or, alternately, change that price to a lower one by devaluation. Running down the country's gold-and-foreign-exchange reserves always brought protests. Devaluation, which makes imports more expensive, usually brought even more. Fixed exchange rates therefore acted as a partial brake on runaway public spending.

Under floating rates, however, all that changed. The political fetters on overspending were removed. Daily changes in the exchange rate are little noticed; even if, as Ambrose Bierce once said, a year is a period of 365 disappointments, and the dollar price of the currency falls by half, there is no landmark event around which opposition or protest can form, nor does the government need to use its exchange reserves to prop up its debauched currency. In the post-1974 world economy, floating exchange rates were widely praised for smoothly effecting an enormous transfer of wealth from oil-importing countries to oil-exporting ones. But the shift from fixed to floating rates also applied a double whammy to the rate of world inflation—it supplied a persistent source of cost increases (in imports) for countries whose currencies weakened, and it removed a major constraint from the purse strings of governments, as figure 7.1 indicates. Moreover, floating exchange rates worked to push money wages upward. In economies for whom exports are important, resistance to paying higher money wages was once based on the fear of losing price competitiveness in world markets; higher wages and fixed exchange rates meant higher export prices. Under floating rates, wages can be boosted without fear, in the secure knowledge that changes in the exchange rate will offset them and keep exports cheap. (When many countries think this way, an international version of *Hot Potato* develops; see chapter 11.)

This chapter and the preceding one have posed the question: In the indexed, floating, deficit-ridden society, why have events once thought *deflationary* now become *inflationary?* What created the backward economy? The time has come to set out a clear answer.

KNOWS GOD

The tool economists use for talking about prices and quantities in markets is the notion of supply schedules—amounts of goods, labor, and capital that people are willing to *sell* at various prices—and demand schedules—amounts of the same things people want to *buy* at various prices. In the right-way economy, supply schedules are stable and relatively unchanging. Most of the action is generated by shifts in the demand schedules. In the backward economy, the dominant force in the economy is shifts in the *supply* schedules, with demand shifts playing a secondary role. Our indexed society has made supply schedules abnormally jumpy. The result is a nervous economy that behaves in ways we find puzzling.

A helpful place to begin is with energy prices. The two major OPEC oil price rises raised energy prices, imposed a heavy tax on Western economies, and made us poorer. This amounts to a contraction in the demand for goods and services, and, as a consequence, for labor and capital. If that were the whole story, we should end it unhappily by saying that demand fell, unemployment rose, recession reared its ugly head—and, as always happens when demand contracts, inflation was *dampened*. That story would be fine for the right-way economy with frozen supply schedules. But it does not fit reality.

In the indexed society, as we saw in the games Zeno played in the previous chapter, a rise in the price of something (in chapter 6, water; in the example here, energy) tows in its wake a rise in the price of everything else—labor, capital, steel, bread, and hot dogs. This is another way of saying that supply schedules, defined as what people offer for sale at various prices, change and contract. It now takes a *higher* price to entice to market the quantities people supplied earlier.

When supply-side effects dominate demand-side changes, we get a combination of reduced economic activity—less spending and production, and more unemployment—*together with* higher prices or a higher rate of inflation. The added inflation comes from the supply schedule: people ask for higher prices for what they sell because they have to pay more for what they buy. This is stagflation—stagnation + inflation—or the "backward economy syndrome." Pin the blame entirely on indexation and what it does to supply.

Higher energy prices were not the chief villain. Blame taxes as well, an even more popular bad guy. In the right-way economy, higher taxes soak up demand and purchasing power, restrain economic activity, and dampen inflation. In the wrong-way economy, higher taxes make things more expensive, either directly by making the price of goods more costly, or indirectly by increasing what it costs businesses to produce these goods. By the chain reaction now familiar to the reader, when a few things become more expensive, soon other things rise in price as well—and stiffer taxes have become an engine of inflation rather than a means of extinguishing it.[20]

In the backward economy, shifts in supply "convert measures intended to be deflationary [devaluation, rising interest rates, excise taxes] into agents of inflation,"[21] and ultimately, of unemployment. In this new and unfamiliar economy, it is as if swinging the rudder hard to port makes the boat turn to starboard—and then begin to sink. This perverse rudder calls to mind the parent who brought a cantankerous child to a psychologist and complained, "I dislike him." "Talk to him," the psychologist counseled, "get to know and understand him." The parent returned a year later. "I understand him," reported the parent. "Now, I can't *stand* him."

Now that we understand the predatory games rampant in the indexed society, and have come to dislike them, how and when will our backward economy right itself? Wolcott Gibbs, who introduced the subject, deserves to close it:

"Knows God."

Thus far we have seen that inflation has emerged through the vigorous actions of people intent on protecting their living standards. In the next chapter, using a psychological theory known as "learned helplessness," we explain people's aversion to inflation as a direct result of their inability to do anything about it. We now turn to this theory and show how the apparent contradiction between the *cause* of inflation—acting to hike prices and wages in response to other such hikes—and the *effect* of inflation—helplessness—can be resolved.

POSTSCRIPT: WHO IS ON THE SUPPLY-SIDE SIDE?

Why did it take economists so long to understand the backward, mutated economy, and in particular, the central role played in it by supply? It was, in fact, known and understood all the time; but, like an inexpert rendition of a Chopin nocturne, perhaps the emphasis was poorly timed or too weak. Imagine for a moment that a dreadful innovation is introduced to the undisciplined discipline of economics. All the ideas and opinions to be taught or written about will be selected by a secret ballot of economists. Only ideas that win a two-thirds majority survive. (The two-thirds provision may be draconic, but should not scientific truth face almost as high a hurdle as a constitutional amendment?) Would anything but a blank page emerge?

The image of economics as a house divided against itself has taken firm hold. If hem lengths ascend as output and employment dip, the repute and esteem of economists do not; they dive along with the economy. A rash of economist jokes has swept the country, rivaling those about other minorities. Even George Bernard Shaw's old saw has been revived: if you placed America's economists end to end, they still would not reach a conclusion.

Recently, when a series of thirty economic propositions were placed before a random sample of the members of the American Economics Association, only five of them won full agreement from two-thirds or more of the 211 respondents.[22] None of the five propositions had anything to do with macroeconomics. Jerome Stein notes that the macroeconomic camp is split among three factions: Keynesians, monetarists, and new classical economics, who deny that Keynesian or monetarist policies can nudge economic activity either up or down.[23] No wonder, then, that economics appears to outsiders as a political party with no platform, or as a house divided against itself.

This is not, however, an accurate picture. At least one proposition exists on which economists have agreed for over a decade—the crucial importance of *supply* factors as the key mechanism underlying the perverse causalities of the 1970s, despite the impression that supply-side economics was born on November 4, 1980.

At the year's end, America's economists undergo a familiar ritual; they meet for three or four days in a major American city to hire, hike, and hype. The centerpiece of the meeting is the annual address of the president of the association. These addresses capture the concentrated wisdom of the man or woman picked to stand at the pinnacle of his or her colleagues' esteem. In the past decade, three of these addresses were given by confirmed Keynesians: Walter Heller in 1974; Franco Modigliani in 1976; and Lawrence Klein in 1977. Each address stated categorically that the root of our problems lies on the supply side, rather than demand side, of the economy.

- In San Francisco on December 29, 1974, Walter Heller favorably cited research by George Perry of the Brookings Institution on the "oil paradox": the *inflation* of costs, and hence of prices, leading to a *deflation* of aggregate demand; in other words, stagflation.[24]
- In Atlantic City on September 17, 1976, M.I.T. Professor Franco Modigliani said that "the serious deterioration in economic stability since 1973 must be attributed in the first place to the novel nature of the shocks that hit us, namely, *supply* shocks."[25]
- In New York City on December 28, 1977, Lawrence Klein said that "anti-inflationary policies of demand restriction run the danger of generating excessive unemployment while holding down the inflation rate." He added, "The Keynesian policy development enabled us to come through an expansive era of more than 25 years without a recurrence of a Great Depression. [But] it carried the situation only so far and undoubtedly underestimated inflation potentials, leaving us now at the point where new systems of thought, drawing more on the supply side, are needed. . . ."[26]

If, then, supply-side economics is taken to mean a belief in the idea that the main source of our economic problems, and perhaps the location of their ultimate solution, have to do with *supply,* then a two-thirds majority might well be mustered, perhaps as early as a decade ago. If, however, supply-side economics is interpreted as the faith that there exist policies (tax cuts, for instance) that unlink the indexed society and shift supply curves outward, and that work quickly enough to be politically viable—having substantial effect during a single administration—then only a small minority of economists would subscribe. Those who espouse such views persuade us that they are absolutely positive—which is, as all scientists know, being wrong at the top of your voice.

Not everyone was impressed by the economists' unity or the addresses of their chosen spokesmen, nor regards the fruits of these meetings as round and ripe. A *Business Week* editorial entitled "The Furniture Movers" railed about the 1977 meeting that ". . . there was no evidence of either humility or competence . . . nor . . . anything resembling a new idea for addressing the major policy dilemma of the industrial West." Like its counterparts the moving men, *Business Week* said, "economists collect money and hours for pushing the furniture around."[27] After the 1981 meetings, *Business Week* called them a "dismal performance" and said "what economists revealed most clearly was the extent to which their profession lags intellectually."[28]

The recovery of economics, at least in the eyes of those viewing the profession from outside it, will likely follow close on the heels of the current economic recovery. Economists, like doctors, are judged on the basis of the perceived success of their prescriptions—even though there may be utterly no connection between the patient's or the economy's health and what has been prescribed for it. One prescription on which economists do widely agree, apart from the importance of supply, is that growth without inflation, if it is to persist, requires a return to the right-way economy through the unhitching both of costs from consumer prices and of the price of one good from the price of another.[29] What they disagree on, though, is precisely how to perform this unhitching, and whether the 1979–83 recession has given us a brief or permanent respite from inflation.

C H A P T E R 8

Help Yourself to
Inflation ... If You Can

"BEWARE the Ides of March," Julius Caesar was cautioned.[1] The warning still holds. Fifty years ago, on March 6, 1933, President Roosevelt declared a nationwide banking holiday; all banks closed for a full week.[2] Cash could not be withdrawn from savings accounts, and storekeepers refused to accept checks. Veteran reporter Alastair Cooke recalls that day well. At the time he was in New York, having agreed to show the town to a friend's fiancée—and without a cent. A hurried trip back to New Haven raised some borrowed cash; enough, he remembers, for dinner and the theater. He and his guest ate at a fine restaurant, they had filet mignon, with kirsch flambé for dessert. The cost per person: $1.10.[3]

Today, Alastair Cooke's dollar and dime would not even pay for the parking time needed to gulp down a shrimp cocktail—let alone buy one. The purchasing power of the dollar is one-fifth of what it was at the end of the Depression. Inflation has had sweeping effects not only on how *Americans* organize their work and business, but upon the world as a whole. Despite the respite from rising prices in 1982 and 1983, which may prove temporary, the postwar inflation is worth our attention in terms of its impact on ordinary people. The specter of inflation may return to haunt us much sooner than we choose to believe.

Economists have largely fenced off the study of inflation's causes and effects within the distressingly narrow confines of their own discipline. We argue in this chapter that what inflation does to people, and what people in turn do to inflation, can best be understood by borrowing and applying a well-tested model from psychology known as "learned helplessness." The crux of this theory boils down to the following scenario. When prices and incomes are stable, people believe, correctly, that they can predict future prices and real incomes and properly allocate their spending over time. Their behavior is regulated by perceptions of personal efficacy and control over their lives. Then, inflation begins and prices rise erratically. The purchasing power of money income declines. The perceived value of the dollar in our minds becomes increasingly vague; the horizon over which we can make economic decisions and plans with reasonable certainty is shortened. The initial expectancy of certainty, control, and efficacy is broken, replaced by its opposite. People learn that in fact they are helpless in the face of inflation and sweeping economic events. This perception is unpleasant and, once learned, hard to change, even if it proves inaccurate.

The resulting helplessness, we contend, can account for much of inflation's psychic costs, and it also helps explain the behavioral process that aggravates price rises once they begin.

Based on the premise that you study measles by searching for lots of spots, we shall refer to the experience of Israel, which has had at minimum two-digit inflation for over a decade—America's inflation touched two-digit levels, barely, for only three consecutive years—and, over the past four years, has had 6 to 7 percent inflation on average *per month.*

OLD WHINE IN NEW BATTLES?

"The importance of money," Keynes once wrote, "essentially flows from its being a link between the present and the future."[4] And, he might have added, between present and past. When the value of money is stable over time, it performs its task of linking past, present, and future values with great ease. But when the value of money fluctuates and shrinks, so does money's usefulness as a helpful bridge across the years of our life cycle.

Is not inflation one of those persistent, recurring phenomena each generation manages to invent from scratch—like the decadence of youth, cold summers, or illicit sex? Is not the complaint of the rising cost of living an old whine in new battles? We think not. Arthur F. Burns calculated that in the 150 years preceding 1939, consumer prices in America *fell* in about as many years as they rose. Since the Revolutionary War, Burns noted, prices never so much as doubled in a forty-year period, let alone quintupled.[5] For Americans, persistently rising prices are a new ingredient whose long-range impact is hard to forecast.

Readers rich in years may recall that a dozen eggs used to cost 57¢—both in 1918 and in 1946. (In between, during the Depression, you could of course buy an egg for two pennies.) In 1946, a pound of sugar cost a bit *less* (8¢) than in 1918 (10¢), but a pound of bacon, at 53¢, cost a cent or two more. For 17¢, you could buy a pound of rice in 1920 and in 1950.[6]

For those who lived the bulk of their lives in the first half of this century, the dollar was a measuring rod, perhaps not quite as stable as a yardstick or a measuring cup, but reassuringly steady over the long haul. Quoting asset values, wages, stock prices, or inheritances in dollars was sufficient to bring a span of a generation into comprehensible relation. The money bridge from past to present was secure, and this gave reassuring predictability to the future as well.

For those whose consuming and producing lives are concentrated in the last half of this century, the dollar has ceased to function as a secure measure of value. Take, for example, baseball players' salaries. In 1981, Dave Winfield was paid an estimated $1.5 million, much more than Willie Mays got in 1969 ($125,000) or, indeed, Babe Ruth in 1931 ($80,000).[7] But, disregarding the tax bite, whose salary was higher in terms of what it could *buy?* Dollars alone can't tell us the answer any longer; we must know what things cost in 1931, 1969, and 1981. In the Age of Inflation, everyone learns to apply versions of this formula:

"Real" Value = Money Dollars ÷ Price Index

When prices are roughly constant, the formula is superfluous. When prices rise, it is essential. This change has major consequences for the behavior of markets and the people who deal in them.

HOW LONG IS A YARD?

To help understand those consequences, imagine that tomorrow the National Bureau of Standards was to call a press conference in Washington and announce: "Each month the length of the yard, foot, and inch will shrink by between 0 and 2 percent. Call us at 301-921-2401 to get the latest metric equivalent." Initially, confusion would reign. People would soon learn to stop comparing (in feet or inches) Junior's height with Dad's when he played varsity basketball. They would shift to an unchanging standard of length if there was one—say, meters.

Canada and Britain have switched to the metric system and adopted the centigrade scale in place of Fahrenheit measures. This onetime shift in physical units caused many people discomfort. Many continue to convert centigrade temperatures to Fahrenheit, and kilometers to miles, years after the switchover (just as in

175

France, a substantial group still thinks in terms of old francs, years after the new franc was created by clipping off two zeros). The consequences of inflation are analogous. Inflation alters a fundamental standard of measurement—the dollar. But unlike a once-and-for-all conversion to the metric system, inflation introduces continual and often erratic changes in the measuring rod of money. It is as if we had to switch to metrics afresh each month or year.

Newcomers to Israel from the United States report less difficulty in switching from Fahrenheit to Centigrade temperatures than in adapting to a new, "rubbery" currency whose value shrinks—even though they make use of money more frequently than they translate temperatures. Conversely, Israeli visitors to the United States claim they adapt much more easily to dollars than to Fahrenheit.[8]

In countries afflicted with rapid inflation, like Israel, people tend to quote prices in dollars rather than in terms of local currency, or they even *use* dollars for transactions. Following the liberalization of foreign exchange regulations in Israel in November 1977, this practice became widespread. Alarmed by this "dollarization"—governments zealously guard their monopoly right over the legal tender, a major source of income, just as Coca Cola jealously guards its patented name for the same reason—the Israeli government banned this practice. The ultimate in "dollarization" is in Panama, whose currency, the balboa, is linked one-for-one to the U.S. dollar—a solution no other country has been willing to embrace.

A problem for America, and for the world, is that America's currency *is* the dollar. When the dollar's

value is unstable, there is nothing else to take its place.*
That, a wit remarked, is what happens with inflation.
Nothing replaces the dollar.

INFLATION IS A DOG'S LIFE

"Man is a pliable animal," Dostoevsky once wrote, "a
being who gets accustomed to everything."[9] A situation
that people do *not* adapt to very well, apparently, is the
perceived inability to predict future events and to control them by their own behavior—a situation that
causes feelings of helplessness. We shall argue that inflation induces this state. "A person or animal is helpless with respect to some outcome," writes psychologist
Martin Seligman, a pioneer in developing this model,
"when the outcome occurs independently of all his voluntary responses." Helplessness is learned when, time
after time, an event occurs irregardless of what we do
to influence it. Learned helplessness, Seligman claims,
produces anxiety and depression, and it saps the motivation to act, even when such action might produce
relief.[10]

Seligman's theory was developed on the basis of lab-
oratory experiments (see the box on page 178). In one
of them, dogs were given shocks in a compartment.
After being conditioned that such shocks were inescapable, they accepted them by lying down and whin-
ing, even when escape was easy. "Once a man or an

*Gold is unsuitable for everyday transactions, and no other country is
willing to stomach the strictures and self-discipline that attend a key currency.

animal has had experience with uncontrollability," Seligman observes, "he has difficulty *learning* that his response has succeeded, even when it is actually successful. Uncontrollability distorts the perception of control."[11]

Learned Helplessness in the Dog

From 1965 through 1969 we studied the behavior of about 150 dogs who had received inescapable shock. Of these, two-thirds [about 100] were helpless. These animals went through [a] striking giving-up sequence. . . . The other one-third were completely normal; like naive dogs, they escaped efficiently, and readily learned to avoid shock by jumping the barrier before the shock came on. There was no intermediate outcome. Occasionally, helpless dogs jumped the barrier between trials. Further, if a dog had been sitting and taking shock after shock on the left side of the box, and the door on the right side was opened at the end of the session, the dog often came bounding across to escape from the box altogether. Since helpless dogs were physically capable of jumping the barrier, their problem must have been psychological.

Outside the shuttle box, too, helpless dogs act differently from nonhelpless dogs. When an experimenter goes to the home cage and attempts to remove a nonhelpless dog, it does not comply eagerly: it barks, runs to the back of the cage, and resists handling. In contrast, helpless dogs seem to wilt; they passively sink to the bottom of the cage, occasionally even rolling over and adopting a submissive posture; they do not resist.[12]

What does learned helplessness have to do with inflation? We suggest the following scenario. For whatever reason—oil prices, budget deficits, or unions—inflation accelerates. The dollar's purchasing power is eroded. Initially, this induces difficulty in predicting *future* income and asset values. As a result, people have trouble dividing their spending between "now" and "later," partly because they confuse nominal and inflation-corrected interest rates. Eventually, this future uncertainty shifts to the present. Rapidly changing prices make it hard for people to know current prices accurately, their estimates of *relative* prices (what one thing costs compared with another) are hence flawed. People come to learn that they cannot efficiently divide up their "now" spending among competing uses. This induces learned helplessness. With it, resistance to price changes decline, effort expended in learning prices drops, and motivation to "do something" about inflation vanishes. As sensitivity to prices diminishes—in economists' jargon, the price-elasticity of demand declines—the variability of prices jumps upward. Increased willingness to pay higher prices means that there is less adjustment to abrupt shifts in supply through quantities purchased, and more adjustment through price shifts. A kind of closed loop results, with individual feelings of declining or reduced efficacy chasing the purchasing power of money downward. Like Seligman's dogs, human beings living under conditions of uncertain inflation come to feel that their own economic well-being has been lifted out of their control. While to some extent they can control the number of dollars they earn—we shall expand on this later—the real value of those dollars is in their eyes uncertain and beyond their control, for two reasons: the rate at which the *general* price level changes is uncertain, subject to wide fluctuations; and the frequent changes in thousands of individual prices makes it hard for people to learn how expensive one thing is relative to another, the knowledge of which is indispensable if income is to be spent wisely.

In Israel, basic foodstuffs and gasoline are subject to price controls. From time to time the Finance Ministry approves price increases. Once, such rises—which can be quite steep—were greeted with angry protests. A premature announcement that gasoline would rise in price at midnight once brought long lines of motorists eager to fill their tanks at lower prices, to gasoline stations. With the passage of time, peoples' reactions have softened. No protests are heard. No lines form at gasoline stations. Announced price hikes are met with apathy. Consumers do not bother altering their spending patterns or even learning the new prices. A state of helplessness has been induced.

An Israeli journalist Leah Porat once asked a group of twenty people whose knowledge of prices were above average—such as trade union leaders and corporate executives—to estimate current prices of basic products like bread and gasoline. The range of their estimates for the price of each item went from about half the true price to double (except for gasoline, which is bought often).[13] Economists once liked to use the concept of "money illusion," mistaking inflated dollars for real purchasing power, in their theories. Today, we observe the opposite—"inflation aversion," or willingness to take a $20.00 wage along with stable prices in preference to, for example, a $50.00 wage with a doubling of prices. Willingness to trade real income for a cut in inflation suggests that the learned helplessness that accompanies inflation is highly aversive.[14]

"Must helpless man, in ignorance sedate, / Roll darkling down the torrent of his fate?" Samuel Johnson asked rhetorically.[15] With inflation, people perceive the answer is yes. One question that has puzzled us is, why are Americans as aversive to inflation as Israelis, even though U.S. inflation rates are a whole order of magnitude smaller? One hypothesis is the deeply-rooted American ethic of individual freedom, which gives everyone the right and duty to pilot his own course. Encroachments on this freedom by inflation, and the perception it is being taken away, apparently exact a high price, even when price rises are quite small.

BE NICE, BE RUDE

All the economic games we portray in this book have one important principle in common: each player's result depends both on what the player does and what others do. How players interact varies from context to context, creating a variety of interpersonal relations. But there is an exception to this principle—one game where each player's "winnings" have nothing to do with the player's skill or decisions but depend solely and exclusively on what *other* people decide to do. We call this game *Emily Post,* after the famous authority on etiquette.

EMILY POST

There are two players, "myself" and "everyone else." A choice is to be made between: (a) Be Nice (behaving with courtesy and consideration toward everyone else); and (b) Be Rude (acting egoistically, ignoring everyone else, shoving in queues, smoking in no-smoking areas, and so on). Suppose that whether I behave strictly according to Emily Post, or precisely in contradiction to her, makes no difference to my well-being; I might save time by elbowing ahead in queues, but I would also suffer from stares and protests that cancel it out. However, my well-being depends crucially on how *others* act toward *me*. If they are nice, I get 10 "points"; if they are rude, I get −10 "points," no matter what I myself do.

How should I choose? (See figure 8.1.)

| | | Others | |
		Be Rude	Be Nice
Myself	Be Rude	−10	10
	Be Nice	−10	10

Figure 8.1 Emily Post
My score in this game depends wholly on what others do and is completely independent of what I do myself.

This is best seen as a continuing game with many successive rounds, where the players have long memories and where a social norm evolves eventually, favoring either Emily Post or Genghis Khan. Note first that this game can be most unpleasant. Solely dependent on others, being powerless to affect the game's outcome (especially if I am only one player out of many thousands and cannot affect social norms by my own actions) is a feeling many people find aversive. In a society where rude behavior is the norm, players learn, like the electrified dog, that they cannot improve their own well-being and are totally dependent on what others do—classic learned helplessness. Feelings of depression and apathy result, which are reflected in further deterioration of standards of behavior. Even in a society where politeness is *de rigeur,* a small number of boors can generate a change for the worse. Retaliation leads to retaliation, and soon everyone is behaving rudely.

How is *Emily Post* related to inflation? Suppose "Be Nice" is "Refrain from Charging Higher Prices and Wages," or, alternately, "Refrain from Paying Higher Prices and Wages." Let "Be Rude" be "Pay, or Charge, Higher Wages and Prices." A feeling of learned helplessness, in an inflation context, develops when people come to believe that they cannot influence the game's outcome but are in the hands of others. Small, limited wage and price increases can quickly spread and become the norm. If everyone were to refrain from hiking prices, and to resist paying them, society might be better off as a whole. The *belief* itself that no one individual can affect the game's outcome for himself is destructive, both in the mental state it induces and in the game's outcome that results from it; so is the belief that there is no reciprocity in behaviors and that hence people cannot influence other people to play responsibly. We are beginning to see clear signs of psychological, political, and social destruction wrought by these beliefs.

THE POLITICS OF SCARCITY

Happily, most Americans' lives are free of enormous, sweeping catastrophes. Most stress arises from "continuous and manifold changes, demands, threats or deprivations, frequently small in scale and embedded in daily life events," argues Marc Fried.[16] He terms such stress "endemic" and attributes a large part of it to stressful social and economic causes. Its striking effects are "the subtle, ominous, subclinical manifestations of apathy, alienation, withdrawal, affective denial, decreased productivity and resignation." Inflation, along with recession, invoke more than a sense of scarcity, Fried says; they cause a sense of insecurity, a sense "of a slowly declining standard of living projected into an unknown future." People become resigned; they "begin to desire what is attainable rather than striving to attain what is desirable." Fried even sees "ominous threats to our democratic society" stemming from the political passivity that learned helplessness induces.[17]

In a controversial report to the U.S. Senate, M. Harvey Brenner, a Johns Hopkins University sociologist, asserted that each 1 percent of unemployment was accompanied by 37,000 deaths a year through suicide, murder, and heart attacks. This study found strong links between unemployment levels and mental hospital admissions, though he found no such link, at that time, with inflation. However, in 1980, after inflation had eroded real wages, Brenner told the *Wall Street Journal* he now thought there *was* such a link. "It's when inflation is combined with other factors, such as reduced GNP or higher unemployment, that it really packs its punch" on the mental well-being of Americans.[18]

Economists, too, attribute psychic damage to inflation. "Even those who are not really hurt by inflation often think they are," Gardner Ackley wrote in 1979, ". . . and if they think they are, they are. So all seek someone to blame—those greedy employers or nasty unions; the bankers, landlords, farmers or foreigners; our economic system, the government, society. A significant real cost of inflation is thus what it does to morale, to social coherence, to people's attitudes toward each other."[19] The doorstep most often chosen for depositing blame is now the government—a distinction once reserved for big business or unions and consistent with the individual's feeling of lack of control, responsibility, or influence.[20] Whatever role governments play in causing inflation, the propensity in politics to equivocate leads people to ask the following question.

"WHO'S IN CHARGE?"

"Now, this is going to hurt for just a few seconds." Dentists know from practical experience that predictable pain is more easily borne than pain whose onset is sudden and unexpected. Knowing what is about to happen prepares us for it. Even for events far beyond our control, we can engage in action that lowers anxiety and gives a feeling of control. Part of peoples' aversion to inflation stems from its unpredictability and people's sense that it lowers their control of their lives. A survey of public opinion in 1978 found that "majorities no longer believe that they are able to exert a great deal of control over providing for their children's education, providing for dependents if they die unexpectedly, accumulating funds for retirement and saving part of their earnings regularly."[21] The same survey found that people have become more dependent on others for legal advice and tax preparation—though more self-reliant for home repairs and minor illnesses.

Physicians still debate whether people should be told the truth when they have cancer. Many doctors, fearing that knowing the truth may sap their patients' spirits, don't tell them. At times, the political system behaves this way regarding our economic prognosis, providing the "patients" with excessively optimistic news and forecasts. The end result likely aggravates uncertainty and helplessness. The fundamental conditions of the country are sound, and he and his son had for some days been purchasing sound common stocks, John D. Rockefeller once pronounced. But the Great Crash of 1929 paid no attention.

THEORY OF RELATIVITY

Learned helplessness induces real, measurable damage to economic activity apart from its psychological toll. The theory of the consumer explains that a rational buyer spends his or her money so that the following equation holds for every type of good purchased,

$$\begin{matrix} \text{Increase in satisfaction} \\ \text{brought by the last unit} \\ \text{of the good} \end{matrix} \quad = \quad \begin{matrix} \text{Dollar price} \\ \text{of the} \\ \text{good} \end{matrix} \quad \times \quad \begin{matrix} \text{"Value" of} \\ \text{a dollar} \end{matrix}$$

where a dollar's "value" is defined as the increase in our happiness or satisfaction that a well-spent dollar can bring. When this equation holds for everything the consumer buys, it is then true that the relative prices of all goods—the price of good *A* divided by the price of good *B*—are equal to the relative contribution of each good to our happiness. In other words, if good *A* is twice as expensive as good *B,* the amounts of *A* and *B* that we buy should be such that the last unit of *A* we buy gives us twice as much satisfaction as the last unit of *B*.

This basic equation tends to break down under inflation. The reason for this was best explained by Milton Friedman in his Nobel prize address. Whereas it is *relative* prices that really matter, he reasoned, what we perceive are absolute, dollar prices. "The more volatile the rate of general inflation, the harder it becomes to extract the signal about relative prices from the absolute prices; the broadcast about relative prices is, as it were, being jammed by the noise coming from the inflation broadcast."[22]

With uncertain inflation, the "value" of a dollar becomes increasingly uncertain. This makes it ever harder to bring prices into accurate relation, and less and less worthwhile to dig up information about prices. "At the extreme," Professor Friedman observed, "economic agents resort either to an alternative currency, or to barter, with disastrous effects on productivity."[23] Some have interpreted indexation as a "crawl away from money, toward barter."[24] And barter systems work extremely poorly in communicating relations among goods.

DIFFERENTIAL HELPLESSNESS

The preceding chapters discussed the anatomy of the indexed society, where all parts of society engage in a fervid race to bind their incomes to prices. Is there not a fundamental contradiction between such a view of society and the view taken in this chapter of apathetic, resigned people who do not bother to *learn* prices, let alone fight to raise their own or keep others from raising theirs. To resolve this clash, we appeal to an extension of Seligman's model. He argues that "if a person has learned in one place, his office for example, that he has control, and becomes helpless in a second place, a train for example, he will discriminate between the different controllability of the two contexts."[25]

We contend that in the context of rising prices, people *in their roles as consumers* become resigned to price rises and pay them abjectly, often finding it difficult to discern between "normal" and "exorbitant" hikes; but *in their roles as sellers of labor and capital, and of goods and services,* these same people may feel highly efficacious in obtaining higher prices, especially when encountering low resistance of buyers. A major source of this asymmetry is government, a major employer, which has traditionally offered weak resistance to wage demands, preferring budget deficits over deficits in political support. This theory is similar to Leibenstein's X-efficiency theory of inflation, where economic agents act to pass on price increases in markets where they are "strong" and passively accept price increases in markets where they are "weak."[26]

What are the implications of differential helplessness for the efficient operation of markets? Free markets operate best, economic theory holds, when there is the following combination: a large number of competing sellers, none of whom has significant control over prices, facing a group of tough, sagacious price-comparing consumers who resist paying a penny more than they have to. If instead differential helplessness is widespread, inflation presents us with the precise opposite. We end up with sellers who jack up the prices of the goods and services and labor and capital they own at the least excuse, and who perceive control over these prices. The sellers face a group of indifferent, apathetic consumers who offer little or no resistance to price increases, who pay more than they have to and don't care. The consequent damage is both psychological and economic. Seemingly competitive markets are in fact little islands of monopoly. Once established, such a state of affairs is very hard to correct.

CONCLUSION

The bitterest pain among men, according to Herodotus, is to have knowledge without power. But, in our complex society, possession of knowledge *is* power. Inflation robs us of clear knowledge of our economic environment in relation to the past, the future, and those around us. In the consequent state of "learned helplessness," we engage in games whose consequences are destructive. To change the game, we require a fundamental change in the way we relate to one another. No single person can alter the game unilaterally; in this sense, feelings of individual helplessness are perfectly justified. But collectively, a coalition of determined individuals can make a difference, ultimately drawing into its fold the chronically skeptical and helpless. Just as we can learn helplessness, we can *un*learn it. Experiments show that people *forced* to act soon regain their belief in efficacy and control.

Another lesson of learned helplessness is, once again, that perceptions can create their own reality. In his study of seven hyperinflations—rates of inflation exceeding 20 percent a year, at least—Martin Spechler notes a common replacement for existing currency (debased and degraded) with a new gold-, commodity-, or land-backed money. Generally, after hyperinflations, governments' gold and silver coffers are empty. The sole asset remaining to them is land, so they "back" their new money with land. Though this is pure illusion—the only true backing of currency is what it can buy—it usually worked. Once people *believe* a currency will hold its value, they refrain from feverishly spending it; this, in turn, generates the very result upon which the belief is founded.[27] (Though we are not among them, this is an argument supporters of a return to a gold standard might well enlist.)

"Economics has a great and increasing concern in motives connected with the . . . collective pursuit of important games," Alfred Marshall once wrote. ". . . in most economic problems the best starting point is to be found in the motives that effect the individual regarded not indeed as an isolated atom, but as a member of some particular trade or industrial group."[28] In the next part we shall examine the underlying motives of one of the most important and intricate of all games—that played by business, labor, and government—and explore the reactions of corporate and labor leaders to a plan for making such games less destructive: a new social contract.

PART IV

Large Groups

We have met the enemy, and they is us!
—*Walt Kelly*

Business, Labor, Government: Why Three's a Crowd

IN ECONOMIC GAMES, it takes two to tangle. We have so far described ways one individual, family member or small group clashes with another, one on one, and we showed why such games are often to the mutual detriment of each player. When we come to analyze the national economy as a whole (the subject of this section) two-player economic games fail to capture a crucial part of the macroeconomic picture. We shall argue that when it comes to maintaining growth, stable prices, and high employment, two—unions *versus* companies—may not be company, but three—unions, companies, and government—is certainly a crowd. The game played by business, labor, and government is portrayed in this chapter as a three-player *Prisoner's Dilemma.* It is this game which in our diagnosis is responsible for both inflation and unemployment. The prognosis and prescriptions for these ills—a new social contract—are the topic of chapter 10.

To understand macroeconomic games, it is helpful to talk to the most powerful and expert players. We therefore wrote to over one hundred top corporate and labor leaders, briefly described the factious economic games we think people play, proposed a new social contract as a possible solution, and elicited their opinions. The reactions and opinions of those who responded are woven throughout this chapter and the following one.[1] Their generally negative responses to the idea of building a new social contract among business, labor, and government confirmed our belief that mutual suspicion and distrust lie at the heart of our economic distress and revealed how immense a task the rebuilding of a nation-wide consensus will be.

THE ECONOMICS OF *FANTASIA*

In order to grasp fully the inner workings—often hidden from full view—of economic games, it is obviously important to understand their structure. But it is no less important to know who is playing. Major misunderstandings arise when a key player is overlooked or conversely when a player is reckoned who does not in fact exist. Unlike in bridge or poker, not everyone seated around the economic bargaining table is an active player, nor does every key player have a visible place at the table. For an illustration of the consequences of not knowing the true roster of players, let us turn to Walt Disney.[2]

The outbreak of World War II and consequent loss of foreign markets, along with accumulated debts, threw Walt Disney Productions into financial crisis. Already owing $5 million to the Bank of America, Walt Disney asked for more. The bank's head, Lawrence Giannini, set stern preconditions for a bailout—chiefly, the cutting and editing of Disney's film *Fantasia* for conventional (rather than selective) release. Walt Disney of course refused. "You bankers loan an umbrella on a sunny day and want it back in the rain," he said. "I'll take my account to another banker."[3] Disney perceived the game as one with at least *three* players: himself, the Bank of America, and other bankers. He believed he could play the bankers off against each other and secure loans on his own terms. Had this been a three-player game, he might have succeeded. As the Bank of America knew, however, there were no other competing banks; it was only a *two-*person game. Disney got his money, but on the bank's terms, and *Fantasia* was cut and edited as it demanded.

A modern version of *Fantasia* exists in economic theory. In macroeconomics, the government is portrayed as an intelligent, impartial institution that seeks only the well-being of its citizens as attained by full employment and price stability. It lacks any semblance of personality, has no narrow interests, and is seen to resemble William Hazlitt's depiction of corporations as feeling neither shame, remorse, gratitude, nor good will. If governments wreak havoc, it is through bungling and ignorance rather than through their single-minded pursuit of selfish bureaucratic interests.

Political scientists have a more realistic view of the government and its role. Ever since Thomas Hobbes's book *Leviathan* was published in 1651, they have viewed the government as an entity with an identity, interests, and the means to achieve them. Two world wars and a global arms race have ratchetted public spending upwards to 30–50 percent of the gross national product. In modern economies, including those that still label themselves "free enterprise," governments are enormous bureaucracies which act both as heavyweight participants in economic games and as omnipotent referees.[4] Charged with providing solutions, governments may in fact form part of the problem. One need not buy Ambrose Bierce's definition of a legislator, "one who goes to the capital of his country to increase his own," to believe that the legislature has objectives of its own just as have capital and labor, not to mention the extensive means to attain them.[5] Unlike Walt Disney, who saw three players where there were just two, modern macroeconomics tends to see two—business and labor—where there are three.

Why should introduction of government as a third player aggravate social frictions and factiousness? We will now show why a three-player *Prisoner's Dilemma* creates a social trap even more pernicious and entangling than a two-player dilemma.

198

"SQUARING THE CIRCLE" IN TRIANGLES

The late Buckminster Fuller claimed that all of nature's structuring is based on the triangle.[6] The structure of our collective economic goals is no exception. At the vertices lie full employment, stable prices, and free collective bargaining.[7] Over the past decade, most Western economies—and most Eastern bloc countries as well—have had difficulty achieving those three goals. Building the three sides of the triangle so that they fit together has proved as hard as squaring the circle. Some have come to question whether it can be done at all.

Our interpretation of these difficulties is also based on an eternal triangle—the three-sided game of *Business-Labor-Government*. When more than two players are involved, it is often helpful to set up the game in its so-called extensive form. This looks like the branches of a tree, where each separate branch shows a particular path along which the game may proceed. Suppose each of our three players picks one of two strategies: "compete" (huge wage demands, big price increases, or large fiscal deficits for labor, business, and government, respectively) or "cooperate" (moderate wage, price, and budget behavior). One game tree that might result is shown in figure 9.1. With each of the three players choosing one of the two strategies, there are eight possible outcomes $(2 \times 2 \times 2)$. The payoffs for each player are shown at the end of each of the eight branches and can be taken to represent "game points" or amounts of satisfaction. The socially rational outcome *(A)* is where business, government, and labor form a pact and jointly agree to behave with moderation. This outcome will not emerge of its own volition, however. More likely, society will find itself at the bottom *(H)*, the worst outcome rather than the best.[8] Here is why.

Suppose society is at *A*. Each of the three players can gain by defecting. Let the defector be labor. Labor will change its behavior from "cooperate" to "compete," giving labor "3" instead of "2" but leaving business and government at *B*, each with 0.

Given labor's defection, it pays for one player in the business-government coalition to defect and switch to "compete." Suppose it is business. When business switches from "cooperate" to "compete," business gains, at government and labor's expense, in moving to *D*. Now, it pays government to change its behavior, from "cooperate" to "compete," moving society down to *H*, a shift which improves government's payoff but worsens those of labor and business.

What is pernicious about three-way *Prisoner's Dilemma* is that it is difficult to achieve a *two*-player coalition, let alone a grand consensus. Each player can gain by unilaterally defecting from a three-way agreement for joint cooperation. When this happens, each player left in the *two*-person coalition can gain by defecting. Finally, whoever is left holding the bag alters his behavior too. And in the end, everyone loses. In this game, what individual players gain by defecting is less than the sum of the losses the defection imposes on the other players. Defection that pays for one pays for all. The total losses from such behavior, when they are added up, put society in its worst possible outcome.

How well does this parable describe what is really

Business, Labor, Government: Why Three's a Crowd

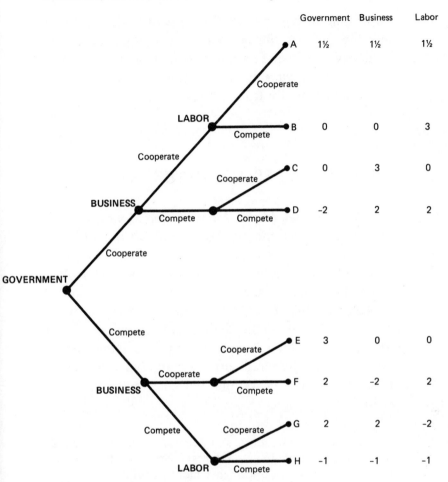

Figure 9.1 Business-Labor-Government

Each player picks one of two behaviors: "cooperate" or "compete." The outcome finishes at the end of one of the eight branches *A* through *H*. "Rational" players will act so that outcome *H* emerges. This result is socially inferior because a change in behavior by each of the players (from "compete" to "cooperate") could make each of them better off (outcome *A*).

happening in the economy? One way to find out is to ask the players themselves—a technique journalists love, psychologists favor, but economists tend to shun. The idea of canvassing the captains of labor and industry came originally from a book review.

BUT CAN YOU SELL IT TO THE TEAMSTERS?

In an earlier book *Minds, Markets, and Money,* the second author traced the psychological roots of macroeconomic conflict and concluded there was a need for a social contract to unite all segments of society.[9] A *New York Times* review suggested rightfully that the author "doesn't explain how to sell [this idea] to the teamsters."[10] We took up the challenge. Rather than sell the idea, we explained it more briefly in a letter sent to more than one hundred corporate and union leaders to elicit their opinions. We put our case in the following words:

America is a free country, and Americans have every right to act to protect their own interests. They can fight to gain higher money wages and higher money profits.

Each individual in society can raise his or her standard of living if he or she has more money to spend. But there is a catch. When the size of the national cake is fixed, one person or group can increase his slice of it, only at the expense of others. And when *everyone* tries to boost his share, the result may actually be less for everyone, as higher wages and prices boost costs. So, what is legitimate and rational for the individual, or group, may ultimately be to the disadvantage of all of us, as members of a community.

Dilemmas of this sort may in principle be resolved by an agreement—a social contract—among all parts of society to refrain from harmful, and ultimately, futile competitive games to boost their money incomes. (Government is, of course, an important party to that agreement; governments, too, compete for shares of the national cake, along with wage earners and stockholders.) Our contention is that without such a plan, we are doomed either to persistent inflation, or to intolerable levels of unemployment caused by battling that inflation with conventional fiscal and monetary tools.[11]

With this, our case rested. Many of those to whom we wrote took the trouble to respond thoughtfully and at length.

MEMORIES THAT WORK BACKWARD

One of the major difficulties in extricating society from the *Prisoner's Dilemma* trap is, as we just noted, the fear that one or more players will defect from a mutual agreement to act moderately. We found ample evidence of such fear in replies to our letter. For example, "I recognize that academics and intellectuals have periodically succeeded in persuading some labor leaders to be seduced into acceptance of a 'social contract' with big business," wrote William W. Winpisinger, president of the International Association of Machinists and Aerospace Workers. "But every time big business is in the ascendancy—as it certainly has been in recent years—the only thing labor gets when it suggests a social contract is the back of a hand . . . with the economy in such a state of disaster for most workers, big business is not the least bit interested. Big business thinks it smells blood. They may yet get blood. But if they do some of it is going to be their own."[12]

At one point in Lewis Carroll's *Through the Looking Glass,* the Queen says, "it's a poor sort of memory that only works backward." Most of us have poor sorts of memories. After a decade of negative-sum economic games, both business and labor look backward at attempts to construct written or unwritten social contracts, and they reach pessimistic conclusions.

For years, a group of eight corporate executives and eight labor leaders, known as the Labor-Management Group, met under the leadership of former Secretary of Labor John Dunlop to seek cooperative approaches to problems such as inflation, unemployment, energy, and so on. When Douglas A. Fraser, then head of the United Auto Workers, resigned from the group on July 19, 1978, he spoke bluntly about business-labor confrontation.

I believe leaders of the business community, with few exceptions, have chosen to wage a one-sided class war today in this country—a war against working people, the unemployed, the poor, the minorities, the very young and the very old, and even many in the middle class of our society. . . . The leaders of industry, commerce and finance in the United States have broken and discarded the fragile, unwritten compact previously existing during a past period of growth and progress. . . . That system . . . survived in part because of an unspoken foundation: that when things got bad enough for a segment of society, the business elite "gave" a little bit—enabling government or interest groups to better conditions somewhat for that segment . . . usually only after sustained struggle. . . . But today I am convinced there has been a shift on the part of the business community toward confrontation, rather than cooperation. . . . Even the very foundations of America's democratic process are threatened by the new approach of the business elite. No democratic country in the world has lower rates of voter participation than the U.S., except Botswana. . . . Even if all the barriers to such participation were removed, there would be no rush to the polls by so many in our society who feel the sense of helplessness and inability to affect the system in any way.[13]

WHO ANSWERS THE ALARM?

Where you stand on an issue depends on where you sit—whether in a corporate armchair or a union hall folding chair. What labor leaders regard as business's exploitation of workers in a weak labor market, corporate leaders regard as a new policy that puts responsibility primarily upon business for generating profits and the investments that flow from them. Jerry McAfee, former president of Gulf Oil, compares business to a fire department charged with dousing economic stagnation.

Consider an analogy: when a town spends money on the training of its fire department, people don't automatically complain that the town cares too much about its firemen. Instead they recognize that everyone in the town has a stake in the quality of the firemen who serve them. In a similar way, the President has formulated a program designed to help the productive sector of society to produce more wealth for the entire nation. Quite simply, President Reagan has given American business the task of creating economic prosperity for all Americans.[14]

Mr. McAfee's fire-department metaphor was recently used by James Tobin of Yale University to damn, rather than praise, the same economic philosophy. In Tobin's version, it is *government* that wields the high-pressure hoses rather than business. He interprets the Reagan administration policy, built on the view that restriction of the money supply—monetarism—is both necessary and sufficient to stabilize prices without generating unemployment, as the following "now hear this" message from government:

"You guys out there had better understand very clearly that your only hope for employment, prosperity, and reasonable economic performance is to cut down on your wages and prices. To continue to inflate as in the past, given our stingy monetary targets, will only lead us into more trouble, and we are not going to bail you out." This is something like the local fire department getting tired of all the careless smokers in the town and saying, "Until this stops, we are not going to put out any more fires."

As Tobin sees it, "the question is whether that is a moral stance for a government to take in a democracy, and if it is not, whether it is believable and whether it will work. Then the question is, are these hardships necessary? Is this the only way that rational people living in a modern society can get rid of a manmade evil, namely a higher rate of inflation than they feel comfortable with?"[15]

OLD TOOLS ARE BEST

Despite Tobin's criticism of reliance on conventional policy tools such as the money supply, many economic leaders who replied to our letter felt that standard fiscal and monetary policy tools were adequate for restoring our economic health without recourse to more drastic, unconventional measures. They worked for us in the past, some reasoned, and can do so again in the future. ". . . let me point out . . . there have been long periods in our economic society of reasonable price stability and low unemployment, such as much of the 50s and 60s,"[16] noted Donald N. Frey, chairman of Bell & Howell. Donald K. McIvor, chairman of Canada's Imperial Oil Ltd., reasoned:

. . . the decade of the 1960s was a time of low inflation and high growth in both the U.S. and Canada. I do not think people were any less free then, nor were they any less eager to pursue their individual interests. And if there was a social contract then, it did not take the form of a plan imposed by government. In short, I do not believe that individual freedom is by itself inconsistent with price stability. Operations of markets have in the past, and in some countries even in the recent past, succeeded in reconciling the demands of individuals with the community's resource constraints, and I see no reason why they cannot continue to perform this function.[17]

Among those who said that conventional policies could do the job, provided they were properly designed and implemented, was Lee Iacocca of the Chrysler Corporation. "We will not be satisfied until we have single-digit interest rates. . . . This is the one most important factor which will put all Americans back to work. We feel we need to drastically reduce our national debt. Reducing defense spending and social programs is one way. And taxes on gasoline should be increased until the debt becomes manageable."[18]

THE BAD NEWS OF RECESSION—
AND THE GOOD

At least one corporate executive agreed that the absence of growth in our national income exacerbates the economic games that are played to divide up that income. In one of his speeches, the chairman of E. I. Du Pont de Nemours, E. G. Jefferson, argued: "The Depression and its human consequences illustrate two points: First, even in the United States, the social fabric can become frayed in periods of economic distress. And second, the health of even great industries cannot be taken for granted. . . . A dynamic economy generates both wealth and opportunity. A stagnant economy reduces options and penalizes virtually everyone, and none as severely as those on the lowest rung of the economic ladder. The task of slicing up an economic pie of constant size causes much stress in a democracy."[19] Other business leaders saw a silver lining in the cloud of stagnation and recession that still hung over us early in 1983, when we wrote to them. They viewed economic hard times as a means of shaking out waste and inefficiency, leaving a stronger, tougher and more competitive economy in their wake. As Donald N. Frey put it:

I do not believe we are doomed to the recent extremes of high inflation or intolerable unemployment. The price of a democratic society carries with it such risks but there are regulators—some of them belatedly applied. For example . . . unionized labor can engage in monopolistic pricing practices and in fact have done so. Heavily unionized industries are paying the price today. They have priced themselves out of the market, and the companies are going out of business. The system is rectifying itself currently, but again the price we are paying for this interference in the free market is less evil than erosion of our democratic society.[20]

WE CAN BAKE BIGGER CAKES

How important is economic growth? Who or what is responsible for the decade-long growth slowdown? How can growth be restored? For most corporate leaders, growth is a religion. We were not surprised, then, by the fervor with which business respondents rejected our premise that "the size of the national cake is fixed." For example:

Lewis W. Lehr, 3M Company: "The human mind . . . is a better resource than any specific raw material. We may run out of something like chromium, but human ingenuity seems inexhaustible. . . . Our reserves in the form of alternate materials and new processes have actually been expanding. They will probably continue to do so if man's mind is left free to experiment and if incentives for technological risk-taking are not destroyed. . . . Even better wings and wheels, roofs and roads, pumps and plowshares, foods and fibers await those who realize it really is a case of mind over matter."[21]

Andrew J. Schroder III, General Foods Corporation: "Our society, by tolerating certain economic policies and priorities, has unnecessarily constrained the growth opportunities of our 'national cake.' I would view the most significant need our society has today to be the revising of those economic policies and priorities to insure that this cake again has the capacity to grow."[22]

David R. Dilley, U.S. Steel Corporation: "We at U.S. Steel do *not* believe the size of the national pie is fixed. Rather, we believe the size of the pie is dependent on the *quantity* of the ingredients. Further, we believe that the taste or quality of the pie depends on the *nature* of the ingredients. It is for this reason that U.S. Steel for many years has sought to bring about an economic climate conducive to saving and investment. Thus, rather than resigning ourselves as a nation to an 'economic pie' of fixed size, we believe we would be far better off as a nation if tax and expenditure policies were highly conducive to economic growth (resulting in more for everyone), rather than conducive to transfers from producers to non-producers (resulting in more for the non-producers but less for the producers)."[23]

BLAME GOVERNMENT OR BUSINESS?

Not surprisingly, business and labor failed to see eye to eye on precisely who is *responsible* for the failure of national output to expand. Business tended to blame government—specifically, its expansion of public consumption at the expense of private investment. "Public policies have stressed consumption at the expense of investment," E. G. Jefferson claimed. "As a result, we have invested inadequately in the modernization and growth of our industry. Somewhere along the line we lost sight of the fact that social programs and improved living standards are attainable only in a highly productive and competitive economy. It is surprising that we made this error, because our history shows clearly that high rates of investment are needed for better living."[24]

Labor, on the other hand, blamed business—specifically, "managerial myopia." Writing in *Foreign Affairs,* the head of the International Ladies' Garment Workers Union, Sol Chaikin, argued: "Investment in financial instruments in lieu of productive outlays is yet another variation of the domestic deindustrialization process. On January 29, 1982, *The Wall Street Journal* reported that rather than expand its high-technology base, Bendix Corporation 'may be content to keep its $500-million pool of cash in short-term investments.' . . . Dr. W. Edwards Deming, often referred to as the prime architect of Japan's postwar boom, has observed: 'Management has failed in this country. The emphasis is on the quarterly dividend and the quick bucks, while the emphasis in Japan is to plan decades ahead. . . . One requirement for innovation is faith that there will be a future.' "[25]

William Winpisinger also pinned the blame on business. "Despite your certainty that 'the national cake' is now 'fixed,' I suggest the American economy will again begin to grow, and the American people will again begin to prosper, when big business is no longer permitted to freely loot America's technology—taking knowhow originally developed by American workers, mostly with American tax dollars, to offshore centers of cheap labor production."[26] Buzzwords like "offshore centers" and "cheap labor" remind us that foreign producers are an integral part of our economic games. In contests between American producers and European and Japanese manufacturers, the government serves as umpire. Its inordinate fondness for the home team often costs us dearly.

THE UMPIRE STRIKES OUT

In the seventh and deciding World Series game, it is the bottom of the ninth inning. Trailing 2 to 1, the team at bat has the winning run at the plate, with two out. The crowd is tense and hushed. Grabbing a handful of chalk dust and swinging three heavy bats, the umpire steps up to the plate. He strikes out on three straight pitches. The game is over.

In baseball, or in any other sport, umpires and referees do not actively take part, at least not overtly. This fanciful scene would likely end with the umpire soon exchanging his black coat for a white coat. In contrast, in our economic games, governments both play in and referee slugging matches between business, labor, and consumers, exporters and importers, environmentalists and developers, and so on. E. G. Jefferson ascribed one weakness of our economy to the government's failings and inconsistency as an "impartial" umpire and rule maker.

We all know consistent, predictable government policy is essential if business is to make the long-term plans necessary to sustain growth. . . . And yet, with our four year Presidential and two year Congressional terms and the lack of harmony between the President and Congress, rapid turnabouts have been the rule rather than the exception. Most recently the helpful provisions of the Administration's 1981 tax relief act were effectively repealed only a year later, all in the name of "reform." It's not easy to play the game well when the ground rules keep changing.[27]

One of the most important ground rules set by government is that governing the battle between domestic producers and their foreign competitors, as expressed in tariffs, quotas, and other restrictions on imports. A familiar scene is the following: business and labor clash to the detriment of each, then race to Washington and ask for higher tariff walls to bail them out. Since cheap imports have only a weak constituency—consumer groups and farm producers, who fear retaliation against their exports—their pleas are often heard and answered. This is most likely to happen in hard times—for example, during the Great Depression. In 1930, intense political pressure brought about the Hawley-Smoot Tariff Act, which raised U.S. tariffs to unprecedented high levels, in response to slowing economic activity. Other countries soon followed suit. The resulting chain reaction of beggar-thy-neighbor import restrictions destroyed world trade and made everyone, including the U.S., worse off (see chapter 11). It is interesting to speculate, as some historians have, how many years of depression might have been saved and how many percentage points of unemployment been forestalled had the "referee" disqualified Hawley-Smoot as an inadmissible and inexcusable unilateral change of rules.

Fifty years later, calls for protectionism are again heard in strength, as business and labor, in rare agreement, ask the government-referee to respond to what they see as other countries' versions of Hawley-Smoot.

Sol C. Chaikin sees imports as a cause of America's de-industrialization, and Ford Motor Company's chairman Philip Caldwell attributes the growth slowdown to heavy imports. According to Chaikin:

Broadly speaking, this country has been following policies which can only lead to intensified deindustrialization. . . . Unrestricted import penetration (during more than a decade of economic stagnation and retrogression) and insufficient new investments have played a vital contributing role in this process. . . . Low levels of real domestic investment in past decades and excessive import penetration deprive American manufacturers of the incentive to expand. Plants become obsolete, further eroding competitiveness. Firms that lack resources die or are swallowed up. Those that have resources produce an increasing share of their output overseas, adding directly to domestic unemployment, diverting capital from domestic investment and making the United States even less competitive.[28]

Philip Caldwell joins Chaikin in decrying America's trade imbalance.

. . . our 1982 worldwide negative merchandise trade balance of $40 billion contributed almost half of our negative GNP growth rate of 1.8 per cent last year, . . . and the government's forecasted negative trade balance of $75 billion for 1983 will comprise a 2 per cent drag on our GNP growth rate this year. In other words, if our trade balance could be in equilibrium this year, the forecasted growth rate of 1.4 per cent could exceed 3 per cent. . . . I sometimes wonder if our economic theories in regard to international trade are not as out-of-date for the realities of today as the Maginot line was at the outbreak of World War II.[29]

Measures that restrict imports have strong appeal as steps that bring immediate short-run results. Myopic legislatures may embrace them, blithely ignoring the long-run costs. E. G. Jefferson commented:

The U.S. has become an intensely adversarial democracy in which each group speaks for its own interests—narrow as they may be—and the differences are compromised in the political process. . . . In economic debates, the outcome is the result of political expediency. Whenever Congress debates major legislation affecting industry, business, consumer groups and labor unions each have their way on a few points, but no group takes responsibility for the final package. In the end no one wins, because the legislation does not recognize our long-term interests.[30]

WORST OF ALL WORLDS

Every theory is built on assumptions that are not quite true. Otherwise it would be narrative, not theory. The unstated assumption underlying our description of business-labor-government games to this point has been that each of the three players is monolithic, united, and all-embracing. This is far from true. For the past thirty years, collective bargaining agreements between union and management have covered only between one-third and one-quarter of all American salaried workers.[31] This implies that side by side with large-scale negotiations between, for example, Ford, General Motors, or Chrysler and the United Auto Workers are thousands of small games in small firms or single plants, where "business" may be the company's sole owner and "labor," the head of a ten-member employee's committee. In some ways, this is the worst of all possible worlds. It creates an environment in which individual agents—employers and employees—are not small and weak enough to lack the ability to gain at others' expense yet are not large enough to facilitate nationwide tripartite agreements that forestall such antisocial behaviors.

An interesting paradigm for such a world is the *Garbage Game* devised by Lloyd Shapley and Martin Shubik.[32] It is useful for showing how a by-product of business-labor-management games can be both inflation and unemployment.

GARBAGE GAME

Each of a dozen families living along a shady suburban street has one large smelly bag of garbage to dispose of daily. There is no garbage collection or city dump, so they must either keep their garbage or dump it on someone else's lawn.

What will be the outcome of this game?

Unless neighborhood relations are in a state of cold war, norms of civilization will likely keep people from dumping garbage on one another. Suppose, though, that the game is played by an entire, crowded city rather than a friendly neighborhood. The anonymity of a million players may well encourage "wholesale" dumping. Will not people get together to form "clean yard" groups or coalitions, agreeing tacitly or explicitly to toss their garbage elsewhere? Shapley and Shubik show there is no stable group of this sort, because "no agreement on garbage disposal can satisfy every group of players to the point where they cannot, by violating it, be sure of doing better."[33] Such a game is said to lack a "core," a concept we discuss in chapter 10.

It has been noted by Clive Bull and Andrew Schotter that inflation—and, they might have added, *de*flation—is analogous to garbage.[34] Suppose oil prices rise, taking dollars out of the economy. All players want to avoid the burden of reductions in their real incomes and are prepared to fight hard to do so. They act to dump their "garbage" onto others and avoid losing income. The primary way this is done is by raising the prices each player controls or influences—the price of goods, the price of labor and capital, and, for the government, taxes. Where the final burden of the oil-price rise lies will depend on how alert, quick-footed, and unscrupulous each player is. As Bull and Schotter point out, coalitions may form—government and business, or government and labor, to dump the burden elsewhere. These coalitions, however, tend to be unstable. Their members can always do better by disbanding them and setting up new ones. This game may last for a very long time—unless society alters its preferences, its standards of behavior, or builds new institutions and mechanisms designed to deal sensibly with the problem. One such institution is an "incomes policy" that dictates "how the various sectors and labor will absorb the real loss in the economy."[35]

Why is the *Garbage Game*—recognized as a version of *Hot Potato* encountered in chapter 6—played so bitterly and earnestly? One answer is provided by Richard Layard. Suppose, as Layard argues, that happiness depends on income and status relative to what you *expected* it to be.[36] In human society, hope (and greed) spring eternal, especially after a couple of decades of rising real incomes. People will therefore resist vigorously an unexpected cut in their real income and status, especially if it means a drop in their position vis-à-vis others, namely, a fall in their relative incomes in comparison with those of their friends and acquaintances. Moreover, the types of behavior invoked to avoid a cut in income (described in chapter 6) are, like the dumping of garbage, socially destructive, whereas actions that generate a *rise* in real income (harder work, longer hours, and higher productivity) may be beneficial to society.

One of the least responsible players may in fact be the government. Governments may act like business and labor in boosting their money expenditures to maintain their real share of resources, by either borrowing more money or simply printing it. Expanding the money supply appears attractive to government for another reason: it facilitates the inflation *Garbage Game* played by others and defers painful readjustment to the new situation. Though desirable in the long run, such readjustment may involve painful cuts in income in the short run; a vengeful electorate with a short memory may choose to punish incumbent governments for being wise and responsible. We noted earlier that between 1976 and 1981, incumbent national governments lost six out of seven elections in Western democracies. The sole losers took solace in having implemented socially responsible but politically costly policies. Others found that voters punished political "realism" and cynicism as well. In politics, the gap between the devil and the deep blue sea may be microscopic, much too narrow for the bulky ship of state to navigate.

There is also an unemployment version of the inflation *Garbage Game*. Suppose the inflation game has damaged productivity growth, relative to that of other countries that dealt with the game more quickly and effectively. This means that in order to maintain competitiveness in international markets, it is necessary for real wages to fall. (In the absence of such a decline, unit costs are high and exports shrink, and with them, jobs.) Attempts of each sector and union to dump real-wage declines onto others will keep real wages high. Those who hang on to their jobs may benefit. But many workers may lose their jobs and become unemployed; employers can no longer afford to employ them since there is no demand for what they produce. The "unemployment" and "inflation" *Garbage Games* go on simultaneously, a war of "all against all," and together generate both more inflation and more unemployment—the so-called stagflation phenomenon.

CONCLUSION

According to Webster's, a bargain is "an agreement between parties to a transaction, settling what each shall give and receive." In economic games among business, labor, and government, players invert the familiar biblical precept (Acts. 20:35) and behave as if it were more blessed to receive than to give. The result: bargains bad for all. Yet despite the familiarity and prevalence of these games, we have not yet achieved the insight of Walt Kelly's cartoon character Pogo, who observed once, "We have met the enemy, and they is us!"

Some readers may be mystified by the apparent contradiction between our call for a social contract—normally associated with those who support wage-price controls, increased government intervention, and higher public spending—and our claim that government *itself,* as a player, is a major source of our economic problems. These two propositions are perfectly consistent. A smaller role for government is *helpful* in building an initial social contract, as the experience of some European countries proves (see chapter 10). If business and labor choose not to cooperate, no statute or stick can force them; if business and labor elect to join forces, no law or legislation is necessary. The adjective "social" in the phrase social contract has less to do with socialism than it does with the common interests of free, interdependent people.

In free market economies, collective bargaining and the price system are the main instruments for regulating economic relationships among players. But, Nobel laureate Kenneth Arrow has observed, "we cannot mediate all our responsibilities to others through prices ... [it is] essential in the running of society that we have what might be called 'conscience,' a feeling of responsibility for the effect of one's actions on others."[37] The social contract is a formal expression of, and aid to, that social conscience. Ogden Nash once rhymed: "There is only one way to achieve happiness on this terrestrial ball,/And that is to have either a clear conscience, or none at all."[38] In our economic games, we seem to have opted for the latter—and it has won us misery, not happiness. There must be a better way. The next chapter uses the game theory concept of the "core," and the experience of several European countries and Japan to search for it.

Include Me Out!

FIVE TIMES in the past forty years, the American government has directly intervened in the process of free collective bargaining in order to stabilize wages and prices.[1] These "incomes policies" were sharp revisions of existing social contracts among wage earners, employers, and bureaucrats. Two of these interventions occurred during wartime emergencies, World War II and Korea. Is the time now ripe for a new, revised social contract, involving formal or informal agreements among business, labor, and government, to refrain from actions that aggravate unemployment and inflation? Should America construct tripartite mechanisms similar to those in Europe? Would such a mechanism damage or annihilate the free enterprise system as we know it? Can existing social institutions, with appropriate renovation and alteration, do the job? Is a major crisis or war the only time Americans are willing to renounce their license to engage in destructive economic games?

In this chapter, we apply some theory—a technical

game theory concept known as the "core"—and practice—experience of other countries and of economic leaders we canvassed—to sketch some answers. Let us move directly to the core of the problem.

SPRINGING THE TRAP

Some economic games contain pernicious social traps. Even when all players unanimously forswear self-serving, socially destructive behavior, the resulting social contract is too fragile to endure because it pays individuals to break the agreement and opt out, as long as others continue to honor it. As we suggested in the last chapter, the only way to spring these traps is to build a social contract that effectively changes the structure of the game or alters the nature of the players themselves. *Prisoner's Dilemma* typifies one such trap.

There is a type of economic game that *appears* to embody such a trap, but in fact does not. In this more amenable game, once a large enough fraction of the players have agreed, whether formally or informally, to prosocial conduct, others quickly join in—and stay in—because to opt out is to lose out. Each individual sees that what is best for him or her is also best for other players too. Given this perception, cooperative behavior quickly becomes the social norm. Here, the problem is one of getting enough players to join a pact of moderation or cooperation. Once this is done, society as a whole attains its most preferred result. No change is necessary in the game structure or in the nature of the players. We label such games "critical-mass" traps. Nuclear physicists tell us that a sufficiently large, critical mass of suitable radioactive material can generate an explosive release of energy. In the same way, a critical mass of people joined in a common behavior can lead to a chain reaction in which that behavior soon becomes ubiquitous. When fewer than the critical number join, the precise opposite behavior may become the rule.

How can one tell the first, pernicious variety of trap from the milder, critical-mass type? It turns out that critical-mass games have a "core"—an idea we shall now explain and illustrate with two very similar games, one of which *(Divide and Rue)* has no core while the second *(Hard Core)* does.

HARD-CORE SOLUTIONS

Game theory distinguishes between two types of games: those in which players may get together to form coalitions; and those in which it is every man for himself, where coalitions are not permitted. The macroeconomic *Business-Labor-Government* is of the first type, since loose coalitions—for instance, between a Democratic administration and labor, or between a Republican administration and business—are possible. A helpful game theory technique can answer the following question: If individuals act rationally, what configuration of coalitions will emerge? Will it be stable or tend to break up into other patterns and groupings? It is first necessary to define what is meant by "rationally," a word that is to behavioral science what mine fields are to infantry.

Individuals are said to be rational if they remain in a coalition only when they cannot do better by acting alone. Leaving a group need not, however, mean becoming a lone wolf; one may join some other group or coalition. Group rationality means that a coalition will break apart if some of its members can do better by forming another grouping—and will stay together if all groups are satisfied they have got the most they can.

The set of coalitions—or "group of groups"—that satisfies group rationality is known in game theory as the "core" of the game. One of the nice properties of the core is that it maintains what economists regard as collective rationality—no person or group could do better without making some other person or group worse off. Unlike apples or nuclear reactors, some cooperative games have no cores. This can result in waste and instability, though not always.

The *Garbage Game* described in chapter 9 lacks a core, for the following reason. Suppose there are ten "dumpers." Nine of them could get together, form a coalition, and dump all their nine bags onto the tenth. The tenth person would of course dump his garbage onto the coalition, which in turn would share it among its nine members: one-ninth of a bag each. This arrangement is unstable. The person left out of the coalition could approach anyone inside it with the following proposition: leave it, join me, and you will be freed of garbage; we will dump our two bags onto the eight people left in the coalition. I will accept the eight bags dumped on us, and your yard will be kept clean. We both gain. You get no garbage. And I get one less bag of garbage than before. A two-person coalition thus forms; then, a three-person, and so on. Coalitions will continue to form and break up in this manner, with no stable arrangement emerging.

The core has been described as "the eye of the storm"—the place where the hurricane of conflict settles down to a quiet balance of equal forces.[2] For someone trapped in a hurricane of social strife, it may be difficult to believe that a core exists or to envisage what it may look like. Here are examples of two games, both of which involve sharp conflict. One is without a core; the other has a core, which is hard to attain but exists nonetheless.

The first game, *Divide and Rue,* has no core. It is a multi-player *Prisoner's Dilemma* where even unanimous agreements to act in moderation are unlikely to hold together.

DIVIDE AND RUE

Each of a large number of individuals must choose between two behaviors: "compete" (secure the maximum for oneself, possibly at the expense of others); and "cooperate" (secure the joint maximum for all, possibly at the expense of one's own gain). Each individual's score depends on what other people choose to do. The scorecard—the number of "points" won for each type of decision—looks like this:

Quick comparison of the "compete" and "cooperate" columns shows that no matter *what* other people do, it always pays to choose "compete." The dominant strategy here is antisocial because when everyone adopts it, society loses as a whole, and collective ratio-

Percent of Others	One Person's Score for:	
Who "Cooperate"	"Cooperate"	"Compete"
0	0	1
10	1	2
30	2	3
50	3	4
70	4	5
90	5	6
100	6	7

nality collapses. Even if everyone in society could be brought to "cooperate," this "grand coalition" would not be the core; it would pay people to defect, quickly bringing the coalition to total collapse. In this type of game, people divide—and then rue it. They do not, however, rue enough to wish to permanently change their behavior, unless some powerful collective incentive is provided.

A similar but significantly different game is *Hard Core;* unlike *Divide and Rue,* it just may have a happy end. The "you flay my back, I'll flay yours" dynamics of *Divide and Rue* has an escape hatch in *Hard Core,* but it take skill, cohesion, and wisdom to open it.

HARD CORE

As in *Divide and Rue,* people choose between "compete" and "cooperate." The scorecard, however, is just slightly different.

Thoughts of someone playing *Hard Core* might be as follows: I am best off playing "compete" unless I am assured that nearly everybody else—at least 90 percent

Percent of Others	One Person's Score for:	
Who "Cooperate"	"Cooperate"	"Compete"
0	0	1
10	1	2
30	2	3
50	3	4
70	4	5
90	6	6
100	8	7

of the others—will "cooperate," in which case it is best for me to do so too. There exists a critical mass (90 percent) of people who, if they behave in a certain manner, soon pull everyone else in to behaving likewise. If less than the 90 percent critical number behave in that way, it is better for everyone—both those outside the coalition of well-behaving people and those inside it—to behave badly. Soon, everyone in society is rude, littering, noisy, or destructively competitive. There is a core in this game. But it is a "hard core," hard to obtain because it includes nearly everybody. It is a stable outcome, because once the critical mass of people emerges, it soon expands to envelop the whole of society, whereupon nobody has any reason to go back to the bad old days and bad old ways.

Very little separates *Divide and Rue* from *Hard Core*—slight alteration in only two numbers. Changing these numbers, or the way they are *perceived,* may be difficult and ultimately frustrating, for such change is futile if even a small part of society has unalterably learned to behave antisocially. To build a core and get society into it, it is necessary to modify the game so that a core exists, to ensure that the modification has been perceived, and to generate the critical mass—a formidable task, but not an impossible one.

TO SAVE OR NOT TO SAVE

Next to relatively short-run concerns about inflation and unemployment, perhaps the greatest long-run failing of the American economy is its low level of private saving and investment. One explanation we advanced for this behavior is the myopic discounting of the future by both those who save resources and those responsible for investing them. There are two other explanations, which turn out to match *Divide and Rue* and *Hard Core,* respectively—each with its own solution.

Suppose that some or all of the benefits of saving accrue to future generations? Will members of the current generation save despite this? Economist Amartya Sen suggests they would not. He reasons as follows. Every person would prefer that all players save one more unit of resources over a situation in which *no one* saved them. Given that others *do* save, however, each person is better off *not* saving—another instance of the "free rider" phenomenon. The end result is that the resources for future generations are not saved; future generations lose out in a game in which they are not asked to take part.[3] This is *Divide and Rue,* where "cooperate" is "save" and "compete" is "not save" or "spend." Sen calls this the "isolation" paradox. It is perhaps typified by Charles Schultz's cartoon character Charlie Brown, who insisted that he loved humanity—it was just other people that he hated. Players who feel that their own well-being is isolated from that of humanity are liable to act to the detriment of other people, and ultimately of themselves. Sen concludes that achieving a socially desirable level of saving will therefore require enforcement.

In contrast, William Vickrey claims no such enforcement would be needed. All that is required, he argues, is unanimous belief in others' goodwill. Once each person has the assurance that other people will indeed save, it pays for that person to do so too, and *continue* to do so. This is analogous to *Hard Core*. Vickrey's "assurance" paradox implies all that is needed to induce and maintain the socially desired outcome is the pervasive assurance that everyone intends to behave in a way that ensures that result.[4]

Who was right—Sen, or Vickrey, or neither? The answer ultimately depends on the motives for saving, the fruitfulness of the investments that saving makes possible, and how these fruits are divided up. High rates of saving over long periods of American history are evidence that tends to favor Vickrey, although it is possible that the post-1973 stagflation may have altered *Hard Core* saving to *Divide and Rue* spending. Perhaps the only true test would be a hypothetical social experiment in which everyone was asked, and agreed, to double the fraction of his disposable income that he set aside for saving for a period of six months or a year. If the new savings rate turned out to be stable and lasting, without further intervention, we might tentatively conclude that saving and investment are a critical-mass problem. If people began sliding back to their old, lower rates of saving, such defections hint at the "free rider" source of the problem.

WHY THREE INTO ONE DOESN'T GO

Economic games can trap us because of their objective structure or because of how we *perceive* that structure subjectively. One reason it is so hard to attain tripartite consensus among labor, management, and government on wages, prices, and incomes is that failure to achieve such consensus is not *perceived* as costly or harmful to our interests. The existing situation, in which every group is at liberty to flay strips from the hide of every other group, is seen as the *sine qua non* of human freedom, liberty, and dignity. As a result, we end up trapped at the very bottom of figure 9.1, instead of right at the top of it where we should be. In the arithmetic of social consensus, three into one doesn't go because players do not fully comprehend the price each of the three players pays for misguided factiousness.

Friedrich Dürrenmatt's play *The Visitor* provides a striking example. A wealthy woman returns to the village of her birth and offers the impoverished villagers a huge sum of money, provided they agree to her gruesome condition—provide a cruel end to one of the villagers who mistreated her. It is all or nothing; if the group of villagers refuse, they and everyone would lose the money. The play develops the moral implications of how the core comes to envelop the most upstanding,

230

moral villagers pressured by others to submit and acquiesce.

Another example is the Marshall Plan. Some observers believe that Marshall Plan aid to Europe created a core of European unity after World War II that ultimately blossomed into the Common Market. Under the plan, a substantial amount of aid was offered by the United States on one condition—that the European countries set up institutions to divide up the aid among themselves amicably and willingly. And those institutions were quickly built.

In both the play and the plan, the likelihood that rivalry and dissent would result in great loss acted as a powerful catalyst for consensus. When no such great loss is perceived by the players—for instance, had the woman offered the villagers an extra 5 or 10 percent to wreak her vengeance, or had George Marshall given Europe the aid unconditionally—there may be no core. Two games devised by Lloyd Shapley and Martin Shubik—one with a core and the other without—serve as good illustrations.[5]

THREE-MILLION-DOLLAR QUESTION

Suppose three brothers inherit $3 million. The will bequeathing it to them stipulates one condition—they must agree unanimously on how it is to be shared among them. If they fail to agree, a smaller sum, $2.5 million, will be split between any two of the brothers who agree how to share it.

This game has no core. To see this, note that an equal three-way split of $3 million is broken apart when two of the brothers put their heads together and agree to split equally $2.5 million, giving each of them a $250,000 profit. Among three brothers, there are three possible two-way splits. Competition among these pairs will break up any two-player coalition. The problem in this game is not that internecine strife is very costly, but that it is not costly enough.

Now, assume that the will has been altered, and the smaller amount distributed to two consenting brothers is only $1.5 million. In this case, a sizable penalty is imposed on the failure to agree. The core in this game is very large indeed. There are a great many ways to divide up $3 million among three brothers, so that each pair shares *at least* $1.5 million (the most they could get if they broke the unanimity and joined forces). For instance: $1 million could go to each of the three, or $1 million, $1.5 million, and $500,000, respectively, and so on. The "contention tax" of 50 percent, or $1.5 million, in this game acts as a strong incentive toward conciliation and cooperation. In general, the fraction of the total prize each faction stands to lose, or *perceives* it stands to lose, from betraying large coalitions has much to do with the existence of a core or its absence.

NATIONS DO THE SPLITS

Is there any evidence that macroeconomic conflict does tax us heavily? Experience of the industrial nations over the past decade shows how everyone loses when economic games degenerate into rancor. There is reason to believe that the cost of factiousness, in terms of needless inflation and unemployment, is very high. Figure 10.1 plots the era of stagflation, 1974–80, comparing it with 1971–73 for seventeen industrial nations, including the United States; the increase in inflation between the two periods is plotted against the increase in unemployment. The countries split into two clear groups: (1) Sweden, Norway, Japan, Austria, the Netherlands, West Germany, and (2) all the rest. The first group succeeded in restraining both inflation and unemployment—West Germany, with its 1920s allergy to inflation, opted for relatively more unemployment; Sweden, with its aversion of joblessness, chose relatively more inflation—but all six were successful in preserving macroeconomic stability. What sets these six countries apart is this: they all have centralized—or synchronized—wage bargaining, together with an informal or formal mechanism for coordinating policies among government, labor, and business. What characterizes the other eleven countries in general is the absence or weakness of such mechanisms. By not acting to mitigate or eliminate the three-way split among business, labor, and government, the United States and ten other countries found themselves on the wrong side of a two-way split: those who dealt successfully with the twin evils of inflation and unemployment, and those who did not.

THOSE WHO CAN

George Bernard Shaw said that those who can, do, and those who can't, teach. When it comes to avoiding macroeconomic conflict, those countries who can, also teach, provided we are willing to learn. We would do well to study carefully their successes.

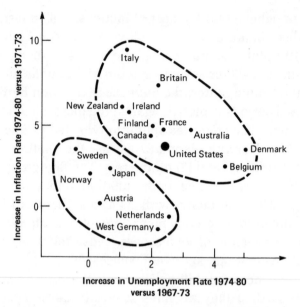

Figure 10.1 Increase in Inflation Rate versus Increase in Unemployment Rate for Seventeen Industrial Countries, 1967–80.
SOURCE: John McCallum, "We Need a Way as Well as the Will," *Financial Post,* November 20, 1982.

Austria: At the initiative of labor unions, a joint council on wages and prices was set up in 1957. The council is comprised of the finance minister and three other government-appointed members, four representatives of labor, and four members of employers' organizations. Though government representatives do have voting power, they have not exercised it for over fifteen years.[6] The council works to achieve consensus agreements on wages and prices between business and labor. It has been notably successful, as figure 10.1 shows. A similar body has existed for years in the Netherlands.

West Germany: No formal incomes policy mechanism exists. Wage bargaining between labor unions and an employers' organization, however, does take place on a national level. Meetings of labor, business, and government officials are held with the common objective of attaining noninflationary growth.

Sweden: Key agreements are hammered out nationally between employers—the S.A.F.—and blue-collar workers—the L.O.—with government intervening from time to time, as it did in 1980, to settle disputes. With nearly half of all workers in Sweden employed in the public sector, the government has now assumed an important role as a player and not just as a mediator.

Norway: Several package deals on wages, prices, and taxes have been hammered out in three-way negotiations, notably in 1973 and 1976. In the 1976 agreement, the government bartered a promise to cut taxes in exchange for promises to keep wage and price increases moderate.

Japan: Earlier in chapter 6, we cited Robert Gordon's claim that since the 1960s, he could find only three episodes where countries halted inflation by demand-management policies without causing recessions. One of these successes was achieved by Japan, in 1976–80. Gordon attributes this success to two factors: a union bargaining structure where contracts last one year only and expire at the same time (see *Happy New Year* in chapter 7), and, perhaps more important, an "implicit social contract" between unions and monetary policy authorities.[7]

In *Business-Labor-Government* described in the previous chapter, government was just another player. This can be misleading. Government is of course much more powerful than either of its two counterparts and has means to force other players to act as it wishes. One labor economist Lloyd Ulman wonders "whether the government should be allowed to sit in on the game, even if it parks its guns outside the door."[8] Despite the European experience, where the government's six-guns stayed holstered or were drawn only on the bad guys, many Americans share Ulman's misgivings.

WE LEARN TO COMPETE

"You cannot have a democratic society without a free market [both labor and goods pricing]," Donald N. Frey wrote us, "and the literature is full of essays to this effect."[9] One of those essays is John F. Bilson's empirical study of 184 states that found positive correlation between real per capita income and the extent of civil liberties.[10]

John F. Sytsma, the head of the Brotherhood of Locomotive Engineers, also opposed our suggestion of a social contract on free-market grounds. "Our government, being a democracy, is based on the free-enterprise system with competition being encouraged at an early age," he wrote us. "Not only would your idea of a 'social contract' be contrary to this learned behavior, but it would also go against the principles of democracy. The competitive free-enterprise system has been challenged on various occasions with the result being the rallying of public support for the retention of our current system."[11] He concluded that "The competitive driving force is an intrinsic ingredient in our society"; and he added that people might not be too readily receptive to the idea of a social contract if it meant forfeiture of a portion of their present or future earning power.

Not everyone agreed. "If the last two years have taught us anything," wrote Owen Bieber of the U.A.W., "it is that laissez-faire is a prescription for disaster. It is time to create the context for renewed growth and for the renewed pursuit of equality and decency."[12] On the other hand, E. G. Jefferson of Du Pont bolstered the case for free markets without meddling government "sheriffs" by citing Winston Churchill, who said that "some see private enterprise as a predatory target to be shot; others as a cow to be milked. But few are those who see it as a sturdy horse pulling the wagon. . . . The sturdy horse of American industry," Jefferson said, "has helped pull this nation forward with remarkable success for more than two centuries."[13]

CATCH-22

A major objection to the social-contract approach is the Catch-22 claim that if government has the muscle to enforce a social contract, it needn't bother—it can simply impose its will regarding wages and prices directly. If it lacks the muscle, the social contract is unlikely to endure. "If a social contract is to be a mere tacit agreement," Abraham Orlofsky, the head of the National

Federation of Federal Employees, wrote us, "it is unlikely to endure under political changes, manipulation and financial stress."[14] As an example, he cited the administration of the Federal Pay Comparability Act of 1970.

Yet other business and labor leaders stressed the importance of making the new social contract *voluntary.* One of them, Irving J. Spitzberg, Jr., of the American Association of University Professors, sees signs that

the language of social contract has [already] emerged in a number of the discussions of the serious problems facing higher education. . . . Thomas Hobbes may be our most relevant contractarian. . . . Hard times have a way of dissolving communities through competition for scarce resources. Universities in retrenchment provide a picture of a war: life becomes nasty, brutish, solitary and short. . . . The major insight to be drawn from the Hobbesian analysis is that security and order require the transfer of certain rights from the individual to the polity, but that society must in return serve the individual's interest. John Locke emphasized both the voluntary nature of decision-making in entering into a contract and the critical role of consent.[15]

To judge whether something is worthwhile, economists tell us to ask two questions: What is it worth? What must we give up to get it? If properly designed, the value of a social contract—what it is worth—should come out far ahead of its cost—what we give up to get it. When it does, for a majority, consent to it will be freely given. Every economy rises and falls according to how well, how hard, and how fully it utilizes its labor and capital. Working harder and better is like marital infidelity—to do it, you need both the desire and the op-

238

portunity. In *The Wealth of Nations,* Adam Smith observes that "it is in the interest of every man to live as much at his ease as he can; and if his emoluments are to be precisely the same whether he does or does not perform some very laborious duty, to perform it in as careless and slovenly a manner that authority will permit."[16]

Adam Smith's words bring to mind unemployment insurance. A study by David J. Smyth asked, "Does the Dole Cause Unemployment?" His answer for the U.S. private nonfarm sector, during the period from 1948 to 1981, is unqualified: "Yes, increases in unemployment benefits do cause unemployment. And the effects are substantial."[17]

One of the purposes of a social contract is to create incentives for people to work—not remain idle—and for others to want to employ them at good rates of pay. "If the unemployed lose their unemployment compensation by accepting a job offer paying about the same, David R. Dilley of U.S. Steel argued, "what incentive is there for them to do so?. . . . if our nation restructured 'unemployment compensation' into 'unemployment loans,' those absolutely unable to find any work would still be able to obtain funds on which to live, and they would repay through payroll deductions when they obtain a job, whereas those able to find work would be inclined to accept employment rather than indebt themselves through unemployment loans."[18] Such major surgery on the existing social contract would require creating more and better jobs and better pay; its effect on public spending might then facilitate such improvements, another instance of a critical-mass game where moving in the right direction generates its own momentum.

When economic games create high unemployment and hard times, as they did during the 1979–83 world recession, some players—especially labor—may change their behavior. For instance, an unusual three-way deal among government, workers, and employers was cut in Italy in March 1983. Under it, labor agreed to take a substantial cut in real wages, in return for government promises to restrain its spending, and presumably mitigate inflation.[19] In the United States, unemployment has brought some unions to change their game goals. Where once fixed contractual wages were sought—with the impact of those contracts on overall employment largely ignored—more and more unions are looking for contracts that ensure job security, even if the price is flexibility on wages.[20]

Governments with muscle to enforce social contracts also have the desire and ability to break them themselves. Britain and Israel offer examples. In 1975, a package deal was worked out in Britain. Under this social contract, labor unions agreed to considerable wage restraint. Asked why he had agreed, labor leader Hugh Scanlon said, "Healy [then finance minister in a Labour government] took us to the edge of the cliff, and we looked over, and didn't like what we saw."[21] The British social contract broke apart when the government hiked taxes. A similar series of events occurred earlier in Israel. A three-way agreement among Histadrut (unions), employers, and government signed in 1970 came unraveled eighteen months later when the government raised taxes to boost its revenues.[22]

PROPER CONDITIONS

"In principle, I believe labor could sit down with government and business, talk through what an anti-inflationary incomes policy would require, reach a consensus and proceed toward implementation," Owen Bieber wrote us. He specified in detail the conditions that would have to be fulfilled. "There would have to be an understanding about 'equality of sacrifice'—owners and managers of capital would have to commit themselves to contributions and sacrifices comparable to those of workers. The most disadvantaged in society would have to be singled out for protection—for example, through a raise in the minimum wage. Labor would want to extend the scope of the contract to include decisions about plant location and relocation, progress toward national health insurance, and compliance with environmental and OSHA (Occupational Safety and Health Act) standards, among others."[23]

Among the leading economists who support a social contract is Nobel laureate Wassily Leontief. "Even the skillful manipulation of taxes and interest rates will not work," he argues, "unless it is accompanied by institutionalized day-by-day cooperation—not simply 'mutual understanding'—between business, labor and government," citing Austria as a prime example.[24] M.I.T.'s Francis Bator is more blunt. Speaking of what he called the "inevitably meddlesome scheme of price oversight and direct mandatory wage restraint," he claims that "there is no other happier choice. People who say otherwise are, in my opinion, fooling themselves."[25]

241

CONCLUSION

"It is a very difficult matter to sit here at this desk and understand the attitude of people toward the emergency with which we are faced," President Harry S Truman wrote in early 1951 to Jonathan Daniels, publisher of the *Raleigh News & Observer*. "Every segment of the economic setup is interested only in its own selfish interests and is making an effort to grab all the traffic will bear. They seem to forget that by taking an attitude of this sort they will wind up with nothing and no country either."[26] Truman's biting letter was written at a time when war raged in Korea, inflation raged in America—1.5 percent per month—and controversy boiled up over Truman's mobilization program, which included wage and price controls. Yet despite the lack of consensus that troubled Truman, the passed buck of halting erosion in the value of the dollar stopped at Truman's desk. Between February and May 1951, prices rose by less than a total of 1 percent, as controls were reinforced and supplemented by stiff monetary and fiscal restraint. In time of crisis, Americans proved they could pull together.

Ford Motor Company's Philip Caldwell said once that "We in the United States have demonstrated to ourselves and to the world that in time of war we can define our national objectives, reach a consensus and get the job done. Isn't it possible to do the same in this period of our history when the weapons and the source of our conflicts are economic?"[27] In peacetime, it is not surprising that calls for sacrifice and self-restraint meet the response movie producer Samuel Goldwyn made famous, "Include me out!" We believe a new social contract can erase the ambiguity of that utterance and change it to "count me in!"

Thomas Hobbes had an interesting perspective on the nature of war and armed conflict which, he said, consists not solely in actual fighting, but rather "in the known disposition thereto during all the time there is no assurance to the contrary." Even without war or external crisis to unite us, we believe a social contract can be fashioned. It will end the disposition toward internal economic wars among us, by providing secure, rational "assurance to the contrary."

The wise words of Johnson & Johnson's James E. Burke provide an apt and optimistic conclusion. "It doesn't seem to me that there is any fundamental conflict in the views you identify—the aspiration of all of us to promote our own interests and the concern some of us have for the community as a whole," he wrote us. "Rather, it is the dynamic process of harnessing individual self-interest that is the primary job of our elected officials.... We already have a social contract," he contended. "It remains for us to prove that we can make it work to the benefit of everyone in society."[28]

PART V

Nations

When one country takes aim at another, it almost always shoots itself in the foot.

Rowland Frazee

PART IV

Nations

CHAPTER 11

Games Nations Play:
Gross Irrational Products

It is the duty of the inhabitants to indicate ... monuments, edifices or places used for artistic, scientific or charitable purposes, historic monuments, hospitals, and places where the sick and wounded are collected, by visible signs, which shall consist of large stiff rectangular panels divided diagonally into two colored triangular portions, the upper portion black, the lower portion, white.

All necessary measures should be taken by the commander of the attacking force to spare such edifices ... on condition that they are not used at the same time for military purposes.

"The Laws of Naval War Governing the Relations Between Belligerents"(1913)

NATIONS, like individuals and groups, play economic games. Of the 160-odd nation-states in the world today, the borders of many were drawn during colonization and decolonization in ways that defied reason and exacerbated economic and political strife. Just as people fight for their share of resources and wealth within their national economy, so do nations compete and cooperate with one another to share the plenties of our planet or to confiscate them from others. In these games, played on a global chessboard, three types of tokens move back and forth—money, goods, and people. Each system of tokens has its own set of complex rules, often changed or violated unilaterally. This chapter focuses on economic games nations play. It examines international money games, trade games, and migration, in turn, and the relationships among them.

RULES OF WAR

Over the centuries, elaborate rules have been worked out governing the most terrible and futile of all games, war. For instance, the black-and-white triangular panels for naval war. Or, the covenant on dum-dum bullets.

In 1863, Russian ballistics experts invented a bullet designed to blow up ammunition wagons that exploded on contact with a hard surface. In 1867, they modified it to explode on contact with soft human flesh. Russia thereupon initiated a convention stating that the object of war, disabling the greatest possible number of men, "would be exceeded by the employment of arms which uselessly aggravate the sufferings of disabled men, or render their death inevitable. . . . The employment of such arms would therefore be contrary to the laws of humanity," hence nations will renounce their use.[1] When, as Byron once said of Napoleon, the dice are the bones of men, there are volumes of complex rules— admittedly, honored more in the breach than in the observance.

International economic games, too, have elaborate rules, designed to regulate the peacetime commercial relations among countries. The objective of the rules is to improve the mutual well-being of all the countries that subscribe to them. Judging by results of the past decade, they have failed badly. The reasons for this failure both resemble, and differ from, the sources of economic stagnation within nations, as we shall note in what follows.

Of all the economic games people play, perhaps none is more esoteric or less understood by nonexperts than what Robert Aliber has called "the international money game."[2] The rules of the game come with their own opaque terminology—arbitrage, agios, counterspeculation, sliding bands, cross rates, SDRs, and Eurodollars for examples. Since World War II, the rules of the game were radically altered twice, in 1947 and in 1973. Each time, decisions of a relatively small handful of heads of central banks deeply affected the lives of billions of people, in ways that became clear only much later.

SELF-REPAIRING, GOOD AS GOLD

Systems that fix themselves have great intellectual appeal. This explains some of the current nostalgia for the old gold standard system that regulated world flows of trade and capital for over a century, until Franklin Delano Roosevelt finally cremated it in 1933. English philosopher David Hume used a simple principle from physics to construct an example helpful in explaining the logic of the gold standard. Water in connected vessels, Hume said, quickly reaches a common level. Similarly, price levels in countries connected by trade also find common levels.

Suppose the only moneys in use are gold coin or bullion, or national currencies made good as gold by government commitments to exchange them for gold on demand at agreed, fixed rates. Now, let one country live beyond its means by buying more from other countries than it sells to them. This will cause gold (or its equivalent) to flow out of the profligate country and into the thriftier ones. These flows of gold help the system right itself. In the spendthrift country, there is deflation. Less money means lower prices and, possibly, higher interest rates. This works to make foreign goods relatively dear, and makes exports cheap and attractive to other countries. In the thrifty countries, the opposite happens. The inflow of money boosts prices. Their citizens now find it both harder to sell abroad and cheaper to buy abroad. Just as water finds a common level in connected vessels, so do prices find a common level in trade-connected countries; under the gold standard, exports and imports balance over the long run, independent of the wisdom or sanity of politicians or kings.

During the gold standard's century-long heyday, 1815–1914, overall prices were relatively stable, with "ups" of inflation offset by "downs" of deflation. The system worked in part because the tail wagged the dog, and the dog was willing to let it. The "tail" was the fixed rate at which national currencies exchanged for gold. The "dog" was the economy and the people with whom it provided a living. Countries were willing to adjust themselves to the fixed gold value of their currencies, instead of vice versa, even if suffering and unemployment were the price they paid. Instead of opposing flows of gold, inward or outward, governments accepted them and at times helped them along by adopting measures consistent with them. Post–World War I England, at the tail end of the gold standard, is a case in point.

Wartime inflation severely eroded what the pound sterling could buy—partly because Britain actively encouraged *Hot Potato* inflation games by selling bonds to pay for the war instead of raising taxes, an error Keynes and others kept Britain from repeating twenty-five years later. The British were adamant in wanting to return to the prewar, pre-inflation gold price of sterling, as befit true believers in the gold standard. To do so, it was necessary to bring down domestic prices sharply, so that what a pound sterling could buy in London shops would match what its prewar gold equivalent could buy elsewhere. The only way to get local prices down was to force wages down.

The man charged with the task of deflating Britain's workers was Winston Churchill. His tough gold standard tail wagged the working class dog severely, at a cost of bitter strikes and joblessness. Though he achieved the goal set for him, Churchill was exiled into the political wilderness. At high human cost, the pound sterling returned proudly to its old, and utterly illogical, prewar gold value.

"MONETARY DISORDERS FUEL WARS"

The interbellum successor to the gold standard was a hybrid, the gold exchange standard. Dollars took up some of the functions of gold; local currencies were given fixed values in terms of gold and dollars. The new system, built on the idea that dollars would now fill many of the roles that gold once did, was formally organized and announced in 1947 at a New England resort called Bretton Woods. In this system, even dollars were not completely immune to changes in their gold value, on rare occasions.

On March 14, 1900, President McKinley set the new gold value of the dollar at $20.67 per ounce. Roosevelt did the same a generation later, somewhat casually picking the figure of $35.00 an ounce. In December 1971, Richard Nixon followed suit by devaluing the dollar 8 percent, to $38.00 an ounce. But in the turbulent 1970s, altering the gold value of the dollar at the same frequency that salmon spawn—once a generation—was no longer enough. Monetary crises in foreign exchange markets (by far the largest market in the world with a global volume of $100 billion a day) grew more frequent. A final series of panics brought rapid change. On March 6, 1973, it was decided to shut them down for three days of repair and renovation. When the "open again for business, thanks for your patience" sign went up, a new monetary system was in place. Its key principle was to let the dog—the economy—wag its own exchange-rate tail again.

Under the new system, the dollar price of francs, pounds, marks, kroner, and pesos "floated" freely, changing daily in response to the forces of supply and demand. No longer would heads of central bank and finance ministers have to meet hurriedly, under pressure from speculators, to patch up new exchange rates. The market would do the job for them.

If one country bought more goods abroad than it sold—for example, Japan, which has been known to run import surpluses—the value of its currency, the yen, would fall; it would take more yen to buy a dollar, and, conversely, a dollar could buy more yen. This would work to make the dollar prices of Japanese goods cheaper, encouraging exports, and to make the yen price of foreign goods more costly, trimming imports. Soon, the import surplus should vanish.

Recall that under the old gold standard, gold flows evened out trade flows by leveling domestic prices across countries. Under floating exchange rates, climbs and dives of exchange rates do this job. Gold standard adjustments at times involved deflation and unemployment. Floating-rate adjustments should, it was reasoned, involve no such social costs. Instead of fixed exchange rates spinning national economies up and down, national economies would move floating exchange rates in the appropriate direction, up or down—eminently more reasonable.

The wisdom of hindsight suggests floating rates are either a bad idea or a good one badly implemented. One of the architects of the system himself is disappointed. "The present world monetary system does not deserve the name," former German Chancellor Helmut Schmidt said.[3] French President Mitterand agreed. "We have to develop a new system as we did at Bretton Woods," he said. "Monetary disorders fuel economic wars between friends."[4] Some economists, notably Columbia University's Robert Mundell, advocate a return to the nineteenth-century gold standard. International economist Edward M. Bernstein is opposed. To restore the gold standard, he reasons, we would need two preconditions: stable prices and costs, and stable exchange rates. But if the United States could achieve such a de-

gree of price and currency stability, Bernstein concludes, we would not need the gold standard at all.[5]

WHY THE FLOATING EXCHANGE-RATE
SYSTEM SANK

The economic wars among "friendly" nations arose in
part from the uncertainty that floating rates permit. The
new rules of the game hammered out in 1973 called for
countries to intervene in foreign exchange markets only
to smooth out fluctuations. But many countries are
known to have acted to nudge their currency's external
value in what they thought was the right direction. The
allegedly undervalued Japanese yen is often mentioned
in this context. Under floating exchange rates, exchange
rates are permitted to bounce within ranges or bands.
It was still found necessary to change these bands from
time to time, which was as jarring a change as a devaluation under the old fixed-rate system. Worst of all, the
tail-wags-the-dog problem persisted, in a new and more
virulent guise. The tail even bit the dog. Here is why.

Trade patterns among countries in theory are supposed to dominate exchange rates and currency flows
among countries. Indeed, the main function of flows of
currencies is to facilitate and expedite flows of goods
and resources. Many experts feel that currency flows
came to dominate trade flows. Money from petrodollars
and other sources skipped from capital to capital, from
currency to currency, in search of higher rates of interest—another economic game nations play—and altered

exchange rates which, in turn, changed trade patterns. It was as if the sled began towing the husky dogs— backward. And that was not how the system was supposed to work.

In theory, floating exchange rates are supposed to insulate one country's economy from the inflation of another country. In the inflation-ridden 1970s, that alone should have bought floating rates immortality. It did not.

QUARANTINING THE INFLATION VIRUS

Rapid inflation in country X means that a unit of X's currency buys fewer and fewer goods. This should quickly make the value of X's currency fall relative to currencies of other countries that have slower inflation. Even if X's prices all double, foreigners buying X's goods pay no more for X's goods in their own money if the exchange rate for X's money falls by half. For instance, when the price of a Jerusalem hotel room doubles, from 1,500 to 3,000 shekels a day, it still costs American tourists $50.00 if the exchange rate climbs from 30 to 60 shekels to the dollar.

In this way, domestic inflation, like incest, is best kept within the family, thanks to the offsetting action of floating exchange rates. Theory proposes but reality disposes. There is evidence that post-1973 inflation rates among Western countries were *more* closely linked than before the switch to floating rates.[6] Though the reasons for this linkage are not clear, use of floating exchange rates to quarantine the inflation virus clearly failed. All they did was furnish an arena for a deadly global interest-rate competition.

INTEREST RATES RATE INTEREST

One of the "property rights" that a sovereign nation enjoys is the right to decide what to do with the size of its money supply. Would anyone deny that America has the right to regulate the quantity of American dollars in order to pursue what it sees as its vital economic interests? The answer is—yes, some do deny it. In our interdependent world, few strategies are costlier than playing international economic games as if there were no partners or opponents.

An underplayed announcement by the U.S. Federal Reserve Board on October 6, 1979, restored interest in interest rates. From now on, it was stated, attention would be shifted away from the growth of the money supply and focused instead on the level of interest rates as the Federal Reserve's primary tool of economic policy. Money would be important only as it affected the rate of interest.[7] Since late 1979, the zigzag graph of American prime interest rates—the rate that banks charge their solidest borrowers—has looked like the New York skyline. Interest rates broke through 19 percent four times during 1980–82, only to fall back. The objective of the monetary authorities was clear and simple. Hiking interest rates makes borrowing more expensive for consumers and for companies, inducing them to spend less and save more. This cools down the economy and slows down inflation.

Did the plan work? It is debatable. Interest-rate surgery brought inflation down to less than 4 percent in 1982, but it sent the American economy into a deep coma, with unemployment touching late Depression levels in November 1982. The surprisingly strong recovery in 1983 still left in its wake unacceptable levels of joblessness. What is certain is that America's recession was exported to Europe. To understand how and why, consider a game all of us have played many times.[8]

CALL BACK

Two people converse on the telephone. They are cut off. Each must decide: "Should I call back?" If both dial, a busy signal results. If both wait for the other to dial, there is silence (see figure 11.1).

What does *Call Back* have to do with interest rates and recession? In the economic games nations play, there are two separate forces or crosscurrents at work that are at times hard to separate. One is the problem of *coordination:* meshing, merging, and matching national economic policies among allies so that they reinforce and strengthen one another. A second is *competition:* contests with friends and rivals for markets and power. In international economic relations, both forces are at work.

The interest-rate game is predominantly a coordination problem. "In the old days," Walter Heller said in 1961, shortly after becoming the head of John Kennedy's Council of Economic Advisers, "we used to say that when the United States economy sneezed the rest of the

	You	
	Wait	Call Back
Wait	Silence	Communicate
Me		
Call Back	Communicate	Busy Signal

Figure 11.1 Call Back: A Game of Coordination

Two people converse on the telephone. The connection is broken. Should I dial or wait? each asks. This is a game of coordination, where the problem is not that of conflict of interest—both have a common interest in renewing the conversation—but of coordination, acting in ways that improve, rather than impair, the well-being of each.

---

world went to bed with pneumonia. Now when the United States economy sneezes, the other countries say, 'Gezundheit!' "[9] The old days are back. By 1981, Federal Reserve Governor Henry Wallich was once again saying, "when we sneeze, the world sneezes, too."[10]

The global teleology of interest rates is straightforward. Very large sums of money lie in liquid deposits in financial capitals—Paris, Frankfurt, London, and New York—ready to move elsewhere in search of slightly higher rates of interest. Countries usually (though not always) welcome migrant money as vigorously as they shun migrant people.

Games Nations Play: Gross Irrational Products

When interest rates in New York are high, they act like a magnet pulling "hot" money out of other currencies and other capitals toward American dollars and New York. Money flows away from marks, pounds, and francs. Demand for dollars rises, and the supply of marks, pounds, and francs grow as all these are exchanged for dollars in foreign exchange markets. With floating exchange rates, high American interest rates work to drive *up* the value of the dollar in terms of European currencies, and what amounts to the same thing, drive *down* the dollar value of marks, pounds, and francs.

When their currencies are worth less, Europe finds itself paying more for dollar-priced imports, especially oil. In the indexed society, this imported inflation soon becomes domestic inflation. If this game were to go on in this way, it would be a transatlantic version of *Hot Potato,* with America exporting inflation to its European partners. European countries, however, react to high U.S. interest rates by shoving up their own. They have virtually no choice. Some countries, like Mitterrand's France, tried to resist and soon found that the heavy selling of francs compelled them to align Paris interest rates more closely with those in New York, like it or not.

What high interest rates do to the American economy, they also do to the French, Belgian, English, and German economies—they slow down economic activity and production and generate unemployment. Moreover, the strong U.S. dollar makes American goods expensive for foreign buyers, and foreign imports cheap for U.S. buyers, further worsening unemployment. An economic game plan set in New York and Washington thus decides the fate of millions of *European,* as well as American, workers.

HELLO, REAGAN?

Europe got on the phone. But the line was busy. Unwilling and unable to cut their own interest rates unilaterally, European countries pressed the United States for a coordinated plan—specifically, for help in preventing the dollar from soaring when Paris and Frankfurt banks tried to hold the line on interest rates. Some efforts at coordination were made at annual economic summit meetings of the heads of state. But America persisted. In some ways this was understandable. In the 1960s, Europe shrilly demanded that America stop printing dollars and get control of inflation, which was spreading to other countries. Like a mother-in-law whose hapless son-in-law could do no right, Europe was equally displeased when America finally took firm anti-inflation action.[11]

In January 1982, the stakes were raised. Japan, West Germany, France, and Britain put their heads together and agreed to "go it alone," after trying futilely to convince the Reagan administration to cut interest rates. With France as the instigator, the four countries sought to cut their interest rates and at the same time keep their currencies from weakening by having their central banks sell dollars.[12] They did not succeed. The army of migrant money, it emerged, could easily overcome the combined divisions of four countries' central banks. No wonder French President Mitterrand complained later, "Rarely have the allies been so indifferent to one another's fate"[13]—clearly referring to one particular ally.

In the end, both sides kept on dialing; no real conversation took place. What the spirit of international cooperation failed to do, domestic politics achieved with ease. Looming congressional elections in November 1982 were preceded by frantic efforts to lower U.S. interest rates in order to stimulate the economy and avert a disastrous defeat.* The combined protests of presidents or prime ministers of six large countries at several economic summit meetings could not budge New York interest rates a single basis point. Protests of American voters were more effective, a meaningful comment on the invisibility of international goodwill's constituency.

The American economy accounts for close to one-third of the free world's gross national product. In the interest-rate episode, America resembled an elephant who climbs into a bathtub and then protests complete innocence when the water spills out over the sides. In late 1981, a London economist warned that "a really severe U.S. recession could knock the rest of the world down as well."[14] It did. What is worse, a world recession could call back again in similar circumstances, unless America and other industrial nations learn to play *Call Back* with greater wisdom, restraint, and coordination.

One bad game, like one good turn, inevitably leads to another. Many countries reacted to the world recession, and the resulting unemployment, by putting new

*Federal Reserve officials vigorously deny any link between the near-panicky efforts to slash interest rates in August and the November elections.

restrictions on imports from other countries. Unlike *Call Back*, this new game involved direct head-to-head conflict. We now leave the international money game, and turn to trade games—often typified by the game of *Brinkmanship*, or *Chicken*.

BLINDMAN'S BLUFF

Slogans or labels are history's way of economizing on time and space and thought in order to keep its drainpipes from clogging. The slogan irrevocably attached to President Eisenhower's secretary of state, John Foster Dulles, is that of the game he relished: Brinkmanship. "The ability to get to the verge without getting into war is the necessary art," he told a reporter from *Life* magazine in 1956. "If you try to run away from it, if you are scared to go to the brink, you are lost."[15]

The structure of *Brinkmanship*, or *Chicken* as it has been called, is this. Each player reasons—I would rather bluff the other person into giving in than be so bluffed myself, but I would rather give in myself than be wiped out along with my opponent. (The label Chicken derives from a hair-raising game teenagers played in the 1950s by racing cars headlong toward one another, with the driver who turned aside first called "Chicken.") *Chicken* is a close cousin to *Prisoner's Dilemma*. The only difference between the two is that in the latter, mutual disaster is preferred to being bluffed and exploited; in *Chicken*, it is better to be exploited than incur mutual destruction (see figure 11.2).

Games Nations Play: Gross Irrational Products

		Aggressor	
		Acquiesce	Challenge
Defender	Yield	2nd Best	Best for Aggressor Next-to-Worst for Defender
	Resist	Best for Defender Next-to-Worst for Aggressor	Worst (Mutual Destruction)

Figure 11.2 Brinkmanship

An aggressor country threatens a defender country. The aggressor must choose between "challenge" (fight) and "acquiesce." The defender must choose between "resist" (fight) and "yield." For each country, if the opponent is steadfastly determined to go to the brink (fight), the best strategy is to yield. By the same token, it is highly profitable to persuade the opponent that one has a sincere determination to fight. Misunderstandings and called bluffs result in war and mutual destruction, the worst of the four possible outcomes for both countries.

The game of erecting barriers to international trade is a blend of *Prisoner's Dilemma* and *Chicken*. Most economists agree that by trading with one another, every country can be made better off when it specializes in producing things it does comparatively well. As Ben Franklin told us, no nation was ever ruined by trade. Even if Japan could produce every product with less labor, capital, and resources per unit than the United States, it would still pay both the United States and Japan to trade. Japan would produce and export things it made at half the cost, say, of things produced in America, and import things it could make at only two-thirds of America's unit costs. A world organized along such lines would be much more efficient than it is now. In a sense, if people and labor are banned from moving freely across borders, permitting free flow of goods and services is a close substitute.

While all countries can benefit from free trade if all engage in it, it is undeniably true that one *individual* country may gain by erecting tariff barriers against the imports of other countries. Such unilateral tariffs act to appropriate some of the mutual benefits of trade from other countries. (The "unilateral" tariff, if it is too high, can of course damage the country imposing it, even when other countries do not retaliate.)

What happens to international well-being when an escalating tariff-wall game is played with one country retaliating against another, and, like quarreling neighbors, they erect even higher trade barriers against one another? Countries may be trapped into this game when they perceive it as *Prisoner's Dilemma*. High tariffs become a dominant strategy when one country pursues both the chance to exploit other countries if the latter do not respond in kind, and the necessity of *avoiding* being exploited if other countries have the same idea. This is probably a mistaken perception. It is worse to retaliate, ultimately, than to grit one's teeth and be "exploited." As in *Brinkmanship* or *Chicken,* successive rounds of retaliation lead to the worst of all outcomes, mutual destruction. When one country takes aim at another, Rowland Frazee, chairman of the Royal Bank of Canada, recently said, it almost always shoots itself in the foot.[16] These days, many countries limp badly, casualties of *Blindman's Bluff.*

RERUN OF THE THIRTIES

How little history teaches us. In the 1930s, many countries engaged in practices such as quotas, exchange controls, and high tariffs in what were called "beggar-thy-neighbor" policies that sought to export unemployment to foreign workers. The result was the destruction of world trade, which harmed everyone. As in *Chicken,* national interests collided tragically and wiped one another out.

To avoid repetition of such games, eighty-eight countries got together after World War II and signed an important treaty, the General Agreement on Tariffs and Trade (GATT), aimed at preventing a recurrence of the 1930s trade debacle. GATT was a sweeping social contract where each signatory country swore to refrain from building selfish, myopic trade barriers. Two GATT-sponsored series of negotiations—the Kennedy Round in 1964–67 and the Tokyo Round in 1973–79—engineered further cuts in trade barriers. The result: the volume of world trade grew more than sixfold in the three decades since the GATT agreement was signed.[17]

Just as nations are interdependent, so are the various economic games they play. The telephone game previously discussed brought on a serious world recession. That, in turn, initiated a fierce, costly version of trade barrier *Chicken*. With GATT rules banning tariff increases, countries found new ways to restrict imports. Japan insisted on opening every crate on its docks and inspecting every item before releasing the goods. France routed Japanese videotape recorders through a small ill-equipped customs house in southern France instead of through modern Le Havre.[18] Why give foreign workers jobs by buying their goods when our workers face serious unemployment? The old, fallacious question of the 1930s was revived. For the first time in decades (except for the oil crunch year of 1975) the real volume of world trade slumped.

A conference—only the third such gathering since GATT was signed in 1948—was called in Geneva in November 1982. Just before the meeting opened, U.S. delegate William Brock said GATT's goal was "to expand trade for the mutual benefit of all countries willing to play by a common set of rules . . . [however] nations will disregard the rules when they perceive such action is in their national interest, and adhere to them when it is convenient."[19] Though America was instrumental in calling the conference, it too had adopted protectionist measures, under pressure from steel and electronics industries and labor unions.

At the Geneva conference, like a stern-faced pastor lecturing his errant unruly flock, the director of the International Monetary Fund J. de Larosière said:

Protectionism has no place in today's world. . . . Interdependence has already gone so far that the point of no return has long since been passed. We have no choice but to continue on this path. Yielding to perceived self-interest can only be self-defeating; the dangers of retaliation are too great.

Playing by the rules laid down by GATT, strengthening them, and intensifying cooperation through the international economic organizations—which, let us not forget, did not exist in the 1930s—will be in the best interests of all economies.[20]

Delegates were not persuaded. The conference broke up in failure, without any agreement. Collective wisdom is, if anything, harder to attain in international forums than it is in games played within individual countries.

Herman Kahn was one of the first to interpret international conflict as *Chicken*. He described a diabolical game strategy used by teenage drivers that Kahn called preemption—visibly and irrevocably removing the steering wheel in mid-game and throwing it away. This is designed to persuade the opponent that you could not possibly turn aside, even if you wanted to, and that he must.[21] Prior to Geneva, many nations had apparently thrown away their steering wheels through commitments to internal pressure groups. The sound of the resulting head-on collision will resound around the world for many years.

ZERO-SUMMIT GAMES

When the international telephone game and *Chicken* turn out badly, when countries shoot each other in the foot as well as themselves, what can be done? There are at least two possible approaches. One is to try to set up world economic games so that they cease to be games, by eliminating the dependence of each country on what other countries choose to do. This is a futile policy, much like amputating a leg to cure a fever. As Ralph Bryant notes in his book *Money and Monetary Policy in Interdependent Nations,* policymakers can, but should not, disintegrate a nation's economy from the global economy by impeding the flow of goods, assets, people, or information across national borders. "In a nirvana designed for nationally myopic policymakers," he reasons, "they would be able simultaneously to retain within the home economy the benefits of good things originating at home, to export as much as possible of their nation's bad things to the rest of the world, to import good things from the rest of the world, and to insulate the home economy from all bad things originating in the rest of the world. But such a nirvana is illusory." Nor can we look to the floating exchange rate system to insulate and isolate us costlessly. "Any dream of achieving nirvana by means of some once-and-for-all decision about the form and degree of exchange variability," he concludes, "is a still more forlorn hope."[22]

A second approach is to try to hammer out social contracts among nations, thus ensuring forbearance from myopic, selfish, and self-defeating policies. One forum where informal contracts of this sort have been worked out is the economic summit meetings held annually in May or June. Since 1975, presidents or prime ministers of the seven major Western powers have met each year for economic talks. Some of these meetings have been dismal failures—for instance, the rancorous Versailles summit in 1982. Others have been more successful—the one in Bonn in 1978, for example.

Against a background of world inflation and rising

energy costs, with large balance of payments surpluses in Japan and Germany and a worrisome American balance of payments deficit, the seven leaders met at Bonn and agreed on a package deal. Germany and Japan made concrete pledges to stimulate the growth of their economies and boost their imports. France, Italy, and Canada also agreed to stimulate growth, although more modestly. The United States agreed to decontrol its oil prices, thus raising the price of energy paid by American consumers and reducing crude oil demand and imports. America and Britain pledged to act to reduce their rates of inflation. All seven countries agreed to liberalize trade.

All the economic summits—not excepting the most recent one at Williamsburg, Virginia, in 1983—recall British Prime Minister Ramsay MacDonald's description of his cabinet—our goodly company of unjust men making other people perfect. Like MacDonald's cabinet, the seven leaders do not often succeed in making other people, or themselves, perfect. But the potential for modestly reducing imperfections is always present. World economic interdependence and economic games leave us no choice but to cooperate and coordinate. As Anthony Solomon, president of the New York Federal Reserve Bank, said recently, "collective actions are often the *only* way for each country to become better off."[23]

So far, we have looked at the games nations play over flows of money and flows of goods. A third arena for international economic conflict—perhaps the most emotional of them all—is the movement of people across borders, the topic to which we now turn.

THE PURSUIT OF HAPPINESS

According to the Declaration of Independence, it is self-evident that the American people have the right to "life, liberty and . . . the pursuit of happiness." Here is a game that would extend this right to encompass the whole world.

PACK YOUR BAGS

In pursuit of happiness and self-fulfillment, people have the right to migrate freely across borders. No obstacles will be placed in their path. The World Bank will provide loans to those too poor to pay for their fare.

Enormous differences in wealth exist among countries. Average real income in the richest countries is up to fifty times that in the poorest. Flows of trade and aid have helped only minimally to narrow that gap. Just as economic inequality within a country causes social instability and strife, so do extremes of wealth and poverty among nations endanger world peace.

A rapid solution would be to organize the present heart-breaking game of immigration, in which people in poor countries battle to surmount high walls erected by people in rich countries to keep them out, along different lines, by smashing down the walls. If people in "have" countries are unwilling to share their fortunes with those in "have-not" lands, then let *people* rather than goods or money flow to equalize the imbalance. If economic well-being were the sole goal of people (which it obviously isn't), and if people could move freely across borders, in theory the only remaining economic inequality would be that due to differences in will, skill, and ability across people, rather than whether they were born in a rich or poor country. Country-specific differentials would be erased by migration.

Pack Your Bags will never happen. Wall-to-wall coalitions across the entire political spectrum exist against it. Among the strongest supporters of strict immigration laws are libertarians and free-market advocates, who in other contexts demand the least possible government intervention. It is hard to pin down their reasoning. The phrase heard most often is "the right to protect our traditional way of life" which would be destroyed by mass influx of people who speak other languages and cherish other cultures.

Perhaps the fundamental issue here is whether people born within a given set of borders have a fundamental "property right" to the riches those borders bestow and whether justice lets them protect that right by banning immigration. Is wealth the product of "generations of honest, hard-working ancestry," in John Marquand's phrase,[24] who labored to make their *own* children, not those of strangers, well off? Or is it the result of bountiful amounts of land, water, and resources supplied by nature and scattered haphazardly and inequitably across the globe? And would the free flow of people across borders drag all countries down to a low, mean existence, or pull most countries up to at least a minimal level of material dignity? Despite the lessons of history, in which mass flows of people uprooted by war and depression proved that immigration can ultimately be a positive-sum game beneficial to hosts and newcomers alike, we continue to treat cross-border movement of people as a zero-sum game with strict rules aimed at preventing foreigners from getting a slice of our pie. The game is not *Pack Your Bags* but *Stay Home.* In discussing international games involving exchange rates and trade flows, it is vital to remember that the rules governing migration games remain unfair and pose a threat both to those who set them and those battling to change them.

CONCLUSION

Physicists explain that nuclei of atoms are held together by a strong nuclear force. This force binds protons tightly together, less than a million millionths of a millimeter apart, even though they bear a positive electrical charge and should therefore repel one another. Nations of the world resemble the protons inside an atom's nucleus. Though they repel one another, the limited space, air, and resources of our planet act as a strong nuclear force to bind them together. The global economic equivalent of the strong nuclear force is both the fruit of cooperation and the disastrous consequences of its absence. But just as atoms break apart with a shattering release of energy, so do nations, as the repulsion of narrow self-interest overwhelms, from time to time, the binding power of common interests.

Like a series of Russian dolls, our economic games are "nested" one within another. Individuals slough burdens off onto other individuals. This leads small groups to do the same, then large groups. Ultimately, whole nations are enmeshed in these games. Can a cohesive world order be constructed at a time when disharmony among individuals dominates our economic relations? In economic games, charity begins at home. Geneva then follows. Someone once said that war decides not who is right but who is left. Economic games nations play in our current unsettled peace will be equally decisive in determining *what* is left, if not *who*.

CHAPTER 12

Hanging Together,
or Separately: Toward a
New Social Contract

" 'SO WHAT!' is a legitimate academic question," King-
man Brewster once told a Yale graduating class. If economic games divide society more than they divide national income, if the economics of factions has shoved
aside the society of common purpose, and if the prize
fund of *Run For Your Money* is in deep deficit—so
what? Perhaps these are all inevitable, though annoy-
ing, by-products of a free democratic society, like traffic
jams or polluted air. Perhaps we should resign ourselves to Robert Ardrey's interpretation of the social
contract, "that the individual is the one and only source
of human fulfillment" and "make elbow room, whatever
the price, for individuality."[1]

We reject this view. Economic games where individual gains are won in large part or wholly at others' ex-

pense now pervade society. Once they are made aware of the price of this kind of "individuality," few people, we believe, are eager to continue paying it.

What, then, can be done? There are four possible options. One is to leave matters as they are, in the faint hope that our economic games, and the spirit of competitive profit seeking, will somehow transform themselves back to their innocuous nineteenth-century versions—a change that is highly improbable. The remaining three choices focus on our economic games and those who play them. We can work to change the nature, values, and behavior of the players. Or, we can change the *rules* of the games. Or, finally, we can change the structure of the games themselves. In this chapter, we shall explore each of these three options in turn.

I. CHANGE THE PLAYERS

In this book, and in a previous one, we sought to merge economics and psychology.[2] But these two disciplines part company over the sanctity of individual preferences and values. Psychologists, especially those with clinical orientation, search for ways to alter people's dispositions and behavior—at their own behest—and to make their lives as members of society more stable and more meaningful. In contrast, economists stand hard, in general, on the maxim that individual preferences are not to be tampered with. One exception is the University of Wisconsin economist Burton Weisbrod. He cites the case of young children, "whom we may consider as persons whose adult utility functions are yet to be shaped.* Society can and does make decisions regarding the development of these utility functions."[3] "Plant green to reap ripe," says an Arab proverb. With children, we do plant green to reap ripe. Weisbrod cites educational and religious frameworks that explicitly aim at shaping preferences in desired directions.

To ameliorate our economic games, how should people change? One possible answer emerges from a game called *Beer Can.*

BEER CAN

Toss your beer can onto the beach or carry it to the trash bin. If you are the only one to litter, you still enjoy a clean beach. When everyone thinks he is the only one, the beach is soon ankle deep in cans.

"Human nature in some economic circumstances is capable of behavior other than the selfish pattern imputed to it by economic theory," wrote economist Jean-Jacques Laffonte. In his mathematical model of *Beer Can,* "a large number of anonymous people" decide daily whether to toss their cans into bins placed every hundred meters or so, or dump them on the beach.[4] "Once," Laffonte argued, "the rule 'do not injure your neighbor's person or his property' worked well. [But] modern times reveal increasing economic interdependencies that are not marketable...." How is it possible, then, he asked, that "[at least in some countries] people do not leave their beer cans on beaches?"[5]

To achieve the socially rational result in *Beer Can,*

---

*"Utility function" is economists' jargon for the relation between the amount of what gives people pleasure or happiness and the quantity of that pleasure.

it is not necessary for people to believe in something impossible or imaginary. To the contrary; what is required is for people to take into account together a constraint they previously ignored or overlooked—the limited amounts of clean sand, clean air and water, and open silent spaces still left to us. Suppose that people can change their behavior, and that social norms do respond to new situations and circumstances. Laffonte suggested that we "try by means of an information campaign to induce a Kantian type of behavior, even if a negligible number of consumers do not comply."[6] Kant, it will be recalled, supplied us with a categorical ethical rule: act such that, if everyone acted thus, you would benefit. It is both amusing and sad that in the sophisticated modern era of missiles, computers, lasers, and genetic engineering, our survival should rest on something as prosaic as the golden rule.

Beer Can is a version of multiperson *Prisoner's Dilemma*. For such games, in the absence of a Kantian norm, Laffonte observed, we can adopt "a repressive policy that necessitates an expensive control system (or requires extremely high penalties) and is not flexible enough to allow fine tuning toward an optimum. Such a policy allows only rules that are prohibitions."[7] In the language of psychology, such a system is built solely on negative reinforcement—withdrawal of rewards— known to be far less effective in encouraging the acquisition of desirable behaviors than positive reinforcement—rewards for doing right.

Now, suppose that economic man assumes that everybody will behave exactly as he does. This reduces the game to only two possible outcomes: everyone litters or everyone refrains from littering. The latter is clearly superior for everyone. "When the economic development of the Middle Ages required honest practices among merchants," Laffonte wrote, "a new ethics helped by some coercive legislation appeared. Even if it may seem dangerous to some humanists, we can predict that future societies will sometimes use the formidable power of modern news media and governmental authority to impose this type of solution."[8]

In this year of 1984, is Laffonte's prescription Big Brother? Or is it collective wisdom? Why is the artistry of *Reach Out and Touch Someone* (see page 63) laudable when it moves fingers toward telephone dials, but deplorable if it is used to keep hands out of the social till?

Some readers may recall an advertising campaign of an earlier day that today seems wonderfully simple and naïve. Coca-Cola handed out large numbers of wooden rulers to schoolchildren, with the golden rule written on them in bright red letters: Do unto others as you would have them do unto you—the biblical version of Kant's imperative. It is remarkable that eight world religions all have closely similar versions of this rule.* If it is per-

* • What is hateful unto you, do not do to others (Judaism).
  • Whatsoever ye would that men should do to you, do ye even so to them (Christianity).
  • Do naught unto others which would cause you pain if done to you (Brahmanism).
  • Hurt not others in ways that you yourself would find hurtful (Buddhism).
  • Do not unto others that you would not have them do unto you (Confucianism).
  • Regard your neighbor's gain as your own gain and your neighbor's loss as your own loss (Taoism).
  • That nature alone is good which refrains from doing unto another whatsoever is not good for itself (Zoroastrianism).
  • No one of you is a believer until he desires for his brother that which he desires for himself (Islam).[9]

vasive in ethical codes, conducive to strong cohesive societies, and virtually mandatory for individual rationality, why then do we observe so few people who practice it? Why are there so few societies where it is the norm?

A small fragment of evidence is provided by a study conducted in Israel. The central problem, it emerges, revolves around the perception of "reciprocation." In March 1979, Jerusalem's Van Leer Institute sponsored an interesting and unusual public opinion poll. The subject and purpose of the poll was the "golden rule."[10] A random sample of Israelis was asked whether they themselves behaved according to it, and whether they thought other people did too.

The results were:[11]

• I act according to the golden rule, but others do not.	57%
• I act according to the golden rule, and so do others.	17
• I do *not* act according to the golden rule, nor do others.	22
• I do *not* act according to the golden rule, but others *do.*	4
	100%

By far the largest segment of the population believes that *it* conforms to Kant's categorical imperative, but others do not. While the *perception* may be well founded for an individual, it is logically impossible for society as a whole. We suspect that a similar poll among Americans would yield similar results. If so, the above findings pose a problem. Given the universality of the golden rule, most people would experience uncomfortable dissonance if they admitted they acted in contradiction to it. Only one-quarter of the Israeli sample responded so, and of this, only one person in twenty-five said he violated the rule but felt others kept it.

People who *already* are firmly convinced that they act in accordance with the categorical imperative are largely immune to persuasion to *behave* in line with that principle, since most people think they act in accordance with their beliefs. It is this "I'm O.K., you're *not* O.K." perception, which, if deeply rooted, is most resistant to changing the ethics of game players. In the four-way division of people shown above in the Van Leer study, the cant of the majority is the toughest to modify in the direction of Kant.

During the 1980–83 recession in the United States, when unemployment brushed close to 11 percent, voices were heard recalling with nostalgia the bitter days of the Depression. In hard times, some said, people shared what they had and helped one another. Society was more cohesive. Perhaps a depression would "shake out" the selfishness of the affluent, effluent society. The Van Leer study bears directly on this view. Only 21 percent of the respondents believed that others acted according to the golden rule in normal times. But fully 80 percent said that other people adhered to the principle in time of war.[12]

Ability of societies to unite and pull together in times of great crisis is beyond dispute. What we must ask ourselves, however, is: Must people be reduced to selling apples on street corners, in order for social norms to change in a manner that a majority approve of *in any event?* "One must not expect miraculous transformations in human behavior," Nobel laureate Kenneth

Arrow cautioned. "Ethical codes, if they are viable, should be limited in scope."[13] Perhaps no more sweeping transformation in human behavior is required than this:

THE ONE-LINE SOCIAL CONTRACT

I'm O.K., and will assume that you're O.K. until proven otherwise.

Thomas Schelling's words on this issue are wise. "A good part of social organization—of what we call society—consists of institutional arrangements to overcome . . . divergences between perceived individual interest and some larger collective bargain. . . . Our morals can substitute for markets and regulations, in getting us sometimes to do from conscience the things that in the long run we might elect to do only if assured of reciprocation."[14] Arrow, Schelling, and the Van Leer study all show how closely economics and ethics are woven together.

In fostering a social climate where individualism and "do your own thing" dominates socialization toward a common American identity, our school system has played a major role. The Bill of Rights has been used repeatedly to support individual rights and to foster the idea that schools can be value-neutral.[15] Once, schools were charged with creating unity and commonality. The melting-pot notion fostered this approach. More and more, however, we use the schools to uphold concern for the individual, whatever the price.

Perhaps, when neutrality of values goes so far as to raise a nation of people more interested in competing for individual gains than learning to share and uphold a common American way of life, we have reached a lower limit beyond which social conscience crumbles and social fabric tears.

Two voices, Dickens and Shaw, rise in dissent. "Do not do unto others as you would that they should do unto you," Shaw urged. "Their tastes may not be the same." Dickens's character Jonas Chuzzlewit says, "Here's the rule for bargains. Do other men, for they would do you. That's the true business concept."[16] Shaw may be whimsy, but, regrettably, Dickens is reality. The gap between "Do unto others. . . ." and "Do others" is as small as a four-letter word and as large as an ocean. If it cannot be narrowed by changes in game players, perhaps it can be closed by modifying the rules of our economic games.

II. CHANGE THE RULES

"Though in the ideal commonwealth men may have been taught or inspired or bred to take no interest in the stakes, it may still be wise and prudent statesmanship to allow the game to be played, subject to rules and limitations," John Maynard Keynes wrote.[17] Given that people will always strive for material gain, what changes should be made in the rules and limitations placed upon our economic games?

"The economic game is a game where the rules are subject to important revisions, say, every ten years," wrote Norbert Wiener, the inventor of cybernetics, "and [hence] bears an uncomfortable resemblance to the Queen's croquet game in Alice in Wonderland."[18] Trapped in a web of changing rules, laws, precedents, and administrative decrees, decision makers at all levels may nod their heads in agreement. Yet in one sense, the rules of our economic games have not been renovated for decades. Our economic system is still founded on the fundamental premise that substantial material reward is indispensable for calling forth human effort and initiative. A recent, abortive attempt was made to modify the rules somewhat—less than people were led to believe—by increasing the after-tax return to effort. The ideology of this attempt was labeled "supply-side economics." It left us, in Shakespeare's words, "Eating the air on promise of supply."[19]

In the economic games we described where my gain comes at your expense, the problem of designing incentives is exceedingly intricate and complex. No system has yet been devised that, in practical terms, provides munificent rewards to those whose sweat and toil enrich both themselves and society, yet punishes or denies rewards to those who seek gain at others' expense. Unlike wine or cars, dollars do not reveal their vintages or ancestries, nor do they tell us in which type of economic game they were won.

Keynes pondered this problem. His views on it, as on many other issues, are worth considering. In 1936, he argued that "the outstanding faults of the economic society in which we live are its failure to provide for full employment and its arbitrary and inequitable distribution of wealth and incomes."[20] Two generations later, these faults are as glaring as ever. To some extent, Keynes claimed the economic games that generate these faults are harmless substitutes for more destructive games. "Dangerous human proclivities can be canalised into comparatively harmless channels by the existence of opportunities for money-making and private wealth," he wrote, "which, if they cannot be satisfied in this way, may find their outlet in cruelty, the reckless pursuit of personal power and authority, and other forms of self-aggrandisement."[21] He continued that "It is better that a man should tyrannise over his bank balance, than over his fellow-citizens; and whilst the former is sometimes denounced as being but a means to the latter, sometimes at least it is an alternative."[22]

On the question of incentives, Keynes spoke clearly and bluntly. "It is not necessary for the stimulation of these activities and the satisfaction of these proclivities that the game should be played for such high stakes as at present. Much lower stakes will serve the purpose equally well, as soon as the players are accustomed to them. *The task of transmuting human nature must not be confused with the task of managing it"* (Our italics).[23] Keynes was right. Large material rewards are neither necessary nor sufficient to call forth entrepreneurial genius and hard productive work. They are not sufficient because human beings have goals other than material comfort. A major source of disillusion in Western economies in this century has been the discovery that historically unprecedented quantities of goods and services have not made us appreciably happier. Nor are large rewards necessary. Intrinsic rewards—doing something for the deed itself, and not for what it brings us—can motivate and energize people far more than extrinsic rewards. If there is a fallacy in the logic of individualistic market economies, it is the worship of the dollars-for-deeds principle. To understand why it is fallacious, we enlist evidence from psychology.

Psychologists distinguish between intrinsic motivation (doing something for its own sake) and extrinsic (doing it for the reward). Children are socialized from an early age to work for extrinsic payoffs. The result, one can argue, is that the drive and cohesiveness that typify an internally motivated person are downplayed, cast aside, and ultimately extinguished. Monetary rewards have a hidden cost, J. C. McCullers reasoned. When extrinsic rewards are offered, especially munificent ones, intrinsic motivation is destroyed.[24] Later, when stirring appeals are made for harder and better work, more production, and more innovation, for their own sakes, it should come as no surprise that there is no response.

A market economy is an autocratic, bureaucratic mechanism that tells people, "Do not do what you want, do what we tell you to do because we pay for it." The result is "alienation, anomie, and a lowered sense of autonomy." As William Ouchi has suggested, when people are socialized to a common, intrinsic goal, "the capacity of the system to measure the subtleties of contributions over the long run is so exact that individuals will naturally seek to do that which is in the common good."[25] This is a close-to-optimal solution to the incentive problem we raised earlier. "The monk, the marine, or the Japanese auto worker who appears to have arrived at a selfless state," Ouchi claimed, "is in fact achieving selfish ends quite thoroughly.... These mechanisms . . . realize human potential and maximize human freedom because they do not constrain behavior."[26]

An increasingly popular diagnosis of capitalism's ailments is the burgeoning size of the public sector. It is argued that feeding the bureaucratic monster swallows, and wastes, huge amounts of resources. Taxes insert bothersome wedges between what individuals give to society and what they take from it. Increasing incentives by shrinking the wedges and slimming down the bureaucracy is urgently needed. We agree with the remedy, though not entirely with the diagnosis. The phrase "social contract" or "incomes policy" has in the past been invariably linked with those who support larger bureaucracies and bigger roles for government. It is, however, entirely consistent to favor a social contract—one of whose expressions is an income-policy pact among labor, business, and government—while supporting a slimmer public sector.

As part of a revised social contract, both the size and influence of government must be curtailed. That is perhaps the one rule change most badly needed. A social contract, interpreted broadly, is simply a clear statement about what game is being played, who the players are, what the rules are, what the players hope to achieve, and how they commit themselves to playing. *Every* society is built on such contracts, mostly unwritten ones. We believe it would be useful to make our social contract clearer and more explicit. If new patterns of individual behavior achieve voluntarily and freely what regulation and decree failed to attain, the result will be a smaller, not larger, role for government.

Tolstoy wrote, in *Anna Karenina,* that happy families are all alike, but unhappy families are unhappy each in their own way. One way some families are unhappy is in unstable, shifting patterns of internal coalitions, with two persons uniting against a third, and with the coalition pairs in constant flux. Nations, like families, experience similar instability when government acts as a powerful player that other players—labor, business, industrial sectors, consumers, exporters, importers, and professional groups—regard as a bountiful direct or indirect source of income, once an alliance is struck. These incomes do not benefit society as a whole, since they are predominantly economic rents (payments above what something is intrinsically worth), and since resources are wasted in search of them. There may be no choice, in the face of such games, but to abolish them.

III. CHANGE THE GAME

Dealing with many of the predatory economic games we have described requires fundamental changes in human behavior, or rule changes needing a degree of consensus often hard to attain. With other games, the problem is simpler—they need to be abolished altogether. Once done, society becomes healthier and the economy, wealthier. Prime candidates for abolition are two types of games in whose creation government acts both as father and midwife: Directly-Unproductive Prof-it-Seeking Activities (DUP), and Directly-Unproductive Bureaucratic-Unprofitable Activities (DUB).

Before defining and describing these games, here is a simple way to measure how pervasive these two games are in our lives. Ask yourself these two questions:

- What part of my waking hours do I spend doing things that benefit me, my family, or my employer but no one else, even indirectly?
- What part of my waking hours do I spend doing things—required by law—that neither benefit me nor anyone else, directly or indirectly?

The answer to the first question yields your DUP quotient; the second, your DUB quotient. Together, they give the DUP + DUB ratio. Our own DUP + DUB number is, we found, distressingly high.

Jagdish Bhagwati defined DUPs as ways of making profit or income that use up real resources but do not produce goods or services, either directly or indirectly.[27] It follows, therefore, that DUPs cause a decline in our overall economic wealth, a decline which can be very large indeed. DUPs are visible, measurable trails left by games that dominate a rent-seeking society. Here are some examples:

- Special-interest legislation (such as tax provisions that encourage overbuilding of apartments or excess exploration for oil and minerals); both the legislation itself, and competition to get it approved, causes great waste
- Licensing mechanisms, where candidates spend heavily to win them

- Competition for contracts, especially large government contracts
- Rate regulation—for instance, interest-rate ceilings that lead to wasteful competition for loans and deposits

Much has been written about resources wasted through government intervention and regulation of markets. This waste is matched by resources spent by those seeking such intervention in order to profit from it. The amount of resources wasted on DUPs rises in step with the rents for which DUPs compete. Anne O. Krueger estimates rents amount to fully 7 percent of India's national income, and rents from import licenses alone amount to an astounding 15 percent of Turkey's gross national product.[28] With such high stakes, it is no wonder players invest heavily to win them—investments that are a net loss to society as a whole.

We used specific economic games to argue that competition is far from an unmixed economic blessing. DUPs are a case in point. The free enterprise system is built on the belief that what you make (in income) depends on what you know. High incomes, it is assumed, imply high contributions to national product. Suppose, however, that in the rent-seeking society, what you make depends largely on *whom* you know. As Anne Krueger observed, the result may be a public insistence on further government intervention and regulation[29]—equivalent to treating alcoholism with a case of Cutty Sark. Perhaps the only way to cut through this tangle is through a social contract in which the rents themselves are eliminated. As long as the rents are in place, people will compete for them, at great cost to society. Volumes have been written on DUBs (bureaucratic waste). Little need be added.

DUPs and DUBs march hand in hand, reinforcing one another. Curtail the size and extent of DUPs, and DUBs will shrink as well.

TO START, AN INCOMES POLICY

A good place to start in changing our economic games is to define their objectives. Each part of society should ask, and answer, a series of questions:

What are my objectives? Are they exclusively for my own and my family's well-being? Are these goals sufficient for long-run contentment? When I act solely to attain these objectives, do I in fact end up frustrating their attainment?

As a nation, do we have objectives? What are they? Is there a consensus about them? If not, how can such a consensus be built? Are there internal conflicts of interest? Are they real or imagined? How can they best be resolved?

The new social contract is built on the answers to these questions.

The structure of our society is like a series of concentric circles, as we noted earlier. It begins with the individual, widens to embrace his or her family, widens further to encompass friends and relatives, and so on until the circle encloses the whole nation. Revising the social contract is best done by working from the inner circle—the individual—and proceeding outward. This is laborious and prone to failure.

An alternate approach is to begin from the largest circle—the nation—and work inward. A national incomes policy, negotiated yearly by representatives of labor and business, refereed by government, with clear goals set for economic and social objectives, and precise policies outlined to attain those goals, would make a good start. Such a policy is a social contract between labor and business, with government acting as source of information and guarantor. It is the macroeconomic equivalent of Kant's categorical imperative. Its objective is to increase the efficiency of free markets, not to curtail them, and to widen our individual freedoms, not to enslave them.[30]

One of the major objections raised by corporate and union leaders to such a social contract, as we saw in chapters 9 and 10, was that it encroaches upon basic freedoms. How easy it is forget or deny that the Statue of Liberty is equally a statute of limitations, which places constraints on the freedom of each person to harm or impinge upon the freedom of others. These constraints form the social contract on which every society is founded and are the core of freedom itself. They find expression in courts of law and in standards of fairness and decency. In calling for a social contract to regulate and modify our economic games, we ask for nothing more than an extension of old and familiar arrangements to the important, economic realm of our lives that is presently in considerable disorder.

To support our case, we shall call to the stand President Herbert Hoover and ask him to read part of his "rugged individualism" speech, delivered on October 22, 1928, at the end of his winning presidential campaign—a speech taken to be a classic statement of optimism and faith in economic individualism. "The very essence of equality of opportunity and of American individualism is that there shall be no domination by any group or combination in this Republic, whether it be business or political. On the contrary, it demands economic justice as well as political and social justice. It is no system of laissez faire."[31] No truer nor surer road to economic justice exists than the free commitment, freely undertaken, to new rules, new behaviors, and new games, that is the essence of a social contract.

In constructing it, the interests of other nations must be taken into account as well, to avoid repetition of the interest-rate-game world recession. "The United States has no ultimate responsibility for the world as a whole," John Sheahan has noted. However, ". . . reduction of real incomes in other countries to lessen our own rate of inflation would seem to be a violation of the sense of any meaningful incomes policy. The point of such a policy is to lessen the human strains and the economic losses associated with inflation. A more fundamental purpose, not necessarily intended but certainly implied in the approach, is an effort to create a better method of reconciling social conflicts. To step on other countries in the process would violate any such principle."[32]

BIAS, SLANT, AND LIGHT

"All writing slants the way a writer leans," E. B. White once wrote, "and no man is born perpendicular, although many men are born upright."[33] For most of the thirty economic games we have described so far, narrow rivalry turns out to be costly and self-destructive. Had we slanted our writing otherwise to include thirty economic games where unbridled competition pays off handsomely for all players, would we not have led readers to a far different conclusion? We plead uprightness. At times, all is for the best in these the best of all economic games. When this holds true, no problem exists, no policy is required, no soul-searching is called for, no brows need furrow.

Given the dismal dividends the past ten years have paid us, few people would agree that this Panglossian perception is wholly accurate. Nor should the surprisingly strong economic recovery of 1983–84 be allowed to overshadow the inflation and recession that preceded—and perhaps even propelled—it. Economic games that turn out well can be left alone. Economic games that turn out badly demand that we ask, Why is this so? What can be done about it? These are the issues toward which this book slants.

We have focused on games where individual gains lead to social losses. In a trivial sense, *every* economic game fits this definition. Because the resources that sustain us are limited, their use by one person or group always deprives someone else, if only future generations. For much of our history, we played such games reasonably well, aided by orderly markets and institutions that gave us the right to keep most or all of what we won. The reason for this success was not the magical machinery of markets. It was rather the benign nature of the games. So long as the number of players was small relative to available amounts of space, air, water, and energy, nature's casino was bountiful. Unlike Las Vegas, more people won than lost. Moreover, the sum total of gains was more than enough to offset the sum total of losses, making it theoretically feasible for society to compensate losers and still pay dividends to winners. And if losers were not compensated in practice, we could shrug off the unfairness either as the homage freedom pays to efficiency, or deny there *was* unfairness by reasoning that in life's lottery, all *start* equally favored, though a few *end* far ahead.

This view is no longer tenable. The economic games we play have changed dramatically, inducing changes in the players themselves. What we now face is a set of economic games where opportunities for individual gains arise primarily through what can be appropriated directly from other players, and where losses exceed gains. Sometime in the 1970s, industrial nations crossed an invisible divide that separates friendly games from malevolent ones. In this new and unfriendly territory, no longer is equality bartered away for added material wealth. We give both away for nothing.

Before the advent of Edison's light bulb, the French had a saying: the game is worth the candle—meaning that the pleasure the game provided exceeded the cost of wicks and wax. If the cost-benefit ratio of our modern economic games tilts heavily in favor of cost, it is not because they are not worth the candle. Rather, it is because we play them in the dark without so much as a candle to see our games, ourselves, and how the two interact. It is time we illuminated the paths of our interrelationships and interdependencies as brightly as we

294

light the streets of our cities. In this regard, we offer a final game.

TAKE MY HAND

Some years ago, the Buffalo Creek burst over its banks and wrecked a small mining community in West Virginia. The people in the community never recovered from the blow.[34] What shattered them was not the destruction of their houses and property, nor even the deaths of loved ones. It was the fact that flood waters swept away the fabric of the community—the network of relationships, love, and support that constitute our social envelope. Loss of this envelope left everyone in this community—relocated in trailer camps with strange neighbors and surroundings—viewing life as without meaning or hope.

One writer has even suggested that people need a certain daily "interaction quota" with other people, which, if lacking, causes physical disturbance much like the deficiency of vitamin C or protein.[35] To illustrate this, we offer an economic game, a fundamental one, in which no money or goods change hands, but which lies at the heart of every sound economy.[36]

TAKE MY HAND

To be strong and happy, each person in society needs to grasp the hand of another person in *each* of his or her hands.

Suppose all the players are arranged in rows or in one straight line. People on the ends have only one other hand to clasp; one hand is empty. Soon they weaken and fall. That leaves the person next to them with only one clasped hand. He too falls. Soon, no one is strong or happy. The game ends badly.

Now, change the structure of the game ever so slightly. Arrange people in one *circle*. The chain is complete. Society is strong, stable, and happy; everyone has two clasped hands—unless one person breaks the chain, which causes the whole system to unravel and end badly as before.

Economies are not as fragile or as delicately balanced as *Take My Hand*. Still, *Take My Hand* is present to some degree in all the economic games we play. Often, we are so wrapped up in the game that we fail to understand its true nature, and we miss the tiny but vital modifications in its structure, or in our behavior, that make the game and those who play it sturdy and viable. Usually, it is the way we link ourselves to other people, and to society as a whole, that requires alteration. Man is a sociable, no less than a reasonable being, the English philosopher David Hume wrote in 1748.[37] The strength of our reason can reveal the true source of our strength, or weakness—the fabric of social bonds that link one person to another.

Take My Hand is an economic game. In it, support passes from hand to hand. Mutual trust and sympathy that flow freely from one person to another, from one group to another, and even from one nation to another, are as essential to economic health as the flow of money, goods, and resources. This truth summarizes our entire book.

CONCLUSION

At the signing of the Declaration of Independence, Benjamin Franklin remarked wryly to his cosigners, "Gentlemen, if we do not hang together, then most assuredly we shall all hang separately." The leaders of revolutionary America and the people they led hung together. America won first its freedom, then wealth, prosperity, and comfort.

Two centuries later, Americans hang separately. They dangle from ropes of dissension, ropes fashioned by divisive economic games that generate inflation, unemployment, inequality, and uncertainty and that imperil both their material and spiritual well-being. That other countries are similarly troubled offers little solace. We need to adapt to new circumstances and new challenges by changing the rules of our economic games, changing the games themselves, and changing the way we play them. There is a way to hang together again. Where there is a way, there is a will.

Let us begin.

NOTES

Chapter 1

1. Chances of a 13-0-0-0 hand in bridge are 158,753,389,899 to 1.

2. All figures are taken from the U.S. Bureau of the Census, *Statistical Abstract of the United States, 1981* (Washington, D.C.: U.S. Government Printing Office, 1981): family income and poverty, p. 905; education, p. 904; cars, p. 911; appliances, p. 766; passports and travel, p. 239; and telephones, pp.562, 892.

3. Gallup Poll random sample of Americans, conducted in August 1979; data provided to authors by the Gallup Organization.

4. "Liquor's Thirst for a Younger Market," *Business Week,* 20 April 1981, 72.

5. Jethro K. Lieberman, *The Litigious Society* (New York: Basic Books, 1981); Lester Thurow, *The Zero-Sum Society* (New York: Basic Books, 1980); Ann Krueger, "The Political Economy of the Rent-Seeking Society," *American Economic Review* 64 (1974): 291–303; Yair Aharoni, *The No-Risk Society* (Chatham, N.J.: Chatham House, 1982); Leif Johansen, "The Bargaining Society and the Inefficiency of Bargaining," *Kyklos* 32 (1979): 497–522; John Kenneth Galbraith, *The Affluent Society* (Boston: Houghton Mifflin, 1958); and Richard Tawney, *The Acquisitive Society* (New York: Harcourt Brace, 1921).

6. Alfred North Whitehead and Bertrand Russell, *Principia Mathematica.* 3 vols. Cambridge University Press: Cambridge, England: 1925–27.

7. J. M. Roberts, M. J. Arth, and R. R. Bush, "Games in Culture," *American Anthropologist* 61 (1959): 597–605.

8. *Games Magazine,* July–August 1982, 9.

9. Oskar Morgenstern, "Game Theory," *International Encyclopedia of the Social Sciences,* vol. 6, ed., David Sills (New York: The Macmillan Co. and The Free Press, 1968), p. 62.

10. John von Neumann and Oskar Morgenstern, *The Theory of Games & Economic Behavior,* 3rd ed. (Princeton, N.J.: Princeton University Press, 1953), p. 41.

11. Martin Shubik, "The Dollar Auction Game: a Paradox in Noncoopera-

tive Behavior and Escalation," *Journal of Conflict Resolution* 15 (March 1971): 109–11.

12. Ibid., p. 110.

13. David N. Hyman, *Public Finance: A Contemporary Application of Theory to Policy* (Chicago, Ill.: The Dryden Press, 1983), p. 100ff.

14. *Business Week,* April 27, 1981, 32.

15. Kenneth Arrow, "General Economic Equilibrium: Purpose, Analytic Techniques, Collective Choice," *American Economic Review* 64 (June 1975): 253–72; James Tobin, "Money and Finance in the Macroeconomic Process," *Journal of Money, Credit & Banking* 14 (May 1982): 171–204.

16. See A. K. Sen, "Isolation, assurance and the social rate of discount," *Quarterly Journal of Economics* 81 (1967): 112–24; and S. A. Marglin, "The Social Rate of Discount and the Optimal Rate of Investment," *Quarterly Journal of Economics* 77 (1963): 95–111.

17. For the contention that the true basis of capitalism is in fact selflessness and "giving," see George Gilder, *Wealth and Poverty* (New York: Basic Books, 1981), chapter 3.

18. Jerome L. Stein, "The 1971 Report of the President's Council of Economic Advisors: Micro-economic Aspects of Public Policy," *American Economic Review* 61 (1971): 531–37.

19. Abba P. Lerner and David G. Colander, *MAP: A Market Anti-Inflation Plan* (New York: Harcourt Brace Jovanovich, 1980).

20. David Lewis, *Convention: A Philosophical Study* (Cambridge, Mass.: Harvard University Press, 1969).

21. See Andrew Schotter, *The Economic Theory of Social Institutions* (New York: Cambridge University Press, 1981).

22. Maschler's proposed solution for cooperative games, the "bargaining set," sprang from his observations of the students' game-playing behavior.

23. Wassily Leontief, *Science* 217, July 9, 1982, 104–7.

24. David Wallechinsky and Irving Wallace, *The People's Almanac* (Garden City, N.Y.: Doubleday, 1975), pp. 565–66.

25. Herman Wouk, *This is My God* (Garden City, N.Y.: Doubleday, 1959).

Chapter 2

1. Edmund Burke, *Reflections on the Revolution in France,* ed., William Todd (New York: Holt, Rinehart and Winston, 1965).

2. Herbert Spencer, *Principles of Biology* (New York: Appleton, 1867), ch. 12.

3. Robert Burns, "To a Louse,". *The Complete Writings of Robert Burns* (Boston: Houghton Mifflin, 1927).

4. Joseph Heller, *Catch-22* (New York: Dell, 1955), p. 107.

5. Lee Ross and Craig Anderson, "Shortcomings in the attribution process: On the origins and maintenance of erroneous social assessments," in Paul

Notes

Slovic, Amos Tversky, and Daniel Kahneman, *Judgment Under Uncertainty: Heuristics and Biases* (Cambridge, Eng.: Cambridge University Press, 1982), pp. 129–52.

6. Ibid., p. 135.

7. H. H. Kelley and A. J. Stahelski, "Errors in perception of intentions in a mixed motive game," *Journal of Experimental Social Psychology* 16 (1970): 379–400; and Kelley and Stahelski, "Social Interaction basis of cooperators' and competitors' belief about others," *Journal of Personality and Social Psychology* 16 (1970): 66–91.

8. Kelley and Stahelski, "Social Interaction," p. 68.

9. "American Bakers: An untested new chief faces a tough turnaround," *Business Week,* September 28, 1981, 38–41.

10. Edmund Phelps, ed., *Altruism, Morality and Economic Theory* (New York: Russell Sage Foundation, 1975), pp. 5–6.

11. Mancur Olson, *The Rise and Fall of Nations* (New Haven, Conn.: Yale University Press, 1982).

12. Kenneth J. Arrow, "Gifts and Exchanges," in Phelps, *Altruism,* p. 24.

13. Morton Deutsch and Paul Kotik, "Altruism and Bargaining," in Heinz Sauerman, ed., *Bargaining Behavior* (Tübingen: J. C. Mohr [Paul Siebeck], 1978), p. 25.

14. Burton Weisbrod, "Comparing Utility Functions in Efficiency Terms," *American Economic Review* 67 (1977): 991–95.

15. Robert Axelrod, "Effective Choice in the Prisoner's Dilemma," *Journal of Conflict Resolution* 24 (1980): 3–26. See also Robert Axelrod, *The Evolution of Cooperation* (New York: Basic Books, 1984).

16. Axelrod, "Effective Choice," p. 19.

17. Ibid., p. 21.

18. Arthur Stein, "When Misperception Matters," *World Politics* 34 (1982): 505–26.

Chapter 3

1. Uri Bronfenbrenner, *The Ecology of Human Development* (Cambridge, Mass.: Harvard University Press, 1979), develops this idea in detail.

2. Letter from Horace Walpole to Sir Horace Mann, September 26, 1781, cited in *My Several Worlds* (New York: Pocket Books, 1956).

3. Gregory Bateson, *Steps to an Ecology of Mind* (New York: Ballantine Books, 1971), p. 241.

4. David Kantor and William Lehr, *Inside the Family: Toward a Theory of Family Process* (New York: Harper & Row, 1976), p. 179.

5. *Current Social Issues: The Public's View* (Washington, D.C.: American Council of Life Insurance, April 1979), p. 15.

6. Daniel Goelman and Jonathan Freedman, *What Psychology Knows that Every Person Should* (Lexington, Mass.: Lewis Publishing Co., 1981), p. 48.

7. *Current Social Issues,* p. 15; Goelman and Freedman, *What Psychology Knows,* p. 49.

8. William G. Ouchi, *Theory Z: How American Business Can Meet the Japanese Challenge* (Reading, Mass.: 1981), p. 9.

9. *Current Social Issues,* p. 15.

10. Gallup Report, 198 (March 1982): 4.

11. George Homans, *The Human Group* (New York: Harcourt, Brace & World, 1950).

12. Lynn Hoffman, *Foundations of Family Therapy* (New York: Basic Books, 1981), p. 191.

13. Hoffman, *Foundations,* pp. 191–92.

14. George L. Wilber, "Migration Expectancy in the United States," *Journal of the American Statistical Association* 58 (1963): 444–53.

15. Ouchi, *Theory Z,* p. 197.

16. *The Bible,* Psalm 68.

17. Hoffman, *Foundations,* p. 10.

18. Virginia Satir, *Peoplemaking* (Palo Alto: Science & Behavior Books, 1972), pp. 158–63.

19. Ibid., p. 30.

20. See Shlomo Maital, *Minds, Markets, and Money* (New York: Basic Books, 1982), p. 276.

21. Morton Deutsch, *The Resolution of Conflict* (New Haven, Conn.: Yale University Press, 1973).

22. Robert Ravich, *Predictable Pairing* (New York: Peter Wyden, 1974), ch. 7.

23. Julian J. Edney, "The Nuts Game: A Concise Commons Dilemma Analog," *Environmental Psychology and Nonverbal Behavior* 3 (1979): 252–54.

24. Ibid., p. 253.

25. Gary S. Becker, "Altruism in the Family and Selfishness in the Market Place," *Economica* 48 (1981): 1–15; and Gary S. Becker, *A Treatise on the Family* (Cambridge, Mass.: Harvard University Press, 1981).

26. Becker, "Altruism," p. 7.

27. Adam Smith, *The Wealth of Nations* (New York: Modern Library, 1937), p. 14.

28. Fred McClafferty, cited in Michael Arlen, "Thirty Seconds," *The New Yorker,* 22 October 1979, p. 63.

29. See Nigel Howard, *Paradoxes of Rationality* (Cambridge, Mass.: M.I.T. Press, 1971).

30. Lauren Wispé, ed., *Altruism, Sympathy and Helping* (New York: Academic Press, 1978), p. xiii.

31. Becker, "Altruism," p. 7.

32. Ibid.

33. Barry Commoner, *The Closing Circle* (New York: Alfred A. Knopf, 1971), cited in Alfred P. French, *Disturbed Children and Their Families* (New York: Sciences Press, 1979), pp. 23–24.

Notes

34. D. H. Robertson, "What does the economist economize?," in *Economic Commentaries* (London: Staples Press, 1956), p. 154.

35. Helga Dudman, "Mrs. Einstein's Flying Raisins," *Jerusalem Post Magazine,* 19 November 1982, 7.

36. Edward Wilson, *Sociobiology* (Cambridge, Mass.: Harvard University Press, 1975).

37. See ibid., and R. Dawkins, *The Selfish Gene* (New York: Oxford University Press, 1976).

38. Jean de Lamarck, *Philosophie Zoologique* (1809; reprint, Monticello, N.Y.: Lubrecht and Cramer, 1960).

39. Jolande Jacobi, *Psychological Reflections: A Jung Anthology* (New York: Harper and Row, 1953), p. 83.

40. Virginia Satir, *Peoplemaking,* p. 3.

41. Dan Greenburg, *How to Be a Jewish Mother* (Los Angeles: Price/Stern/Sloan, 1964), p. 16.

42. Gregory Bateson et al., "Toward a Theory of Schizophrenia," *Behavioral Science* 1 (1956): 251–54.

43. Ibid.

44. A. W. Watts, *Nature, Man and Woman* (New York: Pantheon, 1958).

45. John H. Weakland and Don D. Jackson, "Patient and Therapist Observations on the Circumstances of a Schizophrenic Episode," *Archives of Neurology and Psychiatry* 79 (1958): 554–74.

46. Weakland and Jackson, "Patient and Therapist," in Don D. Jackson, ed., *Communication, Family, and Marriage* (Palo Alto, Calif.: Science and Behavior Books, 1968), p. 113.

47. Charles Lindblom, "The Market as Prison," *Journal of Politics* 44 (1982): 325.

48. Richard Posner, "Utilitarianism, Economics, and Legal Theory," *Journal of Legal Studies* 8 (1979): 136.

49. George Gilder, *Wealth and Poverty* (New York: Basic Books, Inc., 1981), p. 22.

50. Claude Lévi-Strauss, "The Principle of Reciprocity" (1957), in Lewis A. Coser and Bernard Rosenberg, eds., *Sociological Theory* (New York: Macmillan, 1964), p. 85.

51. Ouchi, *Theory Z,* pp. 93–94.

52. Ibid.

Chapter 4

1. David Kantor and William Lehr, *Inside the Family: Toward a Theory of Family Process* (New York: Harper & Row, 1976), ch. 9.

2. Ibid., pp. 126–34.

3. Ibid., pp. 117, 143.

4. William G. Ouchi, *Theory Z: How American Business Can Meet the Japanese Challenge* (Reading, Mass.: Addison-Wesley, 1981).

5. Kantor and Lehr, *Inside the Family*, pp. 146–47.

6. Ouchi, *Theory Z*, p. 72.

7. Kantor and Lehr, *Inside the Family*, p. 119.

8. Ouchi, *Theory Z*, pp. 72, 89.

9. Kantor and Lehr, *Inside the Family*, p. 127.

10. Ouchi, *Theory Z*, pp. 84–85.

11. Kantor and Lehr, *Inside the Family*, p. 127.

12. Ouchi, *Theory Z*, p. 84.

13. Ibid., p. 76.

14. Ibid.

15. Ibid.

16. Kantor and Lehr, *Inside the Family*, p. 2.

17. The story of Softsoap is taken from *Business Week*, 12 January 1981, pp. 76–77.

18. Robert H. Hayes and William J. Abernathy, "Managing our Way to Economic Decline," *Harvard Business Review*, July–August 1980, 68.

19. Dale Mortensen, "Property Rights and Efficiency in Mating, Racing and Related Games," *American Economic Review* 72 (1982): 968–79.

20. *Business Week*, April 13, 1981, 117–18.

21. "Japan Inc. Goes International," *Business Week*, 14 December 1981, 30–32.

22. "Industrial Policy: A Roundtable Discussion," *Manhattan Report* (1983): 24.

23. Virginia Satir, *Peoplemaking* (Palo Alto: Science & Behavior Books, 1972), p. 30.

24. Ouchi, *Theory Z*, p. 88.

25. Ibid.

26. "Getting Business and Research on the Same Track," *Economist* 16 May 1981, 105–6.

Chapter 5

1. "A Russian's prophecy rears its gloomy head," *Business Week*, 29 June 1981, p. 10.

2. *International Financial Statistics, Supplement on Price Statistics* (Washington, D.C.: International Monetary Fund, 1981), pp. 143–44.

3. *World Economic Outlook* (Washington, D.C.: International Monetary Fund, 1982), p. 143.

4. Walter Salant, "The American Economy in Transition: A Review Article," *Journal of Economic Literature* 20 (1982): 569.

5. Shlomo Maital, *Minds, Markets, and Money* (New York: Basic Books Inc., 1982), ch. 6.

Notes

6. These figures are based on press accounts of administration projections in the spring of 1983.

7. Edward Tufte, *Political Control of the Economy* (Princeton: Princeton University Press, 1978), p. 5.

8. *Economist*, 22 August 1981, 11.

9. Ray Fair, "The Effect of Economic Events on Votes for President," *Review of Economics & Statistics* 60 (1978): 171.

10. Tufte, *Political Control*, pp. 9–15.

11. William Nordhaus, "The Political Business Cycle," *Review of Economic Studies* 42 (1975): 169.

12. Fred C. Allvine and Daniel E. O'Neill, "Stock Market Returns and the Presidential Election Cycle: Implications for Market Efficiency," *Financial Analysts Journal*, September–October, 1980, p. 49.

13. Robert J. Shapiro. "Politics and the Federal Reserve." *Public Interest* 66 (1982): 126.

14. James Tobin, *The New Economics One Decade Older* (Princeton: Princeton University Press, 1974), p. 20.

15. Douglas Hibbs, "Public Concern about Inflation and Unemployment in the United States," National Bureau of Economic Research, Conference Paper no. 93, Cambridge, Mass., January 1981, p. 23.

16. Salant, "American Economy," p. 565.

17. Robert J. Gordon, "The Evolution of Macroeconomic Events and Ideas," in Martin Feldstein, ed., *The American Economy in Transition* (Chicago: National Bureau of Economic Research, University of Chicago Press, 1980), p. 110.

18. Arthur M. Okun, *Prices & Quantities: A Macroeconomic Analysis* (Washington, D.C.: Brookings Institution, 1981), pp. 168–69.

19. Walter Salant, "How Has the World Economy Changed Since 1929?" *The Business Cycle and Public Policy, 1929–80,* Joint Economic Committee, 96th Cong. sess., 1980, p. 103.

20. John Maynard Keynes, *The General Theory of Employment, Interest and Money* (London: Macmillan, 1936), pp. 383–84.

21. Keynes, *General Theory*, p. 384.

22. See Edna Ullmann-Margalit, *The Emergence of Norms* (Oxford, Eng.: Oxford University Press, 1977), ch. 3.

23. Keynes, *General Theory*, p. 381.

24. It has occurred to more than one writer that the economy's fluctuations might be causally linked to some recurring cycle in our physical environment. The most famous such theory is William Stanley Jevons's hypothesis that eleven-year economic cycles coincide with, and are related to, sunspots.

25. Joseph Schumpeter, "The Analysis of Economic Change," *Review of Economic Statistics* 17 (1935): 2–10.

26. Nikolai Dmitrievich Kondratieff, "Die langen Wellen der Konjunktur," *Archiv fur Sozialwissenschaft und Sozialpolitik* 56 (1926): 573–600. A condensed translation by Wolfgang Stolper, "The Long Waves in Economic Life," appeared in the *Review of Economic Statistics* 17 (1935): 105–15, and

was reprinted in Gottfried Haberler, ed., *Readings in Business Cycle Theory* (London: American Economics Association, Allen & Unwin, 1950), pp. 20–42.

27. Kondratieff, "langen Wellen," p. 20.

28. Kondratieff, ibid., p. 41.

29. See George Garvy, "Kondratieff, N. D.," *International Encyclopedia of the Social Sciences* (London: Macmillan and The Free Press, 1968), p. 443.

30. Garvy, "Kondratieff."

31. Kondratieff, "langen Wellen," p. 42.

32. Cited by Donald D. Searing, "Rules of the Game in Britain: Can the Politicians be Trusted?," *American Political Science Review* 76 (1982): 239.

Chapter 6

1. Citing work by Arthur Okun and Martin Baily, Walter Salant, *American Economy in Transition,* p. 568, notes that for the United States, the standard deviation (a statistical measure of the degree of variation) of real GNP around its growth trend from 1946–76 was about one-quarter of what it was during 1900–45, and one-half as large as in the peacetime years between 1900–29. Length of expansions during 1854–1937 averaged only twenty-six months, compared to forty-eight months during 1945–75. In the earlier period, recessions averaged twenty-one months; in the later period, only eleven months.

2. The day before taking off for California, Corrigan had broken the speed record for transcontinental flight in an old plane that had failed safety inspection. Did such a skilled and daring pilot really fly the wrong way? "I've told that story so many times that I believe it myself now," Corrigan has said; see David Wallechinsky and Irving Wallace, *The People's Almanac* (Garden City, N.Y.: Doubleday, 1975), p. 1245.

3. "A sea change in the nature of America's macroeconomic problems appears to have occurred around 1965 . . . and has been widely attributed to the political decision to finance the Vietnam War without a tax increase." Alan Blinder, *Economic Policy and the Great Stagflation* (New York: Academic Press, 1900), p. 2.

4. Shlomo Maital, *Minds, Markets, and Money* (New York: Basic Books, 1982), noted some of these wrong-way causalities in the opening pages but did not attempt to explain them in full.

5. Robert J. Gordon, "Why Stopping Inflation May Be Costly: Evidence from Fourteen Historical Episodes." Working paper, Northwestern University and National Bureau of Economic Research, Cambridge, Mass.: February 1981.

6. Ibid., p. 43.

7. Marguerite Kohl and Frederica Young, *Games for Children* (New York: Cornerstone Library, 1972), p. 73.

Notes

8. John Maynard Keynes, *The General Theory of Employment, Interest and Money* (London: Macmillan, 1936), pp. 155–56.

9. Donald Moggridge, ed., *The Collected Writings of John Maynard Keynes*, vol. 19, *Activities 1939–45; Internal War Finance* (Cambridge, Eng.: Macmillan and Cambridge University Press, 1978), pp. 280–89.

10. Ibid., pp. 281–82.

11. Ibid., p. 290.

12. Ibid., p. 292.

13. "Common Stocks Can Hedge Inflation—If You Pick Right," *Business Week*, 24 February 1951, p. 114.

14. Glenn L. Johnson, Frank K. Reilly, and Ralph E. Smith, "Individual Common Stocks as Inflation Hedges," *Journal of Financial and Quantitative Analysis* 6 (1971): 1015–24.

15. Charles R. Nelson, "Inflation and Rates of Return on Common Stocks," *The Journal of Finance* 31 (1976): 471.

16. Eugene Fama, "Stock Returns, Real Activity, Inflation and Money," *American Economic Review* 71 (September 1981): 545–65.

17. Martin Feldstein and Lawrence Summers, "Inflation and the Taxation of Capital Income in the Corporate Sector," *National Tax Journal* 32 (1979): 445–70.

18. Franco Modigliani and Richard A. Cohn, "Inflation, Rational Valuation and the Market," *Financial Analysts Journal* (March–April 1979): 24–44.

19. Ibid., p. 33.

20. Shlomo Maital, "Bulls in the Ivory Tower," *Barron's*, 17 August 1982.

21. Modigliani and Cohn, "Inflation," p. 37.

22. Keynes, *General Theory*, p. 156.

23. Ibid.

24. Burton Malkiel, *The Inflation Beater's Investment Guide* (New York: W. W. Norton, 1982), p. 36, ". . . it is precisely the poor recent performance of equities that provides the price adjustments necessary to produce appropriately higher returns in the future. The issue is not how badly equity investors have done in the past several years—it is what might investors be kicking themselves about five years from now for not having bought today." Or what they think other investors might think others may think they may be kicking themselves for. . . .

Chapter 7

1. W. Arthur Lewis, "Rising Prices: 1899–1913 and 1950–1979," *Scandinavian Journal of Economics* 82 (1980): 425–36.

2. Adam Smith, *The Wealth of Nations* (New York: Random House, 1937), p. 76.

3. Lewis, "Rising Prices," pp. 430–31.

4. Ibid., p. 427.

5. Ibid., p. 435.

6. James Buchanan and Richard Wagner, *Democracy in Deficit* (New York: Academic Press, 1977), p. 182.

7. Lewis, "Rising Prices," p. 435.

8. Smith, *Wealth of Nations,* p. 34.

9. This game was suggested by Richard Layard, "Human Satisfactions and Public Policy," *Economic Journal* 90 (1980):737–50.

10. Personal correspondence from the head of the Legal and Consular Section, Tel Aviv Embassy of the Federal Republic of Germany.

11. John McCallum, "We need a way as well as the will," *Financial Post,* 20 November, 1982.

12. Harvey C. Bunke, "Indexing—It Grows on You," *Business Horizons* 25 (May–June 1982): 3.

13. Phillip Taft, "Collective Bargaining Before the New Deal," in H. A. Millis, ed., *How Collective Bargaining Works* (New York: The Twentieth Century Fund, 1945).

14. Harvey C. Bunke, "Indexing"; and Lloyd C. Ulman, ed., *Collective Bargaining and Government Policies* (Paris: Organization of Economic Cooperation and Development, 1979).

15. J. Huston McCulloch, "The Ban on Indexed Bonds, 1933–77," *American Economic Review* 70 (1980): 1018–20.

16. Rabbi Shlomo Goren, "Inflation in the Light of Halacha [Jewish Law]," broadcast on the Voice of Israel, December 1982.

17. Shlomo Maital, "Plummeting Shekel: Israel is Running the Worst Inflation in the World," *Barron's,* February 23, 1981, pp. 9–20.

18. David Card, "Indexation in Long Term Labor Contracts: A Theoretical and Empirical Analysis" (Working Paper no. 132 of the Industrial Relations Section, Princeton University, August 1982), p. 1.

19. Harvey C. Bunke, "Indexing," p. 5, citing studies by the U.S. Office of Management and Budget.

20. For a fuller analysis of stagflation along these lines, including empirical evidence, see Alan Blinder, *Economic Policy and the Great Stagflation* (New York: Academic Press, 1980).

21. Lewis, "Rising Prices," p. 436.

22. J. L. Kearl et al., "A Confusion of Economists?," *American Economic Review* 69 (1979): 28–37.

23. Jerome L. Stein, *Monetarist, Keynesian & New Classical Economics* (Oxford, Eng.: Basil Blackwell, 1982).

24. Walter Heller, "What's Right With Economics," *American Economic Review* 65 (1975): 20.

25. Franco Modigliani, "The Monetarist Controversy, or Should We Forsake Stabilization Policies," *American Economic* Review 67 (1977): 17.

26. Lawrence Klein, "The Supply Side," *American Economic Review* 68 (1978): 4–5.

27. "The Furniture Movers," *Business Week,* January 16, 1978, 120.

28. *Business Week,* January 1982, 124.

29. Shlomo Maital, "All Roads Lead to Rome: On a Fundamental Macro-economic Equation," Working Paper, Institute for Advanced Studies, Hebrew University of Jerusalem, February 1983.

Chapter 8

1. *Julius Caesar,* act 1, sc. 2, line 18.
2. Milton Friedman and Anna J. Schwartz, *The Great Contraction: 1929–33* (Princeton: Princeton University Press, 1965), p. 3.
3. Alastair Cooke in a BBC broadcast, 1983.
4. John Maynard Keynes, *The General Theory of Employment, Interest and Money* (London: Macmillan, 1936), p. 293.
5. Arthur F. Burns, "Our Inflation in Historical Perspective," *Atlantic Community Quarterly* 19 (Spring 1981): 70–77.
6. Prices are all from the *Associated Press Almanac, 1973* (New York: Almanac Publishing Co., 1973), p. 440.
7. Baseball salaries are taken from: Lawrence Ritter and William Silber, *Money,* 1st ed. (New York: Basic Books, 1970), p. 3, and *The World Almanac 1982* (New York: 1982), p. 861.
8. Sharone Maital, Shlomo Maital, and Steven Plaut, "Behavior Toward Inflation as Learned Helplessness," Working Paper, Technion, Haifa, 1982.
9. Fyodor Dostoevsky, *The House of the Dead* (New York: Dutton, undated).
10. Martin E. R. Seligman, *Helplessness: On Depression, Development, and Death* (San Francisco: W. H. Freeman, 1975), p. 17.
11. Ibid., p. 37.
12. Ibid., pp. 23–25.
13. Leah Porat, "Do You Know How Much You Are Paying?," (Hebrew), *Ha'aretz,* April 5, 1982, 15.
14. Shlomo Maital and Yael Benjamini, "Inflation as Prisoner's Dilemma," *Journal of Post Keynesian Economics* (Summer 1980): 459–81.
15. Samuel Johnson, *Vanity of Human Wishes* (1749).
16. Marc Fried, "Endemic Stress: The Psychology of Resignation and the Politics of Scarcity," *American Journal of Orthopsychiatry* 52, no. 1 (January 1982): 4–19.
17. Ibid., p. 12.
18. T. Petzinger, Jr., "Inflation Can Threaten Your Mental Health," *Wall Street Journal,* 15 May 1980, p. 1.
19. Gardner Ackley, "The Costs of Inflation," *Society* (January–February, 1979).
20. Douglas Hibbs, "Public Concern about Inflation and Unemployment in the United States," National Bureau of Economic Research Conference Paper no. 93, Cambridge, Mass., January 1981, p. 23; and Gallup Report, no. 198, March 1982.

21. *Current Social Issues: The Public's View* (Washington, D.C.: American Council of Life Insurance, April 1979), pp. 11–12.

22. Milton Friedman, "Nobel Lecture: Inflation and Unemployment," *Journal of Political Economy* 85 (June 1977): 467.

23. Ibid., p. 467.

24. "Invisible Handshakes," *The Brookings Bulletin* 17 (Winter 1981): 2.

25. Seligman, *Helplessness,* p. 17.

26. Harvey Leibenstein, "The Inflation Process: A Micro-Behavioral Analysis," *American Economic Review* 71 (1981): 368–73.

27. Martin Spechler, "Ending Big Inflations: An Exercise in Comparative Economic History," Working Paper, Foerder Institute for Economic Research, Tel Aviv University, June 1981.

28. Alfred Marshall, *Principles of Economics,* 9th ed. (London: Macmillan, 1961), p. 23.

Chapter 9

1. The following corporate executives and labor leaders responded by sending personal letters or copies of articles and speeches that are cited in this chapter and the next: Owen F. Bieber, President, United Automobile, Aerospace and Agricultural Implement Workers of America (UAW); Irving J. Spitzberg, Jr., General Secretary, American Association of University Professors; E. G. Jefferson, Chairman, E. I. Du Pont de Nemours & Co.; Lewis W. Lehr, Chairman and Chief Executive Officer, 3M; Andrew J. Schroder III, Senior Vice-President, General Foods Corp.; David R. Dilley, Chief Economist, United States Steel Corp.; William W. Winpisinger, International President, International Association of Machinists and Aerospace Workers; Jerry McAfee, former President, Gulf Oil Corp.; Sol C. Chaikin, President, International Ladies' Garment Workers' Union; Philip Caldwell, Chairman of the Board, Ford Motor Co.; Lee Iacocca, Chairman of the Board, Chrysler Corp.; Donald N. Frey, Chairman of the Board, Bell & Howell; John F. Sytsma, President, Brotherhood of Locomotive Engineers; Douglas A. Fraser, former President, United Automobile, Aerospace and Agricultural Implement Workers of America; Abraham Orlofsky, Secretary-Treasurer, National Federation of Federal Employees; Donald K. McIvor, Chairman, Imperial Oil Ltd.; and James E. Burke, Chairman of the Board, Johnson & Johnson.

2. John McDonald, *The Game of Business* (New York: Doubleday, 1975), ch. 9.

3. Ibid., p. 119.

4. For a theoretical model of "Leviathan" vs. "Of, By, and For the People," natures of government, and an application to California's Proposition 13, see Perry Shapiro and Jon Sonstelie, "Did Proposition 13 Slay Leviathan?," *American Economic Review* 72 (1982): 184–90.

Notes

5. Ambrose Bierce, *The Enlarged Devil's Dictionary*, ed., Ernest Jerome Hopkins (Garden City, N.Y.: Doubleday, 1967), p. 240.

6. Buckminster Fuller, quoted by Calvin Tomkins, "In the Outlaw Area," *New Yorker*, January 8, 1966.

7. Lloyd Ulman, ed., *Collective Bargaining and Government Policies* (Paris: Organization for Economic Cooperation and Development, 1979).

8. For an analysis of three-person *Prisoner's Dilemma*, see Anatol Rapaport, *N-Person Games* (Ann Arbor: University of Michigan Press, 1970).

9. Shlomo Maital, *Minds, Markets, and Money* (New York: Basic Books, 1982).

10. Peter Passell, "Wealth & Whims," *New York Times*, 15 August 1982, Book Review section, p. 8.

11. Partial contents of the letter sent to the corporate and union leaders.

12. Personal communication, January 11, 1983.

13. News release, United Auto Workers, July 19, 1978.

14. Jerry McAfee, "The 1980's: Decade of Unfinished Business," *The Orange Disc* (Spring 1982.), p. 38.

15. James Tobin, "Roundtable on Canadian Monetary Policy," QED (Queen's Economics Department) Newsletter, Queen's University, Kingston, Ontario, Autumn 1982.

16. Personal communication, January 14, 1983.

17. Personal communication, February 3, 1983.

18. Personal communication, March 31, 1983.

19. E. G. Jefferson, "A Time for Courage," address to the Economic Club of Detroit, November 8, 1982.

20. Frey, personal communication, January 14, 1983.

21. Lewis Lehr, "Guest Editorial," *Flying Colors*, 1978.

22. Personal communication, January 19, 1983.

23. Personal communication, January 12, 1983.

24. Jefferson, "Time for Courage" (address).

25. Sol C. Chaikin, "Trade, Investment and Deindustrialization: Myth and Reality," *Foreign Affairs* (Spring 1982): 845–47. Excerpted by permission from *Foreign Affairs*. Copyright 1982 by the Council on Foreign Relations, Inc.

26. Winpisinger, personal communication, January 11, 1983.

27. Jefferson, "Time for Courage" (address).

28. Chaikin, "Trade," pp. 845–47.

29. Philip Caldwell, address to the Bay Area Council, San Francisco, February 9, 1982.

30. Jefferson, "Time for Courage."

31. Richard B. Freeman and James L. Medoff, "New Estimates of Private Sector Unionism in the United States," *Industrial and Labor Relations Review* 32 (1979): 143–74. See also Richard B. Freeman and James L. Medoff, *What Do Unions Do?* (New York: Basic Books, 1984).

32. Lloyd S. Shapley and Martin Shubik, "On the Core of an Economic System with Externalities," *American Economic Review* 59 (1969): 678–84.

33. Ibid., p. 681.

34. Clive Bull and Andrew Schotter, "The Garbage Game, Inflation and Incomes Policy." Presented to the American Economics Association annual meetings in New York, December 28–30, 1982.

35. Ibid., pp. 9–10.

36. Richard Layard, "Human Satisfactions and Public Policy," *Economic Journal* 90 (1980): 737–50.

37. Kenneth Arrow, *The Limits of Organization* (New York: W. W. Norton, 1974), p. 27.

38. Ogden Nash, "Interoffice Memorandum," *I'm a Stranger Here Myself,* 1938.

Chapter 10

1. Daniel Mitchell, "Direct Intervention in Wage and Price Decisions," in M. Ballabon, ed., *Economic Perspectives,* vol. 2 (New York: Harwood Academic Publishers, 1981), p. 27.

2. John McDonald, *The Game of Business* (New York: Doubleday, 1975), p. 119.

3. Amartya K. Sen, "Isolation, assurance and the social rate of discount," *Quarterly Journal of Economics* 81 (1967): 112–24.

4. William Vickrey, "One Economist's View of Philanthropy," in F. G. Dickinson, ed., *Philanthropy and Public Policy* (Chicago: 1962), National Bureau of Economic Research.

5. Lloyd S. Shapley and Martin Shubik, "On the Core of an Economic System with Externalities," *American Economic Review* 59 (1969): 768–84.

6. Information on Austria, West Germany, Sweden, Norway, and the Netherlands is drawn from Aaron Wiener, Eliezer Rosenstein, and Shlomo Maital, "A Framework for the Formulation of Incomes Policy in Israel," Working Paper, Neaman Institute for Advanced Study in Science & Technology, Technion, Haifa, Israel, January 1982.

7. Robert Gordon, "Why Stopping Inflation May be Costly: Evidence from Fourteen Historical Episodes" (Cambridge, Mass.: National Bureau of Economic Research, February 1981).

8. Lloyd Ulman, ed., *Collective Bargaining and Government Policies* (Paris: Organization for Economic Cooperation and Development, 1979), p. 20.

9. Personal communication, January 14, 1983.

10. John F. Bilson, "Civil liberty: an econometric investigation," *Kyklos* 35 (1982): 94–114.

11. Personal communication, January 11, 1983.

12. Personal communication, January 31, 1983.

13. E. G. Jefferson, "A Time for Courage," address to the Economic Club of Detroit, November 8, 1982.

Notes

14. Personal communication, January 17, 1983.

15. Irving J. Spitzberg, Report of the General Secretary, American Association of University Professors, June 25, 1982, p. 2.

16. Adam Smith, *The Wealth of Nations* (New York: Random House, 1937), p. 14.

17. David J. Smyth, "The Effects of Unemployment Insurance Benefits on the Supply of Labor: Does the Dole Cause Unemployment?" Paper presented to the International Institute of Public Finance, 39th Congress, Budapest, Hungary, August 22–26, 1983, p. 14.

18. Personal communication, January 12, 1983.

19. *Ha'aretz,* 6 March 1983, 9.

20. "Labor seeks less," *Business Week,* 21 December 1981, 47.

21. Quoted by Professor H. Clegg in a lecture at Tel Aviv University, December 1982.

22. See Irwin Lipnowski and Shlomo Maital, "Hanging together, or separately: A game-theoretic approach to macroeconomic conflict," Working paper, Technion, Haifa, December 1982.

23. Bieber, personal communication, January 31, 1983.

24. Wassily Leontief, "What Hope for the Economy," *New York Review of Books,* August 12, 1982, p. 34.

25. Francis Bator, "The sins of wages," *Economist,* March 21, 1981, 23.

26. Cited by Robert Donovan, *Tumultuous Years: The Presidency of Harry S. Truman, 1949–1953* (New York: W. W. Norton, 1982), p. 327.

27. Philip Caldwell, address to the Bay Area Council, San Francisco, February 9, 1982.

28. Personal communication, January 13, 1983.

Chapter 11

1. "Declaration Renouncing the Use, in Time of War, of Explosive Projectiles Under 400 Grammes Weight" (1869) in Dietrich Schindler and Jiří Toman, eds., *The Laws of Armed Conflicts: A Collection of Conventions, Resolutions and Other Documents* (Leiden: A. W. Sijthoff, 1973), p. 96. Epigraph to chapter 11 from " The Laws of Naval War Governing the Relations Between Belligerents, Manual Adopted by the Institute of International War (Adopted at Oxford, 9 August 1913) in Schindler and Toman, eds., *The Laws of Armed Conflicts.*

2. Robert Z. Aliber, *The International Money Game,* 3d ed. (New York: Basic Books, Inc., 1979).

3. Edward M. Bernstein, "Back to the Gold Standard?," *Brookings Bulletin* 17 (1980): 8–12.

4. Quoted by Leonard M. Glynn, "Have Currencies Floated Too Long?," *New York Times,* May 8, 1983, 5.

5. Ibid.

6. Steven Plaut, "Transmission of Inflation Under Fixed and Flexible Exchange Rates" (Mimeograph series no. 281, Faculty of Industrial Engineering & Management, Technion, Haifa, Israel, 1982).

7. For discussion, see Shlomo Maital, *Minds, Markets, and Money* (New York: Basic Books, 1982), ch. 6.

8. See Thomas Schelling, *The Strategy of Conflict* (Cambridge, Mass.: Harvard University Press, 1963), p. 77; and Edna Ulmann-Margalit, *The Emergence of Norms* (Oxford, Eng.: Oxford University Press, 1977), p. 77.

9. Walter W. Heller, quoted in the *New York Times,* May 8, 1961.

10. "Why Moneymen Worry," *Newsweek,* October 12, 1981, 42.

11. "High Interest Rates Breed Rising Tension," *International Herald Tribune,* April 30, 1982, 1.

12. "Four Nations Agree on Fiscal Plan," *International Herald Tribune,* January 23–24, 1982, 1.

13. "Mitterrand Calls Allies 'Indifferent' to One Another's Economic Fates," *International Herald Tribune,* 30 May 1982, 1.

14. "New Room for Recovery?," *Newsweek,* December 7, 1981, 31.

15. James Shepley, "How Dulles Averted War," *Life,* 16 January 1956.

16. Rowland Frazee, quoted in *Fortune,* March 22, 1982, 8.

17. *International Monetary Fund Survey,* Dec. 13, 1982, p. 385.

18. Clyde E. Farnsworth, "Amid Slump, Trade-offs in World Trade Seem Unlikely," *New York Times,* November 21, 1982, 5.

19. William Brock in an address to American International Club in Geneva, Switzerland, November 23, press release by U.S. Information Service, November 23, 1982.

20. *International Monetary Fund Survey,* Nov. 29, 1982, p. 381.

21. Herman Kahn, *On Escalation: Metaphors and Scenarios* (New York: Praeger, 1965), p. 11.

22. Ralph C. Bryant, *Money and Monetary Policy in Interdependent Nations* (Washington, D.C.: Brookings Institution, 1980). Cited in *Brookings Bulletin* 17 (1980), p. 7.

23. Anthony M. Solomon. David Horowitz Lectures of 1982, Tel Aviv University, Tel Aviv, Israel, March 4–5, 1982, p. 3.

24. John Marquand, *The Late George Apley* (Waltham, Mass.: Little Brown, 1937).

Chapter 12

1. Robert Ardrey, *The Social Contract* (New York: Fontana, 1972), p. 360.

2. Shlomo Maital, *Minds, Markets, and Money* (New York: Basic Books, Inc., 1982).

3. Burton Weisbrod, "Comparing Utility Functions in Efficiency Terms, or What Kind of Utility Functions Do We Want?," *American Economic Review* 67 (1977): 994.

Notes

4. Jean-Jacques Laffonte, *Essays in the Economics of Uncertainty* (Cambridge, Mass.: Harvard University Press, 1980), p. 49.

5. Ibid., p. 51.

6. Ibid., p. 53.

7. Ibid., p. 53.

8. Ibid., pp. 53–54.

9. David Wallechinsky and Irving Wallace, *The People's Almanac* (Garden City, N. Y.: Doubleday, 1975), pp. 1314–15.

10. Dr. Mina Zemach, *Does the Jewish Population in Israel Act According to the Golden Rule?* Jerusalem: Van Leer Institute, 1980.

11. Derived from results in *Zemach,* ibid., pp. 4–5.

12. Ibid., p. 12.

13. Kenneth J. Arrow, "Social Responsibility and Economic Efficiency," *Public Policy* 21 (1973), p. 316.

14. Thomas C. Schelling, *Micromotives and Macrobehavior* (New York: W. W. Norton, 1978), pp. 127–28.

15. See Stephen Arons, "Separation of School and State: Pierce Reconsidered," *Harvard Educational Review* 46 (1926): 76–104.

16. Charles Dickens, *Martin Chuzzlewit* (New York: Penguin, 1975).

17. John Maynard Keynes, *The General Theory of Employment, Interest and Money* (London: Macmillan, 1936), p. 374.

18. Norbert Wiener, *God and Golem* (Cambridge, Mass.: M.I.T. Press, 1964), p. 91.

19. *Henry IV, Part II,* act 1, sc. 3, line 27.

20. Keynes, *General Theory,* p. 372.

21. Ibid.

22. Ibid., p. 374.

23. Ibid.

24. J. C. McCullers, "Issues in learning and motivation," in M. R. Lepper and D. Greene, eds., *The Hidden Costs of Reward* (Hillsdale, N.J.: Lawrence Erlbaum, 1978), pp. 5–17.

25. William Ouchi, *Theory Z: How American Business Can Meet the Japanese Challenge* (Reading, Mass.: Addison-Wesley, 1981), p. 85.

26. Ibid., pp. 84–85.

27. Jagdish Bhagwati, "Directly Unproductive, Profit-Seeking (DUP) Activities," *Journal of Political Economy* 90 (1982): 988–1002.

28. Anne O. Krueger, "The Political Economy of the Rent-Seeking Society," *American Economic Review* 64 (1974): 294.

29. Ibid., p. 302.

30. See David Colander, "Why an Income Policy Makes an Economy More Efficient," presented to the American Economics Association annual meeting in New York, December 28–31, 1982.

31. Herbert Hoover, address given in New York, October 22, 1928, excerpted in Richard Hofstadter, ed., *Great Issues in American History* (New York: Vintage Books, 1969), p. 342.

32. John Sheahan, "Incomes Policies in an Open Economy: Domestic and

External Interactions," Working Paper, Williams College, Williamstown, Mass., December 1979, pp. 25–26.

33. Cited in Edwin R. Black, *Politics and the News: The Political Functions of the Mass Media* (London: Butterworth, 1982).

34. Kai T. Erikson, *Everything in its Path* (New York: Harper & Row, 1978); cited in Lynn Hoffman, *Foundations of Family Therapy* (New York: Basic Books, Inc., 1981), pp. 106–7.

35. Eliot D. Chapple, *Culture and Biological Man* (New York: Holt, Rinehart & Winston, 1970).

36. This game is based on one suggested by Schelling in *Micromotives*.

37. David Hume, *An Inquiry Concerning Human Understanding* (New York: Bobbs Merrill, 1955), p. 452.

INDEX

Abernathy, William, 89
Ackley, Gardner, 185
acquired characteristics: heritability of, 70
Acquisitive Society, The (Tawney), 9
Affluent Society, The (Galbraith), 9
After You, Garçon (game), 40, 86, 88–91
Aharoni, Yair: *No-Risk Society, The*, 9
Aliber, Robert, 249
alienation, 8, 285
altruism, 23–24, 38–41, 56; as basis of market economies (theory), 75–76; in corporations, 68; in family games, 57–58, 60–69; role of, in society, 69–71
altruistic game players, 59–60, 62–67
American Association of University Professors, 238
American Economic Review, 22
American Economics Association, 168

American Medical International (A.M.I.), 17
Americans: ethic of individual freedom, 74, 181; pulling together in times of crisis, 242–43; *see also* under United States
Anderson, Craig, 33
Anna Karenina (Tolstoy), 287
anomie, 8, 285
antisocial behavior, 225–26, 227
antitrust laws, 24–25
anxiety: produced by learned helplessness, 177
arbitrage, 249
Ardrey, Robert, 274
Armour-Dial, 88
Arrow, Kenneth, 18–19, 38, 220, 280–81
assets, productive, 16–17
"assurance" paradox, 229
attribution theory, 32–35
Austria, 233, 234, 241
autonomy: lowered sense of, 285
aviation history, 126–27
Axelrod, Robert, 41–43

317

GNP; *see* gross national product (GNP)

goals: common, intrinsic, 285–86; egoistic, 50; human, 27, 284

gold, 177*n*

gold-backed money, 190

gold clause, 158–59

gold exchange standard, 251–54

gold standard, 190, 249–51, 253–54; U.S. went off, 158

golden rule, 277; as multi-religious ethical code, 278–80

Goldwyn, Samuel, 242–43

goods: as token in international games, 247–48, 262–69

good will: belief in, 229

Gordon, Robert J., 113, 138, 234

government(s), 58, 195–220; blamed for inflation, 185; control of national income by, 107; curtailing size and influence of, 286; at fault in lack of economic growth, 210–11; as game player, 154, 218, 220, 287; as game player and referee, 24, 198, 212–15, 235–36, 387–88; intervention in collective bargaining, 221; monopoly over legal tender, 176; municipal, 31; peacetime profligacy of, 151; regulation of markets, 289; role of, 118, 197–98, 206, 220, 291; in social contract, 203, 220, 237–40; stabilization policies of, 112–13; weak resistance to wage demands, 189–90

government expenditures, 219; linked to prices, 159–60; *see also* budget deficits

government policy: socially responsible but politically costly, 218; uncertain, 212–13; *see also* policy(ies)

grain-price shock, 105

gratification, deferred, 62

gravity, law of, 119

Great Britain, 240, 260; gold standard, 251

Great Crash (1929), 186

Great Depression, 110, 113, 114, 213, 280

"Great Society," 9

greed, 9, 17, 32

Greenburg, Dan: *How to Be a Jewish Mother*, 71

gross national product (GNP), 9; negative rate, 214; real, 306*n*1; Western industrial economies, 103, 104T

group rationality, 161, 224

groups: natural selection of, 70

Gulf Oil Corp., 205

Haley, Jay, 48

Halley, Edmund, 119

happiness, 284; depends on relative income and status, 217–18; pursuit of, 270–72

Happy New Year (game), 160, 161, 234

Hard Core (game), 223, 226–29

Hardin, Garrett, 30

Hawley-Smoot Tariff Act, 213

Hayes, Robert, 89

Hazlitt, William, 198

health-care industry, 17

Healy, Denis, 240

Heller, Joseph: *Catch-22*, 31

Heller, Walter, 168, 169, 257–58

helplessness, 8, 74, 160, 205; dif-

Index

investor rationality, 17, 148; disavowal of, 146–47
"invisible hand," 38
"isolation" paradox, 228–29
Israel: indexation, 159; inflation, 150, 173, 176, 180, 240; and golden rule, 279–80
Italy, 240, 269; inflation episodes, 138

Jackson, Don, 48, 74
Japan, 211, 220, 260, 263–64; balance of payments surplus, 269; import restrictions, 266; inflation episodes, 138; Ministry of International Trade and Industry (MITI), 91–93; wage-bargaining mechanism, 233, 234
Japanese companies, 82, 83, 84
Jefferson, E. G., 208, 210–11, 212–13, 215, 237, 310n1
Jevons, William Stanley, 305n24
job security, 240; *see also* employment, lifetime
Johansen, Leif: "Bargaining Society, The," 9
Johnson, Glenn, 144
Johnson, Lyndon, 9, 128, 129
Johnson, Samuel, 181
Johnson & Johnson, 243
Jung, Carl, 70–71
justice, economic, 292

Kantor, David, 48, 79, 82, 83, 85
Keeping Ahead of the Joneses (game), 154–57, 160
Kelley, Harold, 34–35
Kelly, Walt, 219
Kennedy, John F., 26, 129; Council of Economic Advisers, 257
Kennedy Round, 265
Kerensky, Alexandr 120
Keynes, John Maynard, 103, 118, 147, 148, 151, 251, 282; budget dictum, 152, 153, 160; *General Theory of Employment, Interest and Money,* 114–15, 141–42; on importance of money, 173; on incentives, 213–85
Keynes' Mutiny, The (game), 115–18
Keynesianism, 115–18, 168; asymmetrical application of, 153; mistaken interpretation of, 115
kibbutz, 68–69
Kitchin cycles, 119–20
Klein, Lawrence, 168, 169
KNBR Bathtub Regatta, 11
knowledge: is power, 189–90
Kondratieff, Nikolai Dmitrevich, 101, 107, 112, 118, 120–23
Kondratieff cycles, 120–23
Korean War, 221, 242
Krueger, Anne O., 289; "Rent-Seeking Society, The," 9
Kuznets, Simon, 120
Kwakiutl, 75

Kahn, Herman, 267
Kant, Immanuel: categorical imperative, 277, 278, 279, 280, 291

labor, 195–220; behavior change in response to unemployment, 240; confrontation with busi-

329

Index

Roosevelt, Franklin D., 162, 171, 249, 252
Ross, Lee, 33
"Rotten Kid" theorem, 61, 65–66, 67–68
Rousseau, Jean-Jacques, 48
rules about rules, 76
rumor(s), 144, 149
Run For Your Money (game), 4–5, 8, 274
Runyan, Damon, 29
Russell, Bertrand, 10
Ruth, Babe, 174

sacrifice, 17
Salant, Walter, 113
Satir, Virginia, 48, 52, 53, 71, 94
saving and investment: private, 228–30; saving/spending balance, 116–18; savings, 142
Scanlon, Hugh, 240
scarcity, 16, 67; politics of, 184–85
Schelling, Thomas, 281
schizophrenia: in families, 71–73
Schmidt, Helmut, 253
school system: and socialization toward common identity, 280
Schotter, Andrew, 217
Schroder, Andrew J., III, 209–10, 310n1
Schultz, Charles, 228–29
Schumpeter, Joseph, 119–20
Science, 22
self-esteem, 17
self-interest, 61, 272–73; in family social contract, 68; harnessing for common good, 243

selfishness, 37; altruism as, 63; in common goals, 285–86
Seligman, Martin, 177, 188
sellers: perceived control over prices, 189
semiconductors, 90–91
Sen, Amartya, 228, 229
Shapley, Lloyd, 216, 231
Shaw, George Bernard, 167, 233, 282
Sheahan, John, 292
Shubik, Martin, 13, 14–15, 17, 216, 231
sliding bands, 249
small business: labor-management relations in, 215–16
small groups, 24; burden shifting by, 272; games played by, 97
"small-world" experiment, 54
Smith, Adam, 61, 151, 154; *Wealth of Nations, The,* 239
Smith, Ralph, 144
Smyth, David J., 239
Snap (game), 141
social bonds, 296
social characteristics: socially inherited, 70
social cohesion, 23, 185
social conscience, 220, 282
social context(s): conflict and cooperation in, 30, 33–34
social contract, 39, 48; advantages of, 76; among nations, 268–69; between unions and monetary authorities (Japan), 234; business and labor relations in, 204–5, 207, 221; changing game structure or nature of players, 222–23; explicit, 286; family, 68, 77; fear of defection in, 203–4; GATT as, 265; government and, 220,

335

Index

stocks; *see* common stocks

stress: in corporations, 79, 85; endemic, 184

sunspots: as cause of economic cycles, 305*n*24

supergames, 62, 72

supply: as key mechanism underlying perverse causalities, 168–69

supply and demand: with floating exchange rates, 162; unhindered, 15–17

supply/demand balance, 115–16, 117–18

supply schedules, 164–66

supply-side economics, 25, 165–66, 167–70, 283

survival of the fittest (theorem), 28–44, 61

Sweden, 233, 234

Sytsma, John F., 236–37, 310*n*1

Taft, Phillip, 158

Take My Hand (game), 295–96

Take Out the Trash (game), 85–86

takeovers, 17, 37

tariffs, 213, 265; restricted by GATT, 265; unilateral, 264; wars of, 4

tax cuts, 25, 129, 142, 169

tax relief act (1981), 213

taxes, 286; effect on inflation, 165–66; high, 125, 129; on profits, 145–46; and paying for wars, 251, 306*n*3

Tawney, Richard: *Acquisitive Society, The*, 9

technology, 211; and indexation, 159

Thatcher, Margaret, 110

Theory of Games and Economic Behavior, The (von Neumann and Morgenstern), 12–13

3M Company, 209

Through the Looking Glass (Carroll), 204

Thurow, Lester: *Zero-Sum Society, The*, 9

TIT FOR TAT (computer program), 42–43

Tnuva (food conglomerate, Israel), 159

Tobin, James, 18–19, 109, 158, 205–6

Tokyo Rounds, 265

Tolstoy, Leo, 144; *Anna Karenina*, 287

trade, international, 4, 213; barriers to, 24–25, 263–66 (*see also* import restrictions; protectionism); competition in, 163–64, 214, 219; efficient, 264; imbalance in, 214

trade flows, 253, 254–55, 270; regulation of, 249–50

trade games, international, 248, 262–69

traffic lights (example), 21

tragedy of the commons, 30

Train Game (game), 52, 55–56, 58

triangle hypothesis, 35, 36F

tripartite mechanisms, 221

Truman, Harry S, 242

trust, 38, 39; in family, 61, 62; in reciprocation, 68; in Type Z corporations, 84

Tufte, Edward, 109

Turkey: economic rents, 289

Index

COLA clauses); as cause of inflation, 150–51, 153, 154–57; changed only once a year (Japan), 161; decline in real, 219; effect of floating exchange rates on, 163–64

Wahrungsreform (Federal Republic of Germany), 156

Wall Street Journal, 211

Wallich, Henry, 258

Walpole, Horace, 48

Walras, Leon, 21

Walt Disney Productions, 197

war: of all against all, 219; government intervention in collective bargaining during, 221; paying for, 251, 306n3; people adhere to golden rule in times of, 280; rules of, 248

Watts, A. W., 73

Weakland, John H., 74

wealth: appropriation of, 8; decline in, through DUPs, 288; disparity in, 270; inequitable distribution of, 283; sources of, 271; transfer of, 163

Wealth and Poverty (Gilder), 75–76

Wealth of Nations, The (Smith), 239

Weisbrod, Burton, 275–76

welfare, 25

West Germany; *see* Federal Republic of Germany

wheat and feed grains: shortage of, 102–3

wheat prices, 103

White, E. B., 292

Whitehead, Alfred North, 10

Wiener, Norbert, 282–83

Williamsburg (Va.) summit, 269

Winfield, Dave, 174

winners, winning (economic games), 9, 39–40, 294

Winning Isn't the Main Thing (game), 39–40

Winpisinger, William, 203, 211, 310n1

Wood, Sir Kingsley, 142

World Council of Churches, 37

world order: cohesive, 273

World Pillow-Fighting Championship, 11

World War II, 113, 127–28, 197, 221

Wouk, Herman, 27

"wrong-way" economy, 106, 125–48; interpretation of, 149–70

X-efficiency theory of inflation, 189

Xerox Corp., 94

Yen, 254

Youngman, Henny, 7

Zeno, 130

zero-sum games, 14, 30, 58; migration treated as, 271–72

Zero-Sum Society, The (Thurow), 9